Social History of Africa

MEN AND MASCULINITIES IN MODERN AFRICA

Recent Titles in
Social History of Africa Series
Series Editors: Allen Isaacman and Jean Allman

Making the Town: Ga State and Society in Early Colonial Accra
John Parker

Chiefs Know Their Boundaries: Essays on Property, Power, and the Past in Asante, 1896–1996
Sara S. Bèrry

"Wicked" Women and the Reconfiguration of Gender in Africa
Dorothy L. Hodgson and Sheryl A. McCurdy, editors

Black Death, White Medicine: Bubonic Plague and the Politics of Public Health in Colonial Senegal, 1914–1945
Myron Echenberg

Vilimani: Labor Migration and Rural Change in Early Colonial Tanzania
Thaddeus Sunseri

"God Alone Is King": Islam and Emancipation in Senegal: The Wolof Kingdoms of Kajoor and Bawol, 1859–1914
James F. Searing

Negotiating Development: African Farmers and Colonial Experts at the Office du Niger, 1920–1960
Monica M. van Beusekom

The Bluest Hands: A Social and Economic History of Women Dyers in Abeokuta (Nigeria), 1890–1940
Judith A. Byfield

Colonial Lessons: Africans' Education in Southern Rhodesia, 1918–1940
Carol Summers

Poison and Medicine: Ethnicity, Power, and Violence in a Nigerian City, 1966 to 1986
Douglas A. Anthony

To Dwell Secure: Generation, Christianity, and Colonialism in Ovamboland
Meredith McKittrick

Genders and Generations Apart: Labor Tenants and Customary Law in Segregation-Era South Africa, 1920s to 1940s
Thomas V. McClendon

MEN AND MASCULINITIES IN MODERN AFRICA

Edited by Lisa A. Lindsay
and Stephan F. Miescher

Social History of Africa
Allen Isaacman and Jean Allman, Series Editors

HEINEMANN
Portsmouth, NH

Heinemann
A division of Reed Elsevier Inc.
361 Hanover Street
Portsmouth, NH 03801-3912
www.heinemann.com

Offices and agents throughout the world

ISBN 0-325-00255-X (cloth)
ISBN 0-325-00254-1 (paper)
ISSN 1099-8098

Library of Congress Cataloging-in-Publication Data

Men and masculinities in modern Africa / edited by Lisa A. Lindsay and Stephan F. Miescher.
    p. cm—(Social history of Africa, ISSN 1099-8098)
  Includes bibliographical references and index.
  ISBN 0-325-00255-X (alk. paper)—ISBN 0-325-00254-1 (pbk. : alk. paper)
  1. Men—Africa, Sub-Saharan. 2. Masculinity—Africa, Sub-Saharan. 3. Masculinity—Africa, Sub-Saharan—History. I. Lindsay, Lisa A. II. Miescher, Stephan. III. Series.
HQ1090.5.A357 M45 2003
305.31'0967—dc21   2002027620

British Library Cataloguing in Publication Data is available

Printed in the United States of America on acid-free paper

07 06 05 04 03 SB 1 2 3 4 5 6 7 8 9

Copyright Acknowledgments

We gratefully acknowledge permission to reprint revised versions of the following articles in this volume:

Luise White, "Separating the Men from the Boys: Constructions of Gender, Sexuality, and Terrorism in Central Kenya, 1939–1959," *International Journal of African Historical Studies* 32, 1 (1990): 1–25.

Dorothy Hodgson, "'Once Intrepid Warriors': Modernity and the Production of Maasai Masculinities," *Ethnology* 38, 2 (1999): 121–150.

We also acknowledge permission to publish the map, which was produced by Karin S. Breiwitz, Center for Teaching and Learning, University of North Carolina-Chapel Hill.

CONTENTS

ILLUSTRATIONS

ACKNOWLEDGMENTS

When the co-editors first met in 1995 in Ann Arbor, we were both completing dissertations dealing with men and masculinity in colonial West Africa. Although it seemed a rather esoteric subject at the time, we became attuned to a growing and exciting body of historical and anthropological work on male gender in Africa. Luise White, who had recently organized the first conference on the subject, urged us to compile an edited volume. We thank her for continuing to nudge us and for her advice, backing, and trenchant analysis over the last few years. We also express our appreciation to Jean Allman and Allen Isaacman, the Social History of Africa series co-editors, along with Jim Lance, our editor at Heinemann/Greenwood, for their support of the project. Dorothy Hodgson graciously shared with us material from her and Sheryl McCurdy's wonderful book on women in Africa, which helped us get started with our own edited volume. Thanks to Emmanuel Akyeampong, Mark Epprecht, Michael Hunt, Gregory Mann, Steven Pierce, and Luise White for reading and commenting on the Introduction. We are also grateful to two anonymous readers for their extensive comments on the whole manuscript. Finally, our contributors deserve special recognition: some for meeting deadlines, others for tolerating our prodding about deadlines; some for sharing new research, others for making available articles that were previously written; some for participating in various African Studies Association panels on masculinity; and all for their goodwill and good work.

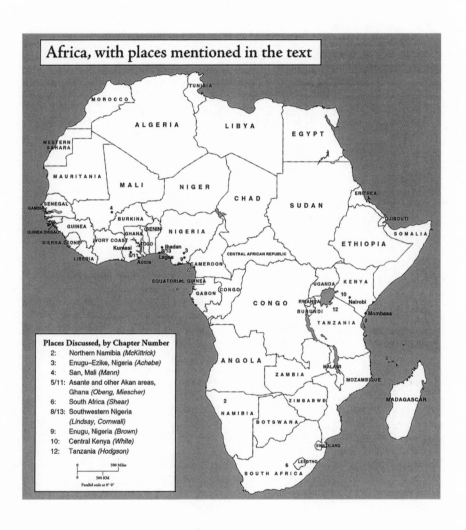

Africa, with places mentioned in the text

Places Discussed, by Chapter Number

2: Northern Namibia (*McKittrick*)
3: Enugu–Ezike, Nigeria (*Achebe*)
4: San, Mali (*Mann*)
5/11: Asante and other Akan areas, Ghana (*Obeng, Miescher*)
6: South Africa (*Shear*)
8/13: Southwestern Nigeria (*Lindsay, Cornwall*)
9: Enugu, Nigeria (*Brown*)
10: Central Kenya (*White*)
12: Tanzania (*Hodgson*)

0 ___ 500 Miles
0 ___ 500 KM
Parallel scale at 0° 0°

MEN AND MASCULINITIES IN MODERN AFRICA

1

INTRODUCTION: MEN AND MASCULINITIES IN MODERN AFRICAN HISTORY

Stephan F. Miescher and Lisa A. Lindsay

Chinua Achebe's *Things Fall Apart*, the most widely read African novel, is generally understood as an explication of early colonialism and its effects in eastern Nigeria. Yet it is also about masculinity. Okonkwo, the tragic hero, kills himself essentially because the new structures of authority and power brought by colonizers exclude senior men like himself. Instead, they provide opportunities for status and accumulation for people previously marginalized from the local power structure, like Okonkwo's son Nwoye, who never was a successful farmer or fighter but who uses mission education to earn a position in the colonial bureaucracy. The novel brilliantly complicates the imposition of colonialism by underscoring divisions within Umuofia society along lines of generation, gender, education, and wealth.

The example of *Things Fall Apart* suggests that the major transformations in African history in the last hundred years (and presumably before) profoundly affected male status and opportunities as well as relationships between men and women, men and men, and women and women. But while gender has become a major research focus in African studies over the last twenty years, men have rarely been the subject of research on gender in Africa. As the field of gender study emerged, the male subject was frequently positioned as given, serving as a backdrop in the examination of women's experiences. Africanist scholars interested in gender issues have only recently begun to address how shifting meanings of gender have affected African men and how understandings and practices of masculinity have been contested and

transformed during the colonial and postcolonial eras. At the same time, however, men and masculinities have been the focus of a growing body of scholarship within the humanities and social sciences. This new field has mainly
theorized masculinity by drawing on studies from Australia, Europe, and
North America with little attention to the rich variety of gendered practices in
Africa.[1]

This collection of essays deals with the construction of masculinities in
modern Africa. Although there has been some work on men as gendered
actors in African history, including two conferences, so far very few mono-
graphs have emerged.[2] The contributions to this volume combine empirical
research on sub-Saharan African history with attention to theoretical issues
surrounding the construction and maintenance of gender relations and identities. Their general concern is with the socioeconomic and cultural transformations of "modern" Africa—that is, in the colonial and postcolonial (or
neocolonial) periods—and the links between those changes and male gender.
Certainly gender relationships and identities were shifting in earlier periods
as well, as Meredith McKittrick's essay in this volume shows (cf. Akyeampong and Obeng 1995; Greene 1996; Ogbomo 1997). Our focus on the last
century enables us to ask questions about the construction and maintenance of
gender in the relatively recent past and examine the dramatic social history
most relevant to contemporary Africa.

Gender constructions are embedded in a dialectic. How men and women
see and represent themselves, and how gender relations are organized and
promoted, are shaped by larger socioeconomic, cultural, and religious transformations. At the same time, notions of gender have an impact on the course
and receptions of these transformations, which include the abolition of
African forms of slavery, the replacement of older structures of political
authority with those derived from colonial systems, the expansion of wage
labor and cash cropping, the introduction of mission-oriented Christianity and
western education, the spread of Islam, as well as migration and urbanization.
To examine these through the lens of gender is to differentiate the experiences
of men within various contexts as well as to probe how inequalities developed
and were sustained, and how power was wielded (Morrell 1998). This exercise is compatible with feminist-inspired histories of women and goes beyond
them as well. If so much of African history has been written with men as an
unmarked category, then destabilizing the male subject can yield insights into
processes previously understood to be outside the realm of gender.[3]

In spite of its concern with power and colonialism, this collection generally
avoids the subjects of "colonial masculinity" and particularly "imperial masculinity."[4] Although our contributors analyze the importance of the colonial
state and its institutions to the formation and maintenance of masculine identities, we are less concerned with contrasting the "manly Englishman" with
the "effeminate" colonial subject (Sinha 1995; but see Shear this volume). As

Africanists, our inquiries are rooted in local dynamics; our primary interest is in *Africans*, generally in relation to each other. We recognize that colonial states and their actors often had a limited reach within African societies, despite their political and coercive power (Cooper and Stoler 1997). Furthermore, given emerging evidence of the *global* context of European ideologies (Stoler 1995), we may do well to rethink how foreign to some African societies the gendered ideals of colonizers were. Thus it makes sense to consider African gender relations as a "patchwork of patriarchies" (Bozzoli 1983), some imposed through colonialism, others locally derived. The power of colonial institutions to shape such patterns varied through time and place, often becoming manifest in indirect or muted ways.

This means that we need to be sensitive not only to innovations and ruptures, but also to the powerful continuities in gender systems that resurfaced in various situations. The African "big man" provides perhaps the most enduring image of African masculinity.[5] Across the continent and for a long sweep of history, ambitious people (usually men) have worked to enlarge their households and use their "wealth in people" for political and material advancement. Iliffe (1995: 94) argues that "the large complex household headed by a Big Man surrounded by his wives, married and unmarried sons, younger brothers, poor relations, dependents, and swarming children" was the "key colonising group" in ancient equatorial Africa as well as in parts of West Africa. In a continual cycle, "big men" were able to gain people and power by distributing resources and providing for their followers. Yet this same process could be counterproductive: during the period of the transatlantic slave trade, Central African "big men" paradoxically traded people to obtain the imported goods necessary to attract more people (Miller 1988); and on the East African coast in the late nineteenth century, financially vulnerable *shirazi* elites attempted to compete with better-financed Arab traders by hosting costly festivals for potential clients (Glassman 1995). Aspirant "big men" responded to changing political and economic circumstances, seizing new opportunities to acquire the person-power necessary where population densities were low and technologies limited. Such improvisation on the "big man" ideal continued through the colonial and postcolonial periods.[6] This archetype shows how exploring understandings of masculinity provides a perspective from which to identify the interrelation between changes and continuities.

CONCEPTS IN THE STUDY OF (AFRICAN) MASCULINITIES

In gender studies, masculinity is a growth industry. While scholars within the "men's studies" paradigm have been concerned with valorizing the experiences of men rather than problematizing gender (cf. Cornwall and Lindisfarne 1994b), Africanists can glean valuable insights from sociological and anthropological treatments of masculinity. Furthermore, the contributors to this volume take their lead from studies of women and gender in Africa, of which there are now many. Thus, although the study of masculinity in Africa is in its infancy, researchers may draw on a range of related material for theoretical insights.

Scholars of women have pointed out that most Africanist (and other) historiography has centered on men's experiences and assumed that they are universal. Political history has tended to be the history of men in politics, economic history has centered on men's economic activities, and so on. This volume emphasizes that histories of men, as well as those of women, must foreground gender. As Luise White has pointed out (1990a), "most studies of African men . . . have tended to make men seem monolithic and homogeneous, either as resistors or collaborators; they have had factions, but no personal reasons for joining them. Men were motivated by land shortages, poverty, and decreasing real wages, but not by their qualms and anxieties about the changing rights and obligations of fatherhood." This volume shows men's private lives as sites of contestation, which often have had important political dimensions. It assumes that domesticity and sexuality are not and have not been exclusively women's issues, and that gendered concerns— overlapping and interacting with broader issues of political economy—are and have been relevant to men *and* women.

We use the term *masculinity* to refer to a cluster of norms, values, and behavioral patterns expressing explicit and implicit expectations of how men should act and represent themselves to others. Ideologies of masculinity— like those of femininity—are culturally and historically constructed, their meanings continually contested and always in the process of being renegotiated in the context of existing power relations. Africa is an important site for studying the social construction of gender, since some scholars have argued that African gender identities have been particularly fluid and contentious, heavily articulated with wealth, age, seniority, and ritual authority (Amadiume 1987; Matory 1994; Oyěwùmí 1997; N. Achebe 2000). Dorothy Hodgson (1999 and this volume) delineates five "generational masculinities" associated with Maasai age sets, and Andrea Cornwall (this volume) presents strategies for "being a man" among members of different generations in a small Yoruba town. It is important to emphasize that there is theoretically no limit to the number of genders in a given society. White (1990a and this volume) asserts that in late colonial Kenya, the state promoted "two male genders, whose literacy and skills informed the ways they conducted themselves as men." Lisa Lindsay (this volume) differentiates between adult and senior masculinity in colonial Yorubaland, even aside from the putative male breadwinner coming into being in some workers' households and the normative "big man." McKittrick (this volume) describes "boys of the king," who enjoyed masculine privileges but were still subject to the authority of a political leader possessing what she calls "super masculinity." "Boy" has been an important social category in many African contexts, implying biological maleness, social (but not necessarily physical) immaturity, and, in colonial situations, racialized inferiority in relation to "men" (Brown and Shear this volume).

Africanist research provides concrete examples of the capacity of gender to transcend biological sex, theorized by European and North American scholars (led by Butler 1990, 1993). Research on Africa shows that in specific circumstances "masculinity without men" (Halberstam 1998) can be ordinary and part of accepted gender experiences, as in the institution of the "female husband" among the Nandi people in Kenya (Oboler 1980), in Igbo societies of Nigeria (Amadiume 1987; N. Achebe 2000), and elsewhere (O'Brien 1977). By "female masculinity," we mean women's attainment of positions or characteristics usually regarded as the preserve of men, like those of the women chiefs in colonial Lesotho, who acted as "honorary men" (Epprecht 1995). In the Igbo "dual sex/flexible gender" system, female and male political/economic hierarchies existed in parallel (Amadiume 1987). The ability of a given woman to "jump" to the male ladder by paying bridewealth and thus gaining access to a wife, or by being designated as "male" for the purposes of inheritance, meant that individuals could change their genders in certain contexts. Nwando Achebe (this volume) provides evidence of a female warrant chief exercising power in a role gendered as male in northern Igboland well into the colonial period. Historical incidents of African forms of (male) homosexualities also indicate that men could embrace and embody qualities associated with femininity, as with young male "wives" in South African "mine marriages" (Harries 1990; Moodie 1988), the "*ngotshana* marriages" of labor camps in early colonial Zimbabwe (Epprecht 1998a), or the *yan daudu* in relation to their male sexual partners in present-day Hausaland of Nigeria (Gaudio 1998).

Although there is not always a connection between physical manhood and sociological masculinity, the relationship between sex and gender is not completely arbitrary. As Elizabeth Grosz (1990: 74) has pointed out, "masculinity and femininity mean *different things* according to whether they are lived out in and experienced by male or female bodies. . . . What is mapped onto the body is not unaffected by the body onto which it is projected." Contrary to a growing literature exploring masculinity outside of Africa (Mosse 1996), and unlike Morrell's overview (1998), we distinguish between manhood and masculinity, at times with attention to local languages. *Manhood* refers to indigenous notions explicitly related to men's physiology, often recognized in terms of male adulthood (see McKittrick this volume). *Masculinity* is broader, more abstract, and often implicit. This distinction helps to explain the limits that were at times placed upon "female masculinity." In the case of the female Igbo "king" (Achebe this volume), her constituents seemingly accepted her authority (backed by the colonial state) only up to a point. When she tried to usurp a masquerade explicitly associated with physical *manhood*, local men rebelled and worked to remove her political power, wives, and associated masculine status.

As noted, on a societal level masculinity can take varying forms. The challenge is to understand how genders emerge and are transformed, and how they relate to each other. How has gender helped to structure stratification and alliances among various individuals and groups? How important are age, class, or generation in delineating gender identities in given contexts? What factors influence the relationships between masculinity and manhood? The most influential elaboration of variation among masculinities has been by sociologist R.W. Connell (1995), who has posited a hierarchy of masculinities, including four levels of masculine privilege: hegemonic, complicitous, marginalized, and subordinated.[7] These categories represent various abilities to enjoy what he calls the "patriarchal dividend," or the "advantage men in general gain from the overall subordination of women" (1995: 79). But not all versions of masculinity have equal power and legitimacy in society. Connell argues that at any given time "one form of masculinity rather than others is culturally exalted" and defines this dominant, hegemonic masculinity "as the configuration of gender practice which embodies the currently accepted answer to the problem of the legitimacy of patriarchy" (1995: 77).[8]

Studying masculinity in African situations requires using Connell's model with caution. Scholars embracing his schema have rightly emphasized that masculinity can have multiple meanings within a society, and that power relations affect which definitions become normative. Certainly such an insight applies to colonial contexts, which included gender norms imposed from outside as well as (often competing) indigenous values and practices. Connell (1995: 77) claims that "*one form* of masculinity . . . is culturally exalted [our emphasis]," meaning hegemonic. We argue, similarly to Morrell (1998), that in colonial Africa it was *not* always obvious which notions of masculinity were dominant, or hegemonic, since understandings of gender depend on the specific context and on different actors' subject positions. The limited power of colonial ideologies, combined with the social flux created by new constraints and opportunities, meant that a multiplicity of competing masculine identities promoted sometimes divergent images of proper male behavior within certain contexts (Miescher this volume). As Andrea Cornwall and Nancy Lindisfarne (1994b: 20) have noted, Connell's model fails to recognize the situations in which "various hegemonic models can coexist." In her chapter, Cornwall pushes that critique even further by detailing a complex array of gender models in southwestern Nigeria and arguing for their continuing interaction and transformation. Similarly, McKittrick (this volume) points out that in nineteenth- and twentieth-century Ovambo societies, "the co-existence of a dominant masculinity based on fatherhood and one based on elite status was of long duration." Our contributors show that African men consciously grappled with different forms of masculinity, engaging with, adopting, and discarding various expectations and images of proper male behavior—images of both local and foreign origin. They confront two central questions linking gender studies with social history more generally. First, under what circumstances were particular dominant masculinities most contested (or most accepted), and why? Second, how did individual social actors engage with a multitude of masculinities, and how did they relate them to their own subjectivities and identities?

In exploring the historical construction of masculinities, we suggest three major methodological and ontological distinctions: we want to know how people in given times and places talked about and characterized gender traits, how gender was embodied in practice, and how actors understood their own gendered identities.[9] First, treatments of masculinity can focus on discourses that express cultural ideas and expectations of those considered masculine, mainly men but at times also women. As shown in this volume, in Ovambo societies "the power to allot and withhold resources and to command others . . . defined the essence of masculinity" (McKittrick); in colonial Mali, marabouts and returning ex-soldiers equated senior masculinity with authority over women and juniors as well as access to exclusive religious knowledge (Mann); Asante dominant masculinity entailed wealth, authority over subordinates, and bravery in warfare (Obeng); Yoruba men expected to wield authority as husbands (Cornwall); and Maasai men were supposed to be pastoralists and warriors (Hodgson). A study of the construction of masculinities in Africa needs to explore which institutions promoted specific notions of masculinity, how they did this, and in what contexts. Does discourse reveal certain hierarchies between different notions of masculinity? How do common assumptions and expectations about men (and women) undergo change? Hodgson's historical treatment of the Maasai term *ormeek* (meaning "modern" and "not Maasai") and its shift from a derogatory appellation for men of subordinate masculinity to a value-neutral or even positive attribute in changing socioeconomic circumstances is a particularly effective use of discourse to understand gender transformations.

Second, notions of masculinity can be approached as expressions of social practice to be observed within specific historical contexts, as practice also reproduces and transforms gender systems. As Dorothy Hodgson and Sheryl McCurdy argue (2001), largely with reference to women, gender is not merely "constructed" but *produced*—by the ideas and actions of women and men in interaction with local and translocal structures and processes. Studies of female husbands or South African mine marriages generally focus on instances in which women or men have *acted* in ways typically associated with the opposite sex, as in Achebe's discussion of the female Igbo king and warrant chief, Ahebi Ugbabe, and Obeng's treatment of Yaa Asantewaa (both this volume). Similarly, Lindsay's chapter suggests that as Nigerian railway men increasingly acted as financial providers in their households, they developed new ideas about the obligations and status of married, working men. The returning veterans described in Gregory Mann's essay attempted to refine notions of respectable masculinity at least in part through the reworking of religious observance. Keith Shear (this volume) suggests that black South African policemen's reputation for brutality may have been fueled by their resistance to emasculinizing treatment by their white superiors. Such investigations raise questions of how men (and women) have negotiated in their daily lives between different, at times conflicting, notions of masculinity. If social transformation is the result of human agency combined with changing circumstances, what are some of the ways in which people have refined masculine norms in modern Africa?

Third, notions of masculinity are reflected in individual experience, identity, and subjectivity. In the examples cited above, how did Yaa Asantewaa, Maasai men identified as *ormeek*, female husbands, black South African policemen, or participants in mine marriages understand their own gendered identities? How do men deal with different notions of masculinity in the course of their life cycles? How important are age, class, or generation in delineating their gender identities? How do gendered practices become part of their self-presentation and self-conception? Emmanuel Akyeampong's (2000) use of highlife song lyrics provides an effective window on gendered subjectivities and emotions: "You like cloth but you don't want children," or "Give me the Bush Girl" make clear urban young men's anxieties about finding a mate in late colonial Ghana. Cornwall's extensive interviews with Yoruba men also reveal tensions between normative male ideals and men's abilities to achieve such ideals in the context of economic insecurity (this volume). A focus on subjectivities suggests that Dunbar Moodie's (1988, 1994) representation of South African mine marriages, analyzed as resistance to proletarianization and urbanization, may be too narrow, being driven by the economic aspects of these relationships. Moodie does not explore whether some miners might have preferred same-sex relationships over conventional marriages, thus embracing a nonstandard notion of masculinity. Moodie and other South African labor historians have dismissed such circumstantial homosexuality practiced in mining and prison compounds as a product of, or response to, the oppressive migrant labor system within capitalism (van Onselen 1976, 1984; Breckenridge 1990). But according to Zackie Achmat (1993: 95), this interpretation ignores "the production and history of desire and pleasure." A serious study of various forms of homosexual relations in African cultures and history is only a very recent endeavor (Murray and Roscoe 1998; Epprecht 1998b; Gevisser and Cameron 1994), which offers the potential to enrich our understanding of gendered subjectivity.

Ideally, the best treatments of masculinity would approach gender through all three lenses, and indeed, discourse, practice, and subjective identity must be conceptualized as connected. The two chapters by anthropologists Hodgson and Cornwall make these links. But the sources available to historians make the excavation of discourses and practices an easier endeavor than reconstructing the subjectivities of people in the past. Although many of our contributors probe the question of how the people they studied understood their gendered identities, clearly we are more comfortable with reporting on what people actually said and did. With his extensive use of oral histories and autobiographical writings, Stephan Miescher is the only historian here to explore confidently his subjects' sense of their own gendered identities. His paper tantalizingly suggests that Ghanaian teachers maintained subjectivities often at odds with their own gendered practices and discourses. This conclusion—that what people said and did could differ from what they thought about themselves—should not be startling, but it does raise serious questions for those of us who base our conclusions largely on people's words and actions. Can we not assume Africans' explicit consciousness of the porousness of gender constructs? Lindsay has suggested that Nigerian railway men in the colonial era strategically employed gendered arguments with British administrators to win certain material benefits, even when those arguments did not necessarily reflect their lives and values (1998, 1999 and this volume). McKittrick, Shear, and Brown describe instances in which certain men were "boys" in one context but "men" in another. How did they define themselves? Understanding individual subjectivities remains a significant methodological challenge for historians of gender and social change in modern Africa.[10]

MASCULINITY IN MODERN AFRICAN HISTORY

A focus on masculinity suggests some reconceptualizations of key issues in African historiography. Although the papers collected here make a start, one must also fill in gaps from the existing historiography not necessarily focused on male gender. As in Chinua Achebe's famous novel, masculinity is an implicit theme of many existing treatments of African history. Combining explicit studies of African masculinity with those in which male gender is a little noted subtheme allows us to begin creating a tentative history of transformations, as well as continuities, in masculinity in twentieth-century sub-Saharan Africa and thus enriching existing political and cultural histories. We acknowledge the preliminary nature of this endeavor and hope that our attempt will encourage others to build on our outline, flesh out its gaps, or challenge its components. The themes noted here correspond to subsections of this volume.

Challenging Senior Masculinity

As suggested by the plot of *Things Fall Apart,* colonial conquest often undermined the authority and power bases of senior men in African communities. What were the specific times and places of such developments? What were the primary issues at stake? Contributions to this volume by McKittrick, Achebe, and Mann show that new opportunities for slave emancipation, financial accumulation and wage labor, religious conversion, and education and literacy among young men and women undermined and challenged the political power and dominant masculinity of older males. Furthermore, they suggest that when men worked, learned, or fought elsewhere and then returned home, they brought with them not only new ideas and things, but fresh conceptions of gender. They sought either to include themselves within local notions of dominant masculinity or to reshape those notions in their own images.

Intergenerational tensions—often overlooked in feminist scholarship—have been closely related to the social and economic transformations of the colonial period and have been crucial in changing definitions of masculinity. It has almost become a commonplace assertion that the new opportunities created by colonialism and commercialization gave junior men the cash to assert autonomy from their seniors. From South Africa to Kenya to Nigeria, men who had once been forced to provide service for their elders as a route to marriage and social adulthood became able to earn money for marriage payments themselves, generally through migrant labor (Beinart 1982; Peel 1983; Bravman 1998) but also through independent marketing or skilled trades (S. Martin 1988; Berry 1985). Moreover, numerous sources attest to the conflicts between the first generation of religious converts and literates and other members of their communities, particularly elders. Chinua Achebe's Nwoye provides a case in point, as does the character Nhamo in Tsitsi Dangarembga's novel *Nervous Conditions,* who so alienates his family while gaining western education that his sister flatly denies any sadness over his death.

In her chapter, McKittrick traces intergenerational relations in Ovamboland, northern Namibia, through the late precolonial period and into the twentieth century, showing that tensions between different generations of men were only enhanced by circumstances produced by colonialism, not created by them. In Ovambo societies, male power was equated with men who had their own livestock, houses, wives, and juvenile dependents—men who were "senior" and who performed the social role of "fathers." Such power was reproduced through their ability to determine the criteria and candidates for becoming "real men" by getting married and setting up their own households. But at the same time, a male initiation ceremony, open mostly to elite sons, provided access to religious and material resources regardless of age. Long-distance trade, the availability of firearms, and political centralization in the nineteenth century redefined masculinity as militaristic, violent, linked to the capitalist world system, and focused on kings. Amid economic and political insecurity, nonelite fathers held back their sons from adulthood to maintain access to their sons' labor. By the early twentieth century, missionaries, colonial officials, labor recruiters, and younger men challenged fathers' roles in the creation of "men" from "boys" and attacked dominant ideas of masculinity. Colonial ethnographies denied fathers any significant role in a matrilineal society, clearing the way for policies designed to turn fathers into migrant laborers with little importance to their families. At the same time, some junior males chose Christianity and labor migration as alternative routes to the acquisition of masculine power. Thus the early twentieth century was a time of crisis over male authority in Ovambo society, with competing notions of masculinity.

Such alternative definitions became more salient with the establishment of colonialism when administrators encouraged cash cropping and labor migration—both of which had profound implications for intergenerational relationships (cf. Mandala 1990). Mann's contribution explores intergenerational struggles by "junior" men (who were often not young) promoting different notions of masculine power within the realm of Islamic practice. His examination of army veterans in Mali expands studies of the *tirailleurs Sénégalais* and enriches our understanding of Islamic politics by looking at them through the lens of gender. Returning home following World War II, veterans of France's African army faced a dilemma of reintegration into their communities' daily lives. While the *tirailleurs* were elsewhere, their age-mates assumed and transformed the position of respectable adult men in a highly gerontocratic society: they married, sired children, and became deeply immersed in local spiritual life. Although a career soldier may have proved his virility, by the time he returned home he had lost his youth. Moreover, a soldier's masculinity remained subordinate (or, according to Connell's schema, marginalized) and closely connected to a heritage of slavery. Seeking reintegration was necessarily a bid for respectability, an assertion of community membership that was highly gendered, requiring fulfillment of certain expectations and improvisations of an adult man's "scripted role." In 1950s San, the town of Mann's study, that script included religious observance, but years of absence frequently denied veterans a spiritual apprenticeship. Instead they had been exposed to new influences and ideas in Europe and the Maghreb. Tensions over religious belief and practice, crucial to senior masculinity, became evident in a 1957 religious riot. Veterans acted as supporters of an Islamic dissident who was beaten and chased out of San because his teachings challenged the marabouts' authority and senior masculinity. Mann argues that this incident represents both a rebellion against senior men by veterans *and* their bid for respectability. Embracing religious innovations, veterans created for themselves a new sense of home that conflicted with local expectations.

Although social, economic, and legal changes brought by colonial rule gave social juniors and women opportunities for autonomy from elder men, the above examples indicate that such challenges often were not easy or successful. In colonial courts, juniors and women asserted claims, even as senior men worked to shape "customary" law in their own interests.[11] Achebe's chapter excavates the history of Ahebi Ugbabe, the only female warrant chief in colonial Igboland (southeastern Nigeria). In the early twentieth century, young Ahebi escaped being dedicated as a slave to the goddess Ohe by running to a nearby town.[12] There, she worked to accumulate cash as well as linguistic skills, occult powers, and political connections. When the British invaded her homeland, Ahebi accompanied them as a guide and translator. From this intermediary position, she was appointed member of the Native Court in 1918 and later had herself confirmed as *Eze* (king), an office previously unknown. Through the 1920s and 1930s, Ahebi ruled as a powerful leader, amassing wealth and wives. Her individual aggrandizement rankled male elders. The final straw broke in 1939, when Ahebi attempted to sponsor a masquerade seen as the exclusive preserve of biological men. Senior men, supported by the British resident, rejected her masquerade. Although she remained in office until her death in 1948, Ahebi never recovered the prestige and influence lost during this incident. Moreover, her abuse of power led local elders to vow that no individual—male or female—would ever rule them again. Ahebi's life story depicts the permeability of gender in Igbo societies, well into the colonial period, but also the limits to such flexibility. When the community determined that Ahebi controlled too much centralized power, they worked to reduce it, as well as her status as a "man."

Studying senior men as gendered actors allows us to see colonialism as the context for two related, but differently weighted, struggles among groups of men: to gain or maintain political or economic power in relation to the colonial, capitalist system and to support patriarchy in the home. This represents the flip side of John Lonsdale and Bruce Berman's (1979) "coping with the contradictions" of colonialism. Their analysis highlights the contradictory position of colonial administrators who had to support European settlers and other colonial interests even while they were required by the exigencies of indirect rule to make compromises with chiefs. At the same time, African male elders found it in their interests to support the state on certain issues, because their power rested on relationships to it, even as their patriarchal authority was undermined by the new opportunities that colonial structures and agents provided to junior men and women.[13] Thus attention to the interplay between gender and age further complicates paradigms of collaboration and resistance and suggests new ways of understanding indirect rule and colonial administration from the vantage point of colonized male elders.

(Re)Making Men in Colonial Africa

Although colonial-era men participated in wage labor or mission Christianity or the army as alternative routes to senior status as formerly defined, many had their ambitions and self-conceptions transformed in the process. In part this resulted from deliberate attempts by colonizers, but men also worked actively to reconcile for themselves the opportunities and constraints of their situations with the expectations of parents and other community members. Again, novels not necessarily about masculinity show this in stark relief: Buchi Emecheta's *The Joys of Motherhood* highlights the divergent expectations about family obligations held by the heroine, her husband, and their many children in late colonial Lagos. While Nnu Ego expects the hardships she has endured on behalf of her older children to pay off with their assistance in providing for the younger ones and for herself and her husband in old age, her two oldest sons instead pursue what seems an unreasonable amount of western education, leave the country, marry abroad, and contribute nothing materially to the family until the time of their mother's funeral.

Although the vast majority of scholarship on colonialism and domesticity in Africa has focused on women, one can observe the effects of colonial efforts on men. Missionaries and administrators worked through institutions like churches, schools, and workplaces, explicitly or implicitly propagating their own ideals of domesticity and men's place in households and marriages.[14] As they intervened in politics, religion, legal systems, agricultural regimes, and labor markets, European actors in colonial Africa worked to remake men; and African men negotiated with women, elders, missionaries, and employers about domesticity and the rights and obligations of men within households (Summers 1999). That this process produced anxieties is revealed in a scene from T.M. Aluko's novel, *One Man, One Wife* (1967: 35), about mission Christianity in southwestern Nigeria in the 1920s. After reluctantly agreeing to send his youngest son to the mission school, a church member exclaimed, "But—TEACHER—YOU MUST NOT TURN MY SON INTO A WOMAN!" Miescher's examination of the lives and subjectivities of mission-trained teachers in southern Ghana focuses on similar issues. In colonial Ghana, Miescher asserts, there were multiple and at times conflicting notions of masculinity, promoted by local and foreign institutions. Mission societies dominated the field of formal education, using schools as sites to shape boys into a certain kind of Christian men. Miescher explores recollections about education by a group of male teachers, trained in Presbyterian institutions during the 1920s and 1930s. He argues that teachers selectively engaged with masculine ideals promoted by their Presbyterian education and those dominant in their hometown societies. These teachers did not perceive some of these notions as hegemonic and others as subordinate. Rather, they created their own synthesis of different cultural practices that were determined by specific contexts. Arranging their lives around contested expectations about their responsibilities and obligations and pragmatic assessments of costs and benefits, these teachers engaged with and complicated ideas about gender, authority, seniority, and Christian education, while redefining themselves as men. Through his careful attention to the ways his subjects understood and articulated their own positions as men, Miescher pushes the study of African gender into interaction with psychology, oral history, and historical memory.

Shear's analysis of the contradictory political and subjective positions held by black South African policemen is situated in roughly the same time period as Miescher's study. But while Presbyterian teachers in the Gold Coast could exercise considerable agency in mediating among masculine ideals, official influence was heavier in South Africa. Shear argues that African policemen represented a key contradiction of the segregationist state: its reliance on African intermediaries to enforce a system that reserved power and resources for whites. This political reality was deeply intertwined with masculinity, as administrators' ambivalence about the role and power of African policemen resulted in measures relating to training, promotions, operating procedures, restrictions on firearms, and uniforms that "effectively emasculated black policemen institutionally and socially." Such provisions ultimately weakened the state's interventionist capacities in African communities, contributed to these intermediaries' contradictory consciousness, and shaped relationships between African policemen and the people they patrolled. Urban residents, consistently subject to night-time police raids and other harassment, characterized "native" constables as "dogs of persons" who were "selling their manhood in working for the Police." Shear suggests that this type of taunt, in conjunction with institutional denigration of their adult masculinity, may have fed into the aggressive violence for which South African police were well known. His essay links the political contradictions of a racialized colonial order with gender in several overlapping ways, focusing on the gendered manifestations of official political anxieties, the intersections of police masculinity with other social categories within African communities, and the potential effects of gendered concerns on relationships between policemen and the black public.

Throughout sub-Saharan Africa, agents, like missionaries and labor recruiters, were important catalysts for transforming men's gendered relationships and identities in the early colonial period. But state officials rarely chose to expend funds and jeopardize relations with African elders, the foundation of indirect rule, by working directly to change households.[15] By the 1940s and 1950s, however, colonial states became more aggressively engaged in social engineering as part of imperial plans to develop African economies and quell unrest.[16] As Frederick Cooper (1996) has detailed, a decisive component of the postwar initiatives was a new attempt to create a stable workforce in certain urban industries. In his contribution to this volume, Cooper lays out in one place a concept that weaves through his extraordinary (and massive) book: that the new labor forces of postwar Africa were particularly gendered. Focusing on colonial discourse about work and reproduction, Cooper argues that European officials conceived of their African labor policies in masculine terms. The majority of workers who received wages in 1945 were male, and as officials thought about work in the ensuing years, they tended to define ever more explicitly the kinds of things that men did as "work" and the kinds of things that women did as something else. Sometimes this was called "customary labor," and—as in the French Code du Travail of 1952—defined as beyond regulators' area of concern. But what worried officials the most was women's role in the reproduction of a male labor force. Drawing on British and French examples, Cooper illustrates the stress on the cultural construction of the proper worker in the early postwar years. He examines one of the most explicit cases of official coding of gender in reproducing a working class, the French program of family allowances implemented in 1956. His focus on official thinking about labor and masculinity suggests some of the ways in which metropolitan gender ideologies shaped the capitalist division of labor and the reproduction of labor power in Africa. It also raises questions of how administrative mandates—saturated with gendered assumptions—were received and transformed by the people who were their objects.

Some historians have begun to answer such questions. White's (1990b) pioneering treatment of prostitution in Nairobi explored the ways in which entrepreneurial women responded to "industrial men's" needs for housing and other aspects of social reproduction. Timothy Scarnecchia's (1994) research on colonial Harare suggests that their access to "family housing" allowed stabilized male workers to exert power over wives and relatives. Because those women and family members were not officially designated as "workers," they were effectively deprived of access to jobs and housing in the city.[17] Lindsay's Nigerian case (this volume) is not so stark, but nonetheless emphasizes the ways in which access to wage labor shaped men's relationships with others and their gendered identities. Drawing on a study of railway workers in southwestern Nigeria from the late 1930s to the mid-1960s, she argues that steady paychecks, as well as the demands of working for the railway, helped to transform arrangements within workers' households, causing men to take on increasing proportions of family expenses as well as greater self-conceptions as breadwinners. Railway men's wives also supported the construction of the male provider image because it suited their own financial strategies. Lindsay examines a particular debate between Nigerian trade unionists, led by railway workers, and the colonial administration. In their discussion of family allowances and family wages, both sides described workers as domestic providers. This overlapping discourse pointed to the development of new kinds of masculine self-conceptions among Nigerian wage workers, in relation to both their wives and their employers.

Brown's essay tells an analogous story, which resonates with Shear's treatment of South African policemen. In their construction of the "African worker," she points out, colonial officials and employers feminized and infantalized African men within the racialized political structure of colonialism. Brown uses a case study of mine workers in the Enugu Government Colliery, southeastern Nigeria, to argue that historians of Africa need to pay more attention to how labor affected African workers' construction of masculinity and how this informed their decisions to engage in individual and collective action. Unlike most historians of West Africa, Brown foregrounds race as a crucial factor in the colonial encounter. She argues that gender was constantly created and re-created both through the work experience, where African men had their most intimate contact with a racialized European masculine power, and in the roles that these men were able to assume because of their work (and pay) in the broader society. By focusing on the period from 1930 to 1945, a time of intensified state intervention in African family life as well as war-era mobilization, Brown's essay shows how men drew strength from their positions in home communities to challenge emasculating treatment in the workplace and were empowered by the specialized nature of their work. These men resolved the conflict between their degrading work experience and the masculinization of coal mining as a skill by cultivating a moral code in which notions of "justice," entitlement, democracy, and the social responsibilities of the state played a prominent role.

The contributions by Brown and Lindsay chart the ways in which miners and railway men interpreted and acted upon the changing imperatives and opportunities of industrial work and point to the limits of the colonial state and employers in promoting hegemonic masculinities.[18] They and other contributors (see Shear) complicate the Fanonesque assertion that colonialism entailed the subjective emasculation of colonized men (Fanon 1967). While this may have been part of the story, men's (and women's) identities could be multiple and situational. The coexistence of competing dominant masculinities meant that men could pursue distinct but interrelated strategies for being a "big man," even under the constraints of colonialism.

Gendered Nationalisms

But if colonialism was at times perceived as an assault on African masculinity, and certainly had gendered implications, then what were the gendered expectations and aspirations of male nationalists? To what extent were nationalist movements about remaking gender and masculinity? More and more evidence is emerging of women's importance in African resistance to colonial rule and their participation in nationalist movements. Well known is the Aba Women's War of 1929, in which women launched a revolt in southeastern Nigeria in response to rumors about the inclusion of women in colonial taxation, among other grievances.[19] Recent studies have highlighted women's importance in the nationalist struggles of Ghana (Manuh 1993), Tanzania (Geiger 1997), Kenya (Presley 1992), Mozambique (Urdang 1989), and Zimbabwe (Staunton 1990). Ellen Kuzwayo's autobiography (1985) provides a vivid account of women's leadership in the South African anti-apartheid struggle. Yet in all of these cases, men dominated the political and military organizations, and indeed they seemed to view women as auxiliaries to the "real" fighters. Ingrid Sinclair's (1996) controversial film *Flame,* focusing on two fighters in the anticolonial struggle of Zimbabwe, dramatizes the difficulties women faced in the guerrilla movement and following liberation. Susan Geiger (1997) suggests, too, that in Tanzania women's participation in nationalist activities did not provide them with significant entrée into political decision-making after independence.

African nationalist projects seem to have been largely gendered as male, in spite of women's participation, but only a few scholars so far have examined male anticolonial activities in terms of gender (Lindsay 1999; Scarnecchia 1996; Epprecht 1995). Based on memoirs of men who participated in or were jailed for the Mau Mau rebellion of the 1950s, White's chapter foregrounds constructions and reconstructions of masculinity in Kenyan nationalism and its repression. White reports that in Mau Mau autobiographies men wrote about being men—about defining gender, about courtship, about whose task it was to cook, and fetch water. Men wrote about being husbands, lovers, and fathers—gendered expectations that were an integral part of their political struggles. These men were not the only people in central Kenya concerned with the conduct of African masculinity, since colonialists, as Cooper's essay argues, had been obsessed with the needs of working men for years. Long before Mau Mau, colonialists had put men to work within particularly gendered milieux. Post–World War II officials designed policies to make sure that Africans with "respectable" employment had family lives, with appropriate housing, and others did not. Similar divisions existed among the Mau Mau forest fighters: the educated men wanted companionate marriages, and the illiterate ones, the Kenya Riigi, banned rank and conjugal relationships. In government detention camps, however, "rehabilitation" involved the consolidation of identities into one officially sanctioned type of masculinity. There men, as well as women, were reconstructed through doing domestic work, guided by a British vision of calm and productive African families. Thus men on both sides understood Kenyan politics to be partly driven by ideas about male gender and domesticity. A longer version of this article was originally published over ten years ago, but we include the revised essay here because it so provocatively implicates gender in the racial politics of the Mau Mau era and because it remains a seminal example of how attention to masculinity can uncover previously unperceived layers of stories that historians thought they knew.

Obeng's contribution examines Asante (modern Ghana) nationalist struggles as occasions for women and junior men to assume political leadership, usually the preserve of senior men. Obeng contrasts the leadership of Yaa

Asantewaa, the queen mother of Edweso, during the 1900 Asante uprising against British colonial rule with the National Liberation Movement between 1954 and 1957, in which "youngmen" led the opposition to Nkrumah's Convention People's Party. These two historical moments illuminate the reconfigurations and representations of masculinities as negotiated and contested terrain within Asante understandings of cultural and political leadership. In Asante, political and military leadership were intertwined with ideologies of senior masculinity, making it unusual for women or junior men to wield widespread authority. Both Yaa Asantewaa, a woman, and youngmen, the *nkwankwaa,* tried to take on the attributes of dominant senior masculinity—including bravery, royalty, and religious authority—to rally a unified military or electoral effort. Obeng argues that Yaa Asantewaa was successful because she was a senior person herself, because she was of a royal lineage, and because she was connected with religious power. The Asante youngmen of the 1950s, however, struggled to gain the authority of senior masculinity. Even though they were biologically men, they were social juniors, and their attempts to gain royal and religious legitimacy were insufficient to give them widespread political support. Obeng's essay shows that the production and reproduction of gender in Asante related not only to an individual's biology but also to his or her imbrication in a pool of sociocultural attributes, such as lineage, status, religion, economics, and age, which became particularly salient in moments of crisis and nationalist activism.

Masculinity and Modernity

Understanding nation-building as an enterprise saturated with gender imagery suggests an examination of the gendered implications of postcolonial developments, including economic decline, political crisis, and "globalization." How have the political and economic transformations of the late colonial and postcolonial periods created new, dominant and subordinate models for male aspirations and behavior? Are we witnessing another crisis of African masculinity, as Ayi Kwei Armah suggested as early as 1968 in his novel *The Beautyful Ones Are Not Yet Born*? Armah's hero, "the man," was profoundly alienated from society as well as his family because of his refusal to take part in Ghana's culture of corruption. His wife taunted him for his inability to provide, and indeed his uselessness at home paralleled the impotence of political reformers.

On the other hand, African "big men" have honed the attributes and perquisites of dominant masculinity in much of postcolonial Africa. Popular culture in particular provides what has now become almost a stereotype, at least for West and Central Africa: the wealthy and powerful patriarch, with business and government networks in the city and perhaps some rural links to "his people" as well, perhaps only one wife but certainly eyes for many, dispensing gifts and largesse in exchange for particular services or general deference.[20] A common comic trope is to portray such a man as impotent or unable to control his wife or wives. Yet it seems that the humor is based on the very real conflation of wealth, power, and a certain form of masculinity dominant among the wealthy elites of postcolonial Africa. In the novel *Xala*, Ousmane Sembène narrates how El Hadji Abdu Kader fails to consummate the marriage to his third wife. Following this personal fiasco, the powerful El Hadji loses not only the function of his manhood, but also his friends, two of his wives, his wealth, and finally his reputation and status among Dakar's *nouveaux riches*. The "penis snatchers" of West Africa, who have surfaced in many recent news stories, also recognize this connection between political and economic power and male sexuality.[21]

David William Cohen and Atieno Odhiambo's (1992) portrayal of the life and legacy of S.M. Otieno suggests another "new" type of masculinity: what we might call the "modern" or "cosmopolitan" African man. Otieno was a western-educated lawyer, quoter of Shakespeare, maker of a cross-ethnic, companionate marriage. Certainly a "big man" in the sense of commanding power and wealth in postcolonial Kenya, Otieno nevertheless asserted a break with older models of patriarchy by choosing, as his wife claimed, to be buried away from his ancestral homeland and out of the control of his Luo patrilineage. That the courts ultimately did not allow this to happen underscores the contested nature of this type of identity. As in earlier times, elders continued to evoke Luo "customary law" to preserve their prerogatives in the face of challenges by men (and women) deriving their wealth and position from the modern state or the capitalist economy.

Hodgson's essay (this volume) shows that ideas about "modern" men and their validity as men have not been limited to the postindependence period and have changed over time. Maasai in Tanzania have had a long history of engagement with the complex, overlapping cultural processes and material structures of "modernity." For Maasai men in particular, the encounter with modernity has been an uneven and deeply ambivalent process. What is it like, Hodgson wonders, to live in a world where a certain configuration of masculine attributes—being a nomad, a pastoralist, a warrior—persists for more than a hundred years in defining who you are to other people? How do men whose masculinity is shaped by such configurations experience and reconcile the contradictions that are produced? Finally, what happens when none of these pursuits are possible anymore, when the props that sustained men as "traditional" in a "modern" world collapse? To address these questions, Hodgson explores the historical articulation of "modernity" with the changing production of Maasai masculinities. She frames her analysis in terms of the shifting meanings and referents of "traditional" Maasai masculinity and *ormeek* masculinity. Although Maasai have multiple masculinities, she uses "traditional" masculinity to refer to the hegemonic masculinity nurtured and reinforced by colonial and postcolonial policies, based on pastoralism and warfare. *Ormeek*, in contrast, is a Maa word that emerged in the early colonial period as a derogatory label for "modern" (and somewhat effeminate) Maasai men and thus refers to a historically subordinate masculinity. As Hodgson shows, *ormeek* masculinity has become socially valued over the last few decades and in present circumstances challenges "traditional" masculinity as a normative model. Thus she calls attention to the changing relationship between political and economic transformations, and gender identities and norms. Her case study offers a counterpoint to the "modern" masculinity of someone like S.M. Otieno.

Like Hodgson, Cornwall is also concerned with men and their masculine identities in changing times. Based largely on ethnographic fieldwork, her chapter examines the reconfiguration of masculinity in Ado-Odo, a small town in southwestern Nigeria, over the past several generations and particularly during the recent period of economic hardship. While the conflation of "man" and "husband" seems to have been constant over time, life histories of different generations point to significant changes in expectations of men as husbands and of men's abilities to realize such expectations. Cornwall concurs with Lindsay and Brown that the 1940s and 1950s witnessed an increased emphasis on Nigerian men as financial providers in their families. But when women earned money as well, or when men's economic opportunities diminished, men became less able to control their wives than previously. By the 1990s, in the wake of structural adjustment programs, discourses on masculinity offered models that many of today's young men struggle to emulate. Caught between discursive domains that create variant images of masculinity, from responsible provider to insatiable lover, youths find that becoming a man is fraught with complications. Accused by wives of being "useless" and passed over by would-be girlfriends for lacking the economic potency to satisfy them, young men find themselves in a position of diminishing control. Cornwall's essay argues that the notion of "hegemonic masculinity" conceals more complex negotiations of masculinity within competing domains of discourse that offer distinctively different ways to be a man.

CONCLUSION

The above examples illustrate the centrality of a gender analysis to understanding historical and current issues on the African continent. Africanists, and not only those who study women, should remember the old North American feminist slogan, "The personal is political." For it is only by examining the varied motivations and subject positions of the actors—many of which stem from their lives as spouses, parents, sons and daughters, girlfriends and boyfriends— that we can tease apart the meanings of contemporary and historical events. Knowing that there is no "normative" African man or static relation of power

(Hodgson and McCurdy 2001: 16) helps us to understand what may otherwise seem contradictory or puzzling: why some men collaborated with colonial conquerors (to take an easy example) or why, when other jobs were available, Igbo coal miners or even Presbyterian teachers put up with insulting treatment from their employers. Why did (male) Nigerian trade unionists demand family allowances when they rarely supported wives and children? Why did Maasai men at first denigrate and then embrace western education and literacy? Why did ex-soldiers in Mali support a Muslim cleric who criticized men's treatment of women? In the broadest terms, the answers to all of these questions relate to the historical and contextual variability of men's gendered identities and the ways in which these identities interact with, and are structured through, relations of power in a given society. Attention to masculinity—indeed, to gender in its broadest sense—helps us understand the ways in which Africans in given contexts formed, or took for granted, certain kinds of alliances in certain circumstances. Conversely, in its interactions with age, seniority, race, class, politics, and religion, gender can also delineate points of social fissure, where potential alliances failed to take hold or broke down. How can we understand modern African nationalisms, for instance, without attention to the gender politics that both shaped and took inspiration from them?

Because gender is so closely related to the operation of power, studying masculinity (and femininity) reveals the strengths *and* weaknesses of colonialism in Africa. Administrators, missionaries, and employers were in some instances able to reach the most intimate spaces and practices of colonized men and women: dictating who would fetch water in Mau Mau rehabilitation camps, or sending policemen into sleeping South Africans' bedrooms, or offering opportunities for young men to challenge their fathers' authority. But there were limits to such colonial interventions. Presbyterian teachers may have been constrained in their public comportment, but in private many acted in ways their missionary employers would have decried. British authorities could install Ahebi Ugbabe as an Igbo chief, but they could not force the community to accept her appropriation of a male ritual. Zulu policemen could terrorize, but they could not contain the taunts about their masculinity. And, conversely, colonial racism denigrated African men, but it did not prevent assertions of powerful masculinity outside of its gaze.

This back-and-forth between the relative importance and insignificance of European regimes, whether political or cultural, undermines the idea of "hegemonic masculinity" so fashionable in western-oriented studies of gender. Scholars of masculinity outside of Africa should take from the contributors to this volume a healthy skepticism about ranking various forms of gender identities and norms, even as the multiplicity of masculinities is clear. Africa may be unique as a site of multiple, competing, and interacting ideas about gender—or it may not be. Comparative research, perhaps even with African themes at its center, would be welcome.

Moreover, a recognition of heterogeneous masculinities leads to funda-mental questions about societies and history. If one works to understand how and why particular gender norms become dominant, or are contested, such an exercise entails probing the very nature of social change. What kinds of polit-ical, economic, religious, occupational, or other transformations are linked to gender changes? What are the key pressure points? Furthermore, looking at how individual social actors or given social categories engage with multiple gender norms helps us to theorize personal agency. In any given context, what is the relationship between social structure and individual practices? When is gender flexible, and when is it not?

These essays firmly establish the importance of gender—male and female—to the social and political transformations of twentieth-century Africa, as well as to the historical experiences of African men and women. They bridge the gap between examinations of (generally ungendered) men and studies of gender by demonstrating how gender relations are produced, reproduced, and transformed through the discourse, practices, and subjectivities of men and women in inter-action with local and broader structures and processes. Gender relations are no marginal concern and definitely are not restricted to women. They have shaped and been shaped by men and women's involvement in the spread of wage labor, education, religious practices, resistance and nationalism, "development," and economic crisis. Gender—along with age, seniority, race, class, and status—is thus crucial to understanding the history of modern Africa, its women, and its men.

NOTES

1. This literature is growing and includes Tosh (1999), Dinges (1998), Brod and Kauf-man (1996), Kimmel (1987, 1996), Connell (1995), Bederman (1995), Cornwall and Lind-isfarne (1994a), Roper and Tosh (1991), Segal (1990), Hearn and Morgan (1990); but see Sinha (1995).

2. In 1990, Luise White organized the conference "Towards a Gendered History of Men in Africa" at the University of Minnesota. A colloquium, "Masculinities in Southern Africa," was held at the University of Natal, Durban, in 1997. Compare Morrell (1998, 2001) and the articles published in a special issue of the *Journal of Southern African Stud-ies* 24, 2 (1998). Helen Mugambi and Tuzyline Jita Allan are editing a collection of essays, *Contending Masculinities: Perspectives on Maleness in African Culture and Literature.*

3. For a similar argument about including the study of masculinity in another field, see Zalewski and Parpart (1998).

4. Sinha (1995), McClintock (1995), Dawson (1994), and Mangan and Walvin (1987).

5. There have also been "big women" (Akyeampong 2000).

6. For the continuities of the "big man" in precolonial and colonial Ghana, see McCaskie (1995) and Miescher (1997a); for southwestern Nigeria, see Barber (1981, 1991), Peel (1983), and Lindsay (1998).

7. For earlier formulations of this model, see Carrigan et al. (1985) and Connell (1987).

8. Ouzgane and Coleman (1998: para. 15) provide a useful summary of Connell's exe-gesis.

9. This distinction draws on Kühne (1996).

10. For a useful beginning, see Vaughan (1991, 1994).

11. Mann and Roberts (1991), as well as Chanock (1985), Moore (1986), Schmidt (1992), Miescher (1997b), Bravman (1998), and Allman and Tashjian (2000).

12. European conquerors justified their interventions in Africa through reference to slavery and slave trading, and abolition was often one of colonial governments' first initiatives (Miers and Roberts 1988). Although most slaves in Africa were women (Robertson and Klein 1983), abolition efforts focused on men. Gendered consequences of emancipation are only beginning to be explored. See Romero (1986), Wright (1993), Scully (1997), and Haenger (2000).

13. Compare Lovett (1989) and Schmidt (1992).

14. On domesticity, see Hansen (1989, 1992) and Hunt (1990, 1999); compare Comaroff and Comaroff (1997), Miescher (1997a), Scully (1997), and Lindsay (1998, 1999).

15. For the varying but generally restrained actions of early colonial states to change gender and household arrangements, see, inter alia, Chauncey (1981), Mann (1985), and Schmidt (1992).

16. Hunt (1988, 1999), White (1990b), Scarnecchia (1994), and Lindsay (forthcoming).

17. For colonial Zambia, see Chauncey (1981) and Parpart (1988, 1994).

18. Compare Moore and Vaughan (1994) on the attempt to promote the notion of a "progressive farmer" as part of a colonial development discourse on agricultural masculinity in 1950s Zambia.

19. Ifeka-Moller (1975), van Allen (1976), and Mba (1982).

20. For Nigeria, compare Waterman (1990) on the ways in which Nigerian *juju* music reflected and reproduced notions about "big men," as well as Barber (1981, 1991) and C. Achebe (1966).

21. Compare Jean-Pierre Bekolo's film, *Quartier Mozart* (1992).

REFERENCES

Achebe, Chinua. 1959. *Things Fall Apart*. New York: Anchor Books.

———. 1966. *A Man of the People*. London: Heinemann.

Achebe, Nwando. 2000. "Farmers, Traders, Warriors and Kings: Female Power and Authority in Northern Igboland, 1900–1960." Ph.D. dissertation, UCLA.

Achmat, Zackie. 1993. "'Apostles of Civilised Vice': 'Immoral Practices' and 'Unnatural Vice' in South African Prisons and Compounds, 1890–1920." *Social Dynamics* 19, 2: 92–110.

Akyeampong, Emmanuel K. 2000. "'Wo pe tam won pe ba' ('You like cloth but you don't want children'): Urbanization, Individualism and Gender Relations in Colonial Ghana, c. 1900–39." In *Africa's Urban Past*, D. M. Anderson and R. Rathbone, eds. Oxford: James Currey.

Akyeampong, Emmanuel K. and Pashington Obeng. 1995. "Spirituality, Gender and Power in Asante History." *International Journal of African Historical Studies* 28, 3: 481–508.

Allman, Jean and Victoria Tashjian. 2000. *"I Will Not Eat Stone": A Women's History of Colonial Asante*. Portsmouth, NH: Heinemann.

Aluko, T. M. 1967 [1959]. *One Man, One Wife*. London: Heinemann.

Amadiume, Ifi. 1987. *Male Daughters, Female Husbands: Gender and Sex in an African Society*. London: Zed Books.

Armah, Ayi Kwei. 1968. *The Beautyful Ones Are Not Yet Born*. Boston: Houghton Mifflin.

Barber, Karin. 1981. "How God Makes Man in West Africa." *Africa* 51: 724–45.

———. 1991. *I Could Speak Until Tomorrow: Oriki, Women and the Past in a Yoruba Town*. Washington, DC: Smithsonian Institution Press.

Bederman, Gail. 1995. *Manliness and Civilization: A Cultural History of Gender and Race in the United States, 1880–1917*. Chicago: University of Chicago Press.

Beinart, William. 1982. *The Political Economy of Pondoland, 1860–1930*. Cambridge: Cambridge University Press.

Bekolo, Jean-Pierre. 1992. *Quartier Mozart* (film, Cameroon, distributed by California Newsreel).

Berry, Sara. 1985. *Fathers Work for Their Sons: Accumulation, Mobility and Class Formation in an Extended Yoruba Community*. Berkeley and Los Angeles: University of California Press.

Bozzoli, Belinda. 1983. "Marxism, Feminism and South African Studies." *Journal of Southern African Studies* 9, 2: 139–71.

Bravman, Bill. 1998. *Making Ethnic Ways: Communities and Their Transformations in Taita, Kenya, 1800–1950*. Portsmouth, NH: Heinemann.

Breckenridge, Keith. 1990. "Migrancy, Crime and Faction Fighting: the Role of the Isitshozi in the Development of Ethnic Organisations in the Compounds." *Journal of Southern African Studies* 16, 1: 55–78.

Brod, Harry and Michael Kaufman. 1996. *Theorizing Masculinities*. Thousand Oaks, CA: Sage.

Butler, Judith. 1990. *Gender Trouble: Feminism and the Subversion of Identity*. New York and London: Routledge.

———. 1993. *Bodies that Matter: On the Discursive Limits of "Sex."* New York and London: Routledge.

Carrigan, Tim, R. W. Connell, and John Lee. 1985. "Toward a New Sociology of Masculinity." *Theory and Society* 14: 551–604.

Chanock, Martin. 1985. *Law, Custom and Social Order: The Colonial Experience in Malawi and Zambia*. Cambridge: Cambridge University Press.

Chauncey, George, Jr. 1981. "The Locus of Reproduction: Women's Labour in the Zambian Copperbelt, 1927–1953." *Journal of Southern African Studies* 7, 2: 135–64.

Cohen, David William and E.S. Atieno Odhiambo. 1992. *Burying SM: The Politics of Knowledge and the Sociology of Power in Africa*. Portsmouth, NH: Heinemann.

Comaroff, John L. and Jean Comaroff. 1997. *Of Revelation and Revolution: The Dialectics of Modernity on a South African Frontier*, Vol. 2. Chicago: University of Chicago Press.

Connell, R. W. 1987. *Gender & Power: Society, the Person and Sexual Politics*. Stanford, CA: Stanford University Press.

———. 1995. *Masculinities*. Berkeley and Los Angeles: University of California.

Cooper, Frederick. 1996. *Decolonization and African Society: The Labor Question in French and British Africa*. Cambridge: Cambridge University Press.

Cooper, Frederick and Ann Laura Stoler, eds. 1997. *Tensions of Empire: Colonial Cultures in a Bourgeois World*. Berkeley and Los Angeles: University of California Press.

Cornwall, Andrea and Nancy Lindisfarne, eds. 1994a. *Dislocating Masculinity: Comparative Ethnographies*. London and New York: Routledge.

———. 1994b. "Dislocating Masculinity: Gender, Power and Anthropology." In *Dislocating Masculinity: Comparative Ethnographies*, A. Cornwall and N. Lindisfarne, eds. London and New York: Routledge.

Dangarembga, Tsitsi. 1988. *Nervous Conditions*. Seattle, WA: Seal Press.

Dawson, Graham 1994. *Soldier Heroes: British Adventure, Empire and the Imagining of Masculinities*. New York and London: Routledge.

Dinges, Martin, ed. 1998. *Hausväter, Priester, Kastraten: Zur Konstruktion von Männlichkeit in Spättmittelalter und Frühen Neuzeit*. Göttingen: Vandenhoeck & Ruprecht.

Emecheta, Buchi. 1979. *The Joys of Motherhood*. New York: G. Braziller.

Epprecht, Marc. 1995. "Women's 'Conservatism' and the Politics of Gender in Late Colonial Lesotho." *Journal of African History* 36: 29–56.

———. 1998a. "'Good God Almighty, What's This!': Homosexual 'Crime' in Early Colonial Zimbabwe." In *Boy-Wives and Female Husbands: Studies of African Homosexualities*, S.O. Murray and W. Roscoe, eds. New York: St. Martin's Press.

———. 1998b. "The Unsaying of Indigenous Homosexualities in Zimbabwe: Mapping a Blindspot in an African Masculinity." *Journal of Southern African Studies* 24, 4: 631–51.

Fanon, Frantz. 1967 [1952]. *Black Skin, White Masks*, Charles Lam Markmann, trans. New York: Grove Press.

Gaudio, Rudi P. 1998. "Male Lesbians and Other Queer Notions in Hausa." In *Boy-Wives and Female Husbands: Studies of African Homosexualities*, S.O. Murray and W. Roscoe, eds. New York: St. Martin's Press.

Geiger, Susan. 1997. *TANU Women: Gender and Culture in the Making of Tanganyikan Nationalism, 1955–1965*. Portsmouth, NH: Heinemann.

Gevisser, Mark and Edwin Cameron, eds. 1994. *Defiant Desire: Gay and Lesbian Lives in South Africa*. Johannesburg: Ravan Press.

Glassman, Jonathan. 1995. *Feasts and Riot: Revelry, Rebellion, and Popular Consciousness on the Swahili Coast, 1856–1888*. Portsmouth, NH: Heinemann.

Greene, Sandra E. 1996. *Gender, Ethnicity, and Social Change on the Upper Slave Coast: A History of the Anlo-Ewe*. Portsmouth, NH: Heinemann.

Grosz, Elizabeth. 1990. "Inscriptions and Body-Maps: Representations and the Corporal." In *Feminine, Masculine and Representation*, T. Threadgold and A. Cranny-Francis, eds. London: Allen & Unwin.

Haenger, Peter. 2000 [1997]. *Slaves and Slave Holders on the Gold Coast: Towards an Understanding of Social Bondage in West Africa*, Christina Handford, trans. Basel: P. Schlettwein Publishing.

Halberstam, Judith. 1998. *Female Masculinity*. Durham, NC: Duke University Press.

Hansen, Karen Tranberg. 1989. *Distant Companions: Servants and Employers in Zambia, 1900–1985*. Ithaca, NY: Connell University Press.

———, ed. 1992. *African Encounters with Domesticity*. New Brunswick, NJ: Rutgers University Press.

Harries, Patrick. 1990. "Symbols and Sexuality: Culture and Identity on the Early Witwatersrand Gold Mines." *Gender and History* 2, 3: 318–36.

Hearn, Jeff and David Morgan, eds. 1990. *Men, Masculinities & Social Theory*. London: Unwin Hyman.

Hodgson, Dorothy L. 1999. "'Once Intrepid Warriors': Modernity and the Production of Maasai Masculinities." *Ethnology* 38, 2: 121–50.

Hodgson, Dorothy L. and Sheryl McCurdy, eds. 2001. *"Wicked" Women and the Reconfiguration of Gender in Africa*. Portsmouth, NH: Heinemann.

Hunt, Nancy Rose. 1988. "'Le Bebe en Brousse': European Women, African Birth Spacing and Colonial Intervention in Breast Feeding in the Belgian Congo." *International Journal of African Historical Studies* 21: 401–32.

———. 1990. "Domesticity and Colonialism in Belgian Africa: Usumbura's *Foyer Social*, 1946–60." *Signs* 15, 3: 447–74.

———. 1999. *A Colonial Lexicon: Of Birth Ritual, Medicalization, and Mobility in the Congo*. Durham and London: Duke University Press.

Ifeka-Moller, Caroline. 1975. "Female Militancy and Colonial Revolt: The Women's War of 1929, Eastern Nigeria." In *Perceiving Women*, S. Ardener, ed. London: Malaby Press.

Iliffe, John. 1995. *Africans: The History of a Continent*. Cambridge: Cambridge University Press.

Kimmel, Michael S., ed. 1987. *Changing Men: New Directions in Research on Men and Masculinity*. Beverly Hills, CA: Sage.

———. 1996. *Manhood in America: A Cultural History*. New York: Free Press.

Kühne, Thomas. 1996. "Männergeschichte als Geschlechtergeschichte." In *Männergeschichte, Geschlechtergeschichte: Männlichkeit im Wandel der Moderne*, T. Kühne, ed. Frankfurt/Main and New York: Campus Verlag.

Kuzwayo, Ellen. 1985. *Call Me Woman*. San Francisco: Women's Press.

Lindsay, Lisa A. 1998. "'No Need . . . to Think of Home'? Masculinity and Domestic Life on the Nigerian Railway, c. 1940–61." *Journal of African History* 39, 3: 439–66.

———. 1999. "Domesticity and Difference: Male Breadwinners, Working Women and Colonial Citizenship in the 1945 Nigerian General Strike." *American Historical Review* 104, 3: 783–812.

———. Forthcoming. *Working with Gender: Wage Labor and Social Change in Southwestern Nigeria*. Portsmouth, NH: Heinemann.

Lonsdale, John and Bruce Berman. 1979. "Coping with the Contradictions: The Development of the Colonial State in Kenya, 1895–1914." *Journal of African History* 20, 4: 487–506.

Lovett, Margo. 1989. "Gender Relations, Class Formation, and the Colonial State in Africa." In *Women and the State in Africa*, J.L. Parpart and K.A. Staudt, eds. Boulder, CO: Lynne Rienner.

Mandala, Elias C. 1990. *Work and Control in a Peasant Economy: A History of the Lower Tchiri Valley in Malawi, 1859–1960*. Madison, WI: University of Wisconsin Press.

Mangan, James A. and James Walvin, eds. 1987. *Manliness and Morality: Middle-Class Masculinity in Britain and America, 1800–1940*. Manchester: Manchester University Press.

Mann, Kristin. 1985. *Marrying Well: Marriage, Status and Social Change among the Educated Elite in Colonial Lagos*. Cambridge: Cambridge University Press.

Mann, Kristin and Richard Roberts, eds. 1991. *Law in Colonial Africa*. Portsmouth, N.H.: Heinemann.

Manuh, Takyiwaa. 1993. "Women and their Organizations during the Convention Peoples' Party Period." In *The Life and Work of Kwame Nkrumah*, K. Arhin, ed. Trenton, NJ: Africa World Press.

Martin, Susan M. 1988. *Palm Oil and Protest: An Economic History of the Ngwa Region, South-Eastern Nigeria, 1800–1980*. Cambridge: Cambridge University Press.

Matory, J. Lorand. 1994. *Sex and the Empire That Is No More: Gender and the Politics of Metaphor in Oyo Yoruba Religion*. Minneapolis: University of Minnesota Press.

Mba, Nina Emma. 1982. *Nigerian Women Mobilized: Women's Political Activity in Southern Nigeria, 1900–1965*. Berkeley: Institute of International Studies.

McCaskie, T. C. 1995. *State and Society in Pre-Colonial Asante*. Cambridge: Cambridge University Press.

McClintock, Anne. 1995. *Imperial Leather: Race, Gender and Sexuality in the Colonial Context*. New York and London: Routledge.

Miers, Suzanne and Richard Roberts, eds. 1988. *The End of Slavery in Africa*. Madison, WI: University of Wisconsin Press.

Miescher, Stephan F. 1997a. "Becoming a Man in Kwawu: Gender, Law, Personhood, and the Construction of Masculinities in Colonial Ghana, 1875–1957." Ph.D. dissertation, Northwestern University.

———. 1997b. "Of Documents and Litigants: Disputes on Inheritance in Abetifi—a Town of Colonial Ghana." *Journal of Legal Pluralism* 39: 81–119.

Miller, Joseph C. 1988. *Way of Death: Merchant Capitalism and the Angolan Slave Trade, 1730–1830*. Madison, WI: University of Wisconsin Press.

Moodie, T. Dunbar, with Vivienne Ndatshe and British Sibuyi. 1988. "Migrancy and Male Sexuality in the South African Gold Mines." *Journal of Southern African Studies* 14, 1: 228–56.

Moodie, T. Dunbar, with Vivienne Ndatshe. 1994. *Going for Gold: Men, Mines and Migration*. Berkeley and Los Angeles: University of California.

Moore, Henrietta L. and Megan Vaughan. 1994. *Cutting Down Trees: Gender, Nutrition, and Agricultural Change in the Northern Province of Zambia, 1890–1990*. Portsmouth, NH: Heinemann.

Moore, Sally Falk. 1986. *Social Facts and Fabrications: "Customary" Law on Kilimanjaro, 1880–1960*. Cambridge: Cambridge University Press.

Morrell, Robert. 1998. "Of Boys and Men: Masculinity and Gender in Southern African Studies." *Journal of Southern African Studies* 24, 4: 605–30.

———, ed. 2001. *Changing Masculinities in a Changing Society*. London: Zed.

Mosse, George L. 1996. *The Image of Man: The Creation of Modern Masculinity*. New York: Oxford University Press.

Murray, Stephen O. and Will Roscoe, eds. 1998. *Boy-Wives and Female Husbands: Studies of African Homosexualities*. New York: St. Martin's Press.

Oboler, Regina Smith. 1980. "Is the Female Husband a Man? Woman/Woman Marriage Among the Nandi of Kenya." *Ethnology* 19, 1:69–88.

O'Brien, Denis. 1977. "Female Husbands in Southern Bantu Societies." In *Sexual Stratification: A Cross-Cultural View*, A. Schlegel, ed. New York: Columbia University Press.

Ogbomo, Onaiwu W. 1997. *When Men and Women Mattered: The History of Gender Relations among the Owan of Nigeria*. Rochester, NY: University of Rochester Press.

Ouzgane, Lahoucine and Daniel Coleman. 1998. "Postcolonial Masculinities: Introduction." *Jouvert* (electronic journal) 2, 1.

Oyěwùmí, Oyèrónké. 1997. *The Invention of Women: Making an African Sense of Western Gender Discourses*. Minneapolis: University of Minnesota Press.

Parpart, Jane. 1988. "Sexuality and Power on the Zambian Copperbelt, 1926–1964." In *Patriarchy and Class*, S. Stichter and J. Parpart, eds. Boulder, CO: Westview Press.

———. 1994. "'Where is Your Mother?' Gender Urban, Marriage, and Colonial Discourse on the Zambian Copperbelt, 1924–45." *International Journal of African Historical Studies* 27, 2: 241–71.

Peel, J.D.Y. 1983. *Ijeshas and Nigerians: The Incorporation of a Yoruba Kingdom*. Cambridge: Cambridge University Press.

Presley, Cora Ann. 1992. *Kikuyu Women, the Mau Mau Rebellion, and Social Change in Kenya*. Boulder, CO: Westview Press.

Robertson, Claire and Martin A. Klein, eds. 1983. *Women and Slavery in Africa*. Madison, WI: University of Wisconsin Press (reprint 1997, Heinemann).

Romero, Patricia W. 1986. "'Where Have All the Slaves Gone?' Emancipation and Post-Emancipation in Lamu, Kenya." *Journal of African History* 27: 497–512.

Roper, Michael and John Tosh, eds. 1991. *Manful Assertions: Masculinities in Britain Since 1800*. London and New York: Routledge.

Scarnecchia, Timothy. 1994. "The Politics of Gender and Class in the Creation of African Communities, Salisbury, Rhodesia, 1937–1957." Ph.D. dissertation, University of Michigan.

———. 1996. "Poor Women and Nationalist Politics: Alliance and Fissures in the Formation of a Nationalist Political Movement in Salisbury, Rhodesia, 1950–6." *Journal of African History* 37, 2: 283–310.

Schmidt, Elizabeth. 1992. *Peasants, Traders, and Wives: Shona Women in the History of Zimbabwe*. Portsmouth, NH: Heinemann.

Scully, Pamela. 1997. *Liberating the Family? Gender and British Slave Emancipation in the Rural Western Cape, South Africa, 1823–1853*. Portsmouth, NH: Heinemann.

Segal, Lynne. 1990. *Slow Motion: Changing Masculinities, Changing Men*. New Brunswick, NJ: Rutgers University Press.

Sembène, Ousmane. 1976 [1973]. *Xala*, Clive Wake, trans. Westport, CT: Lawrence Hill.

Sinclair, Ingrid. 1996. *Flame* (film, Zimbabwe, distributed by California Newsreel).

Sinha, Mrinalini. 1995. *Colonial Masculinity: The "Manly Englishman" and the "Effeminate Bengali" in the Late Nineteenth Century*. Manchester: Manchester University Press.

Staunton, Irene. 1990. *Mothers of the Revolution: The War Experiences of Thirty Zimbabwean Women*. Bloomington, IN: Indiana University Press.

Stoler, Ann Laura. 1995. *Race and the Education of Desire: Foucault's History of Sexuality and the Colonial Order of Things*. Durham and London: Duke University Press.

Summers, Carol. 1999. "Mission Boys, Civilized Men, and Marriage: Educated African Men in the Missions of Southern Rhodesia, 1920–1945." *Journal of Religious History* 23, 1: 75–91.

Tosh, John. 1999. *A Man's Place: Masculinity and the Middle-Class Home in Victorian England*. New Haven and London: Yale University Press.

Urdang, Stephanie. 1989. *And Still They Dance: Women, War, and the Struggle for Change in Mozambique*. New York: Monthly Review Press.

van Allen, Judith. 1976. "'Aba Riots' or 'Women's War': Ideology, Stratification and the Invisibility of Women." In *Women in Africa: Studies in Social and Economic Change*, N. Hafkin and E. Bay, eds. Stanford, CA: Stanford University Press.

van Onselen, Charles. 1976. *Chibaro: African Mine Labor in Southern Rhodesia, 1900–1933*. London: Pluto Press.

———. 1984. *The Small Matter of a Horse: The Life of "Nongoloza" Mathebula, 1867–1948*. Johannesburg: Ravan Press.

Vaughan, Megan. 1991. *Curing Their Ills: Colonial Power and African Illness*. Stanford, CA: Stanford University Press.

———. 1994. "Colonial Discourse Theory and African History, or Has Postmodernism Passed Us By?" *Social Dynamics* 20, 2: 1–23.

Waterman, Christopher. 1990. *Juju: A Social History and Ethnography of an African Popular Music*. Chicago: University of Chicago Press.

White, Luise. 1990a. "Separating the Men from the Boys: Constructions of Gender, Sexuality, and Terrorism in Central Kenya, 1939–1959." *International Journal of African Historical Studies* 23, 1.

———. 1990b. *The Comforts of Home: Prostitution in Colonial Nairobi*. Chicago: University of Chicago Press.

Wright, Marcia. 1993. *Strategies of Slaves and Women: Life Histories from East/Central Africa*. New York: Lynne Barber.

Zalewski, Marysia and Jane Parpart, eds. 1998. *The "Man" Question in International Relations*. Boulder, CO: Westview Press.

PART I

CHALLENGING SENIOR MASCULINITY

2

FORSAKING THEIR FATHERS? COLONIALISM, CHRISTIANITY, AND COMING OF AGE IN OVAMBOLAND, NORTHERN NAMIBIA

Meredith McKittrick

"BOYS ARE THEIR FATHERS' FRIEND"

This chapter examines changes in ideas and practices of masculinity in the Ovambo societies of present-day northern Namibia during the nineteenth and early twentieth centuries. It argues that while the composition of elites in Ovambo societies and the characteristics of men who epitomized dominant masculinity changed during this time, the importance of fathers to reproducing and defining "men" remained strikingly consistent and came under sustained assault only after colonial conquest. Despite the fact that colonial officials here—as elsewhere—relied on alliances with older African men to uphold their rule, those same older men found their position challenged by colonial ethnography, the policies grounded in such ethnography, and the extension of men's wage labor careers into middle age. The existence of matrilineal inheritance of property and matrilineal succession to kingship in this region led colonial ethnographers and, later, scholars to downplay the importance of fatherhood in Ovambo societies. Still, fathers were profoundly important, particularly to junior men. Fathers reproduced dominant masculinity by ushering young men into full male adulthood through the redistribution of livestock resources. At one level, therefore, male power resided in fathers, both social and biological, who protected and nurtured junior men. This was a dominant masculinity structured along the lines of generation; theoretically, what Mandala has called "social age" (Mandala 1990: 154) paralleled biological age, and senior male status was thus open to all men as they grew older.

But there was considerable differentiation even among "fathers" of similar ages. While masculinity, the biological category of "men," and male power converged at the level of ideology, this correlation was imperfect in practice. In the mid-nineteenth century, the qualities of ideal men were tested and refined through a male initiation ceremony open mostly to the sons of elites; participation in this ceremony granted men control over ritual practices such as rain-making regardless of age and gave them an advantage in accumulating resources in people and cattle as they grew older. Idealized conceptions of masculinity therefore justified and normalized not only inequalities between men and women, but also stratification among men.

Scholars have noted the potential for multiple masculinities, even hegemonic masculinities, to coexist (Cornwall and Lindisfarne 1994: 20). Within Ovambo societies, the coexistence of a dominant masculinity based on fatherhood and one based on elite status was of long duration, not simply the product of a moment of crisis. The presence of multiple masculinities produced tensions but did not demand an immediate resolution in favor of one or the other. Instead, these tensions produced an ongoing dynamism in male gender identities that changed understandings of masculinity and yet outlasted those changes. Political centralization, Christianity, migrant labor, and colonial rule all allowed young men new scope to redefine prevailing notions of masculinity, reduced junior men's dependence on fathers in some respects, and yet ultimately reinforced the dominance of an elite group of men over other men and all women. And fathers continued to play a profoundly important role in the lives of young men, largely because their dominance was framed in an ideology of affection and deference that obscured the economic power men continued to wield over their sons. Such personal relations were understood as outside institutions of legal kinship and politics which were buffeted by changes in the nineteenth and twentieth centuries and which attracted the attention of colonials. As one informant (Ankumbo interview) said, "We belong to our mother's clan, but fathers are more important." Or as another put it (Nangolo interview): "Boys are their fathers' friend."

FATHERS AND KINGS

In the first half of the nineteenth century, masculinity within Ovambo societies was embodied partly in "fathers," who represented male power and determined the criteria and the candidates for becoming men. Although Ovambo societies were matrilineal in inheritance and royal succession, they were patrilocal, and fathers had a central role in their children's lives. It was fathers who named their offspring, ransomed a child captured in war, offered a sacrifice if a child became sick, and paid for male and female initiation. They often gave gifts of property to their children before their death.[1] Young men usually obtained from their fathers livestock that allowed them to begin their own herds, demonstrating their readiness for marriage and placing them on the road to male adulthood (McKittrick 1996; Salokoski 1992: 139). A young man frequently created his first household in his father's field and would commonly seek land and settle in the vicinity of his father rather than joining his mother's people, who were often distant and might be virtual strangers.[2] Fathers were therefore the personification of and the path to full manhood. Fatherhood was also a metaphor for other vertical relationships between men. Subjects called the king *tate*, or father, and relations between dominant and subordinate men were understood as parent–child relations regardless of blood ties.

The power to allot and withhold resources and to command others, whether male or female, defined the essence of masculinity in Ovambo societies, for it resided mostly in men. But not all men had an equal share of this power. This is seen most clearly in the institution of male initiation, which divided men into those closer to and farther from women. Although theoretically open to anyone, male initiation was not universal; its high fees largely restricted it to sons of the wealthy. Members of this elite generally had more wives, more cattle, and better farms than uninitiated men. They also claimed monopolies over many aspects of ritual power. When initiated men performed *omadhila*, an annual ceremony to call the rain, women and uninitiated males of any age risked death or madness if they watched.

Male initiation legitimated an elite male power that superseded a more universal male authority based on fatherhood. Initiates were put through tests of courage and endurance and could thus claim that their exalted position was based on the possession of ideal male qualities: they were stronger, braver, and more disciplined than other men.[3] And yet because the sons of elite men had greater access to initiation, the ceremony also reinforced power a paternal line already possessed. Nor was this the only example of male social stratification replicated through fathers. Although kingship was inherited matrilineally, most markers of male status were not. Fathers frequently passed ritual authority and the position of *elenga*, or royal adviser, to their sons (Mwatotele interview; Amutana interview; Amadhila interview; also Tönjes 1911: 111). The sons of kings themselves became members of the nobility. Even in Ombalantu, a society without a king, "titles"—markers of senior status— were inherited paternally.[4] Village headmanships, based on clan membership and usually inherited matrilineally, also could flow from father to son if community members consented (Shihepo interview; Amutenya interview).

Throughout the nineteenth century, the social dominance of "fathers" was challenged by a force that laid claim to many of the same bases of power even as it drew on new ones. Most Ovambo societies underwent a process of centralization at this time. Older notions of dominant masculinity were appropriated by leaders known as *aakwaniilwa* (sing. *omukwaniilwa*)—now translated as "kings"—who claimed superior ritual powers and amassed greater resources in people and cattle than anyone else in the community, and by the relatives of kings who controlled large districts, often with a great deal of autonomy. By the 1860s, control over imported commodities and militarization allowed these kings and their relatives to create new networks of patronage and shifted the power to define dominant masculinity and to make men of boys, away from fathers to the court.

Nineteenth-century kings were largely initiated men, and they increasingly asserted control over the land, its fertility, the lives and well-being of their subjects, and the appointment of village headmen. They drew elite men and male and female ritual leaders into their service.[5] By mid-century female initiation, controlled by women in some areas and by women and men in others, was linked to kingship, as was male initiation, rain-making, planting and harvest ceremonies, and salt-gathering. At the same time, some kings began to embody a kind of supermasculinity by virtue of their greater share of "masculine" wealth: they had larger herds than other senior men and attracted large numbers of clients, both male and female, to their courts.[6] In all kingdoms "boys of the king"—some who were physically grown men—took up residence at the palace and served as messengers and other low-level assistants. Kings took more wives than other men and exerted exceptional power over their wives. They also controlled male dependents' acquisition of wives. Ngandjera king Amunyela Shaaningwa, who ruled in the late 1850s or 1860s, reportedly forbade his guards to dress well or rub themselves with ochre-tinted fat lest they attract his wives; a traveler in the 1860s similarly said that the "boys" of a neighboring king were not allowed to grease themselves.[7]

This stratification was contested. Other Ngandjera traditions assert that King Amunyela was the first monarch to take more than one wife, with dire consequences: he was killed in a war and his kingdom's greatness ended.[8] Disastrous results are attributed to the expanding power of kings elsewhere as well: some were accused of causing famine and abusing their powers over the land, while others were said to have killed their subjects indiscriminately.[9] Perhaps the most famous tradition in the region comes from Ombalantu, whose political centralization was truncated, probably in the first half of the nineteenth century, when a king caused his subjects to starve and tricked and killed his advisers, the elites who once had embodied dominant masculinity. His subjects revolted, killed him, and abolished the kingship.[10]

Both residents and outsiders portrayed Ombalantu as a society that had returned to a pre-kingship system of political governance based on male clan and household leadership. The contrasting responses of Ombalantu and its centralized neighbors to the forces that visited the region in the latter half of the century reveal the consequences of centralization for constructions of masculinity and authority. While kings eager to expand their political author- ity welcomed traders bearing firearms and other European goods and engaged in raids to obtain cattle and slaves as payment, people in Ombalantu shunned such trade and the missionaries who came in its wake. The expanding colo- nial world affected the region long before formal conquest in 1915, and it reshaped the terrain on which masculinities were constructed and understood. Military might, imported goods, the experience of wage labor, and member- ship in the Christian church each affected what it meant to be a man in turn- of-the-century Ovambo societies.

COMMODITIES

In the 1850s, European traders began offering clothing, firearms, horses, and a variety of consumer goods in exchange for ivory, cattle, and slaves. In the more decentralized Ombalantu, the markers and representatives of male power remained largely unchanged. But elsewhere, long-distance trade and the availability of firearms created a cycle of warfare and economic stratifica- tion. These events had a profound impact on male identities. Boys increas- ingly took crucial steps toward manhood within the walls of the palace. The centrality of the king to male identity cut across lines of wealth and status but reproduced these hierarchies within the court. One missionary described this process:

> The sons of the prominent and the wealthy . . . prefer to be close to the ruler of their land from an early age. . . . During the various military campaigns, they are afforded ample opportunity to prove their courage and bravery. It is seen as a token of the king's special goodwill if he awards a young man a better-quality rifle . . . ; this rifle, however, never becomes the personal property of the young man concerned, and it can be taken back by the king whenever he pleases. Naturally the bearer of such a rifle considers himself to be an *elenga* of the future. In a very short period, he assembles his own group of servants, who accompany him on all his trips in the service of the king, and thus contribute considerably to his rising in the esteem of his peo- ple. (Tönjes 1911: 111–12)

A gun culture linked to male power emerged in late nineteenth-century Ovambo kingdoms. Bravery in battle had long been an element of ideal mas- culinity, but the desire for costly commodities militarized masculinity. The resulting elite male culture incorporated goods such as horses, guns, and clothing into the textures of both mundane daily life and momentous ritual events, even including those that made girls into women. Kings sent men on

Photo 2.1. An undated photo of Uukwambi Chief Iipumbu's army (taken before 1932, when Iipumbu was deposed), from the National Archives of Namibia, shows the prevalence of firearms, European-style shirts, and cloth (worn as loincloths or skirts) among men close to the palace. (Courtesy National Archives of Namibia)

horseback to female initiation ceremonies, and men fired guns at their conclusion.[11]

Elite masculinity in late nineteenth-century Ovambo kingdoms was militaristic, violent, and closely linked to the capitalist world system. European commodities largely replaced a need for wealth in people to construct male power, and the importance of social connections was increasingly limited to a group of male soldiers. The men of the palace and *omalenga* were deeply feared and resented because of their predations; prisoners of war, once enslaved by elites, were by the 1880s often sold to Portuguese traders in exchange for alcohol and firearms, as were the king's own subjects.[12] Powerful men no longer viewed their roles as protectors of the land, and the land became less fertile. The period from 1880 to 1915 saw at least three famines with massive mortality, recurring droughts, bovine pleuropneumonia, and rinderpest; it was also marked by devastating floods and locusts that ruined crops in years when drought did not. The rich, accused of disloyalty and witchcraft, frequently were expelled and robbed of their property, while the poor fled to relatives in neighboring societies when famine and cattle disease left them destitute.[13]

Households managed these crises partly by holding back young men and women from adulthood, thereby retaining their labor power and delaying payment of livestock for bridewealth, female initiation, and wedding feasts. Female initiation was delayed, with some women remaining "girls" until their thirties;[14] at the same time, polygyny among the older elites increased. Male initiation was marginalized as elites were formed in the king's court rather than at the ritual leader's forest shelter, and with it ceremonies that had ensured the land's fertility also began to vanish. Many young men found that their fathers, who had once been their primary protectors and patrons, would not or could not assume this role any longer. A "riddle" first recorded around 1900 expresses the tensions that could emerge between generations of related men: "A thorn pricked me in my father's cattle pen; I went into slavery even though my father has cattle"—a devastating critique of fathers' refusal to devote resources to their children's protection (Kuusi 1974; cf. Harries 1994: 97–8). While a few young men, primarily kings and their advisers, rose to a status once linked ideologically to age, economic stratification ensured that, for many, the trappings of elite masculinity were far beyond their reach.

CONTRACTS

In the closing years of Ovambo autonomy, the system of male social mobility centered on the king began to disintegrate. Raiding decreased, possibly because of Portuguese colonial aggression and tighter controls on selling firearms and ammunition to Africans.[15] In 1906, a German Lutheran missionary wrote from the highly militarized state of Uukwanyama that the association between a man's status and his favor with the king was weakening because of male labor migration to German South West Africa.[16]

Some younger men began to negotiate the route from boyhood to manhood by engaging more directly with the institutions, rather than just the commodities, of colonialism. Missions and migrant labor promised a measure of independence from local male power brokers, although they inevitably ensnared men in new relations of dependence. While missionaries preceded labor recruiters by several decades, the system of labor migration expanded faster than the church. By the early 1880s small numbers of Ovambo men worked in colonial industries such as mining. In the ensuing two decades, many more were recruited to work at the Swakopmund harbor and to build railways. Between 1907 and 1910 the number of Ovambo migrants in South West Africa increased dramatically, from about 1700 to more than 6,000 at any given moment; a smaller but indeterminate number also worked in Angola (Moorsom 1989).

Initially, these workers—almost exclusively young men, often impoverished—sought from wage labor the means to become senior men within the existing terms of masculinity. They particularly wanted cash and goods to trade for livestock, which not only marked them as men but also gave them the means to pay bridewealth and land rent in kingdoms where this was required, or to offer "presents" to fathers and the king to ensure future favor when they asked to be allowed to marry or to be given land to establish a household. They also kept some manufactured goods for themselves, appropriating the new markers of elite male status that had emerged as a result of trade with Europeans. But while wage labor can be seen as offering an opportunity to operate outside local hierarchies of men, it was fraught with risk, and junior men's willingness to migrate also reflected their vulnerability and desperation. The journey was dangerous, and, once at labor centers, men found few measures in place to protect their lives in hazardous work on railroads, in harbors, and in mines. Conditions were no better on isolated European farms, where laborers could die of malnutrition or disease or be beaten to death by their employers.[17] Still, despite the risks, a missionary noted in 1911 that for the past thirty years, "thousands of young people have left Ovamboland every year to work for the whites living in Hereroland."[18]

The sudden presence of a group of relatively young men who owned clothing and cattle and had incurred few or no local social obligations to obtain them helped reshape the parameters of dominant masculinity. To an extent not seen even with raiding and long-distance trade, male wage labor outside the region dramatically and conclusively defined the external world as male. Women rarely accompanied men, and there were almost no wage labor opportunities for them. And within the realm of men, those who returned from stints as wage laborers formed a distinct culture that other young men sought to emulate by becoming migrants themselves.

A missionary opined hopefully that migrant labor gave some their first contact with Christianity and made them "new men."[19] Returned migrants seldom talked about the ways in which African men working for whites were feminized and made junior: forced to do women's work, called "boy," and beaten for slight or imaginary offenses. Rather, upon their return home they displayed the culture of the urban areas where they worked and used imported goods to signify their new prosperity. Some spoke haltingly in their native tongue or impressed others with the German they had learned. They wore their hats cocked at an angle and tucked handkerchiefs into their breast pockets. They socialized together and regaled listeners with tales of eating rice and drinking coffee and liquor.[20] When they established households, these men usually sought to retain the trappings of migrants, trading cattle for the goods young laborers brought home and later appropriating a portion of their grown sons' wages through "gifts." Their life trajectories became a template for what men "should" do: by the 1930s, labor migration was practically universal, an accepted and expected part of every man's life which marked the path to manhood (Andowa interview; Iishitile interview).

In the long term, however, migrant labor did not give men independence from fathers and kings. By the 1920s, young men were expected to pay tribute to both in the form of goods purchased with wages. The practice, called paying *omutenge*, or burden, had been optional in the mid-nineteenth century. But in an economy where cattle ownership had become concentrated in the hands of the elite and then decimated by disease, and where wages were so low that two or three contracts were necessary to buy one beast, young men became even more dependent on the goodwill of elder males for cattle, and the practice of *omutenge* became a way for senior men to assert some control over junior men's wages (McKittrick 1996, also Chanock 1991: 77). And as Ovambo from Angola poured across the border to settle in Namibia between 1915 and 1945, desirable farms became scarce and a young man hoping one day to start his own farm needed to court the king's favor well in advance by offering a substantial gift (Angala interview). Thus in the early decades of South African colonialism, labor migrancy reshaped ideas of hegemonic masculinity, but the economic impact of colonialism also reinforced the power of both fathers and kings (Harries 1994; Lovett 1994; Schmidt 1992; Mandala 1990).

CHRISTIANITY

Finnish Lutheran missionaries first arrived in the floodplain in 1870; in subsequent decades other societies followed. Their initial relationships with the kings who invited them were stormy.[21] Kings viewed missionaries as a necessary bridge to European traders and commodities as well as a threat to royal power. While missionaries formed close ties to kings and other elites and made very few converts during their first twenty years, they competed with monarchs for the loyalty of the same group of people—men. Missionaries strove to convert those who epitomized dominant masculinity—kings, elites, and wealthy household heads—and they defined the difficulties of Christianization as a problem of dominant Ovambo masculinity. The biggest obstacle to conversion, they argued, was the "pagan's" attachment to marrying more than one wife—"pagan" here being male and elite by default.[22] Missionaries also lamented the fact that young men who might occasionally attend school nevertheless preferred to spend their time at the palace pursuing indigenous routes to male social mobility.[23] Problems unique to female converts, such as the need to divorce a polygamous husband or the desire to participate in female initiation, were addressed much later.

Missionaries eventually realized that their friendships with male leaders were not going to lead to conversions. They therefore invited boys to live with them at the mission station, drawing them away from both their fathers and the king. While some young men floated between life at the station and that at their fathers' houses, others cut ties to their families to live with the missionaries (Pelema and Kaanandunge interview; Amutana interview). One of the first Ovambo pastors recalled that it was commonly believed that the white missionaries were mythical beasts who stole children, casting a spell on them so they

Photo 2.2. Ndonga King Kambonde, his head wife, and son, from a 1911 ethnography by Rheinish missionary (and later SWA Native Commissioner) Hermann Tönjes. While the head wife's status is marked with more traditional ornaments (and perhaps imported beads and metal objects), the son's is marked by an ammunition belt and Kambonde's by a full suit of European clothing. (Courtesy National Archives of Namibia)

would "leave their parents and follow the wagons of white people."[24] These youth were known in Ovamboland as *Aanamatemba*—children of the wagons.

The first "followers of the wagons," baptized locally by Finnish missionaries in 1883, were men between the ages of 18 and 26. These six converts lived with the missionaries for four to eight years, meaning that they were at least partially cut off from the proximity to kings and fathers whom most young men of their age still relied upon for resources to mark them as "real men."

The men first asked to be baptized in central Namibia. The missionary rejected this strategy, which would have negotiated a path of peace between obedience to Christianity and to the local elite. To the missionary, these baptisms were to be a movement away from indigenous masculinities based on loyalty to fathers and kings. Requests for baptism were refused until the converts finally asserted that "they would give up everything; they would suffer anything if that was necessary. . . . Now they didn't say that they were scared of the king or anyone else's harassment. Two of them who were already engaged to two fiancees were ready to give up one of them."[25]

In exchange for their sacrifice, these men were inducted into a world of signs and symbols increasingly associated with masculinity. They were baptized in white clothes made by the missionary's wife; after the ceremony they ate sweet buns and drank coffee—goods associated with the world of European traders and colonial labor centers, which had become the near-exclusive domain of men. They were literate—reading came to occupy an important place in the construction of Christian masculinity. A later convert remembered that when a missionary gave him a book, it made him "a proud man."[26] Reading eventually became another component of the exotic experiences and knowledge—foreign languages, unusual foods—which marked male status in later years.

These first-generation converts were no longer the children of their fathers but were brought into the orbit of new fathers, biblical as well as mission: "None of their ancestors, not even the adult citizens, has taken the same road that they are taking. In spite of their fathers, mothers, or other relatives, these youngsters have followed God's way like the father of the religion, father Abraham."[27] The missionaries were not the only ones who saw theirs as an enterprise aimed at tearing males away from the things that made them proper Ovambo men. Elderly women watching the baptism saw it as feminization rather than an alternative masculinity; they observed ominously that the missionaries were now putting men through female initiation.[28]

Many of the young men also saw their conversion as an acceptance of a new set of male guardians. One found his loyalty secured by the bread and cloth missionaries gave him—goods that symbolized both the status of kings and the expanding culture of labor migration—and covertly attended school and church services: "Deep in my mind, I felt that I now belonged to the whites. . . . I did everything in secret because I knew that if my father found out what was going on in my life he would punish me." The moment of his conversion came when he fell into a trance in the forest. He recalled seeing "a group of men with peaceful faces. . . . They were guarding me as a father guards his child. . . . I was now a worshiper of God—God who sends his peaceful men as protectors in times of difficulties."[29]

This convert does not relate whether he reconciled his new faith to his relationship with his father; both he and his brother became preachers who eventually were stationed in areas far from their family home. Many men sought a compromise between the demands of Christianity and those of Ovambo masculinity, but a boy's decision to associate or live with missionaries almost always caused some degree of tension in a father–son relationship (Amupala interview). One informant remembers that when he "sneaked away" to live with a missionary he was teased by his friends, who called him "a boy who left his father for missionaries." Ultimately he returned to his family (Iitembu interview).

Yet as Christianity spread to encompass entire nuclear families rather than a few disobedient sons, it sometimes strengthened father–son bonds. This was the case with Kaukumba, a "witch doctor" who served the Kwanyama king, and his son Nghoshi. Although missionaries trumpeted the conversion of Kaukumba, who took the name Noah, as a significant victory, his son recalled that the man brought his entire polygamous family to church. At first, Kaukumba's son was less taken with Christianity than his father. But when his desire to learn to read led to baptism, his father asked that he choose the name Sem for himself to mirror the biblical father–son relationship. Sem's new identity as a Christian reinforced his older identity as his father's son; when his father moved to an area without a school, Sem set aside his ambition to continue his education and moved with him, because "even though I was a married man, I did not want to live away from my father."[30]

The process of resisting the church, embracing it, and reconciling it with local ideas of masculinity spanned generations. In 1874, a wealthy religious leader, Auala, gained the favor of the Ondonga court, which awarded him the farm of a deceased king—a considerable and desirable property. The farm came with a title, and so the surrounding villages also fell under Auala's rule, compounding his wealth and standing. With his large herds, many wives and children, and ties to the court, Auala personified dominant masculinity in these decades, and not surprisingly he had little use for missionaries—even less use than the king, who forbade people to be baptized or to build square houses but who nonetheless needed a steady supply of European goods to maintain the loyalty of men like Auala.

This contact was more than idle curiosity for at least some of Auala's children. When he divorced one of his wives, she moved to a village near a mission station, and one of Auala's sons took the unusual step of leaving his father's house and going to live with his mother, "in search of the words of God." He was baptized as Vilho in 1901. Vilho's future wife had a similar background. Born to the son of an Ondonga king famed for his hostility to missionaries, she grew up at her mother's house near the church after her father died. The missionaries offered economic assistance to the family and drew her into their orbit; she was baptized Loide in 1896. After Loide's husband reverted to paganism and divorced her, and after Vilho's first wife died, Loide and Vilho married and had a son they named Leonard.[31]

Born into a family that had to some extent traded the privileges of its fathers for those of life at the mission station, Leonard had a pampered childhood. He was raised by two Finnish missionaries who had no children of their own, given to them as an act of friendship by his own parents. By his own account, Leonard was the terror of the neighborhood as a child; by the tender age of ten he was destroying property and trying to seduce girls. He was aware of his elite status: "As a little boy, people spoke of me as very handsome. I was always dressed in nice clothes. . . . Whenever we played with other children, they made me their king, or I made myself their king, or their pastor, or their teacher, or their headman." The fantasies and games of children said a great deal about how different routes to male dominance converged. The rightful role for a boy born to Christian parents of noble ancestry, living with the missionaries and dressed immaculately in European clothes, was as much a king or headman as a teacher or pastor.

When Leonard was about four years old the new king of Ondonga, a mere teenager himself, was baptized. King Martin had a complex relationship with mission-style Christianity, continuing many of the rites and practices considered necessary for an Ovambo king and even taking an additional wife; yet he was also lauded as the missionaries' greatest success.[32] But his open affiliation with the church drew Christian and indigenous masculinities together. Martin selected his "boys of the king" from the ranks of both the Christian elite and the old aristocracy. When Leonard was 15, he was summoned to live with the king.[33] With firm claims to male status accorded by affiliation with the church and that which came with ties to the court, Leonard seemed to embody the new hegemonic masculinity, as did King Martin. Yet he sought Martin's permission to engage in contract labor in the south as well.

Leonard Auala wavered between Christian and "pagan" behavior in his young adulthood. He enrolled in the seminary upon his return to Ovamboland, dropped out, enrolled again some years later, and became a teacher. His membership in the educated Christian elite offered him one of the few waged jobs in Ovamboland and permitted him to avoid further labor migration.[34] As he wrote his life story in 1942 he was in training to become a pastor; 18 years later he would become the first black bishop of Ovamboland. It was a position that in many respects granted him more power than his illustrious ancestor Auala had had, but one that he probably would not have won without pedigrees from both the aristocracy and the Christian elite.

By the time Leonard Auala became bishop, court-based masculinity still survived, but its power was altered and vastly diminished. Four decades of colonial rule, population pressure that restricted space for grazing and farming alike, rapid Christianization, and an entrenched system of migrant labor had damaged elites' hold on the resources and knowledge that represented the power of the old dominant masculinity. "Traditional" leaders—headmen and kings—owed their positions to the colonial government and were increasingly distrusted and even despised by their subjects for their role in collecting taxes, enforcing colonial laws, carrying out unpopular "development" projects, and rounding up forced labor to build roads and staff the Native Military Corps during World War II (McKittrick 1995: 160–65; Hayes 1998). Ritual specialists also were increasingly irrelevant in a world where more people were members of a conservative Lutheran church that discouraged indigenous adaptation. By the 1950s, male and female initiation, rain-making, planting, and harvest ceremonies—once controlled by kings and their "doctors"—were either extinct or ignored by many.

COLONIALISM AND CONCLUSION

The South African officials who ruled South West Africa after World War I established a formal colonial administration in Ovamboland but ruled with very few European personnel. They developed a system of governance that resembled "indirect rule," removing troublesome leaders and selecting cooperative men with some claim to "traditional" bases of authority to carry out the government's orders. Ovamboland officials, particularly the long-ruling Native Commissioner, C.H.L. Hahn, compiled a body of ethnographic information about Ovambo societies that was supposed to ensure the survival of "native customs" despite the fact of colonial overrule. Central to the notion of tribal traditions was matrilineality, which seemed to hold a particular fascination for Hahn. He extrapolated from matrilineal kingship and property inheritance that "a man is not a blood relation of his children"[35] and that "strictly speaking the father has no powers over his children."[36] He also stated that a father could raise no objection if a maternal uncle claimed his child—although I have never found a record of such an occurrence in the colonial archives.[37]

Even as Hahn told his wide audience that fathers were "traditionally" irrelevant to their children, Ovambo fathers were spending more and more time away from their rural homes on labor contracts. By the 1940s, expanded needs for consumer goods and increasingly fragile subsistence economies meant that men's careers as migrants extended well beyond marriage. This exacerbated tensions within households; many women claimed that their husbands refused to support them financially or had effectively deserted them, while significant numbers of men seem to have established lives and families in southern labor centers (McKittrick 1997).

Despite their extended absence, fathers continued to mediate the transition from junior to senior male status by virtue of their control over cattle and land. The practice of giving "gifts" to fathers in exchange for the goods needed to become a man continues even today. Nor was this seen as a simple material transaction; informants stressed that both parties conducted the exchange out of affection as much as a desire to get something in return. For young men it was a way of expressing "a son's pride at being a son."[38] During World War II, when men were recruited or coerced into joining the Native Military Corps, most of them listed their fathers as the recipients of their pay.[39]

Why did fathers remain so important in this matrilineal society where they supposedly had no institutional control over or role in their children's lives, while in many patrilineal societies where they had a formal legal role in their children's lives they ended up (literally or figuratively) "working for their sons" (Berry 1985)? Fathers' access to certain types of wealth and resources was the basis of their dominant masculinity, just as wealth undergirded other forms of male power. But their role was understood outside the legal institution of maternal kinship and the formal relations of politics; instead, fathers' authority was expressed in terms of affection and emotion. Even when junior men gained new routes to wealth and status, these idioms of deference and affection persisted. Like gender, generation contained within it hegemonic ideals; these opened the way for a persistent, dominant masculinity based on notions of social seniority. At the same time, by virtue of fatherhood's very invisibility to European administrators (the same invisibility that allowed officials to sanction the extended absence of older men without concern), it remained outside the scope of the colonial state. *Omutenge*, the practice of sons giving gifts to their fathers before marriage, is not mentioned in a single colonial record or ethnography, despite its crucial role in perpetuating labor migration.

As the colonial period progressed, fathers' importance to their sons' economic security actually expanded in some respects. Lucrative jobs in the diamond mines began to be passed from fathers to sons (Ankumbo interview). And as the church's emphasis on nuclear families and its ban on divorce were more widely accepted, strains began to show in the practice of matrilineal inheritance, which had often resulted in a wife and her young children being expelled so that the father's house could revert to his maternal relatives. Today matrilineal inheritance of land is the exception rather than the rule, and news of a widow being "chased" from her dead husband's farm is routinely met with community condemnation.[40] Population pressures have made it more difficult for sons to settle close to their fathers, since often no farm is available, yet the notion that sons should live near their fathers never died. Thus my research assistant, who is 34, once explained to me that he would one day inherit his father's farm, while his older brother was establishing his farm on an adjoining vacant property (the family lives in one of the most recently settled areas of Ongandjera, so that some vacant land is still available). His claim that this was "traditional" says much about continuities in the importance of fathers in defining and perpetuating notions of masculinity, even as the meaning and substance of dominant masculinity have changed.

NOTES

1. Amadhila interview; Angombe interview; Kalenga interview; Aipumbu and Kafe interview; Salokoski (1992: 48–9).

2. Amadhila interview; Augustus interview; Kamulunga interview; Estermann (1976: 77). A proverb urged men to stay in their own village if they wanted a good field, since it was there that they had ties (Kuusi 1970: 177). Fathers also often served as intermediaries between their sons and the king when their sons sought land (Amutenya interview).

3. Women who were ascribed such qualities were said to be like men. For example, Henok Haufiku notes in his life story that his mother was "a woman in appearance but she was a man in action" and proceeded to recount her considerable fighting abilities (National Archives of Finland (NAF), Finnish Missionary Society (FMS) Collection, Ha2, Ambomaan Pappisseminaarin Oppilaiden Elämäkerrat 1942, autobiography of Henok Haufiku). And yet it is important to note that the association of male characteristics with women did not necessarily imply any recognition that such women had a claim to resources or power that were generally associated with men.

4. NAF, FMS, K. Himmanen, "Ehistori lj'Ombalantu" (unpublished manuscript, n.d.), 16.

5. Traditions of kingship are recounted in Williams (1991); National Archives of Namibia (NAN), A450 v. 9 f 2/34; Helsinki University Library (HUL), ELC mf 56, Daniel Nameya; Möller (1974: 122).

6. The German missionary Hahn (grandfather of the future Ovamboland native commissioner) wrote in 1851 that early European travelers to Ovamboland reported the Ondonga king had 106 wives—probably referring to both actual wives and girls living with the king as dependents (the female equivalent of "boys of the king" (Hahn 1984: 509).

7. NAN, A 450 v. 9 f 2/34, "Notes on Ongandjera chiefs"; Andersson (1969: 299).

8. NAN, A450 v. 9 f 2/34, handwritten notes on Ongandjera chiefs; also Amwaama interview; Louw 1967: 22–4.

9. NAN, A450 v. 9 f 2/34, notes on Uukwambi kings; "Ehistori lj'Ombalantu," 7; Williams (1991).

10. "Ehistori lj'Ombalantu," 7–8; Williams (1991: 135–7).

11. HUL, ELC, mf card 8, Akilofel Amupembe, Uukwambi.

12. For example, NAF, FMS, Martti Rautanen Diary, Sept. 26, 1880, and Oct. 10, 1881.

13. The life histories of people born between 1900 and 1915 are replete with accounts of movement over long distances, death from guns or famine, and enslavement at the palaces of aristocrats. The diary of Finnish missionary Martti Rautanen also details individual cases of expulsion and robbery through the 1880s to the 1910s.

14. Loeb (1962: 237); Mallory (1971: 129). Also Elago interview and Negongo interview.

15. Rheinish Mission Society (RMS), Feb. 1906 report, 26.

16. RMS, Feb. 1906 report, 26.

17. Tönjes (1911: 88); AVEM, RMG, Feb. 1906 report, 27.

18. Tönjes (1911: 88).

19. RMS, Feb. 1906 report, 27; also NAF, FMSA, Ha 2, autobiographies of Erastus Shilongo, Moses Shilongo, Paulus Nailenge. I am grateful to Richard Stites for translating Moses Shilongo's autobiography from Swedish.

20. AVEM, RMG, Feb. 1906 report, 27.

21. Two Catholic missionaries who came briefly to Uukwanyama were killed on accusations of poisoning the king in 1885 (Pelissier 1977: 425).

22. Helsinki, Archives of the Finnish Mission Society, 1882 annual report. All Finnish translations by Niina Valtanen.

23. RMS, 1894 annual report, 77.

24. NAF, FMS, Ha2, Sakeus Iihuhua autobiography.

25. Helsinki, Archives of the Finnish Mission Society, 1882 annual report.

26. NAF, FMS, Ha2, Sakeus Iihuhua autobiography.

27. Helsinki, Archives of the Finnish Mission Society, 1882 annual report.

28. Ibid. Baptism and female initiation ceremonies had no obvious similarities, perhaps aside from superficial ones such as dressing in special clothing, singing, and eating afterward. The women instead may have been commenting on the public nature of the ceremony: while boys were initiated in groups in the forest, far from the eyes of women and uninitiated males, female initiation was largely a public event, held before the eyes of the community—much as this early baptism would have been.

29. NAF, FMS, Ha2, Sakeus Iihuhua autobiography.

30. NAF, FMS, Ha2, Sem Kaukumba autobiography.

31. NAF, FMS, Ha2, Leonard V. Auala autobiography.

32. Amutana interview; NAF, FMS, diary of Martti Rautanen, Oct. 9, 1916.

33. NAF, FMS, Ha2, Leonard V. Auala autobiography.

34. NAF, FMS, Ha2, Paulus Shiyagaya autobiography.

35. NAN, NAO, Vol. 20 f 11/1, 1937 annual report, 20.

36. NAN, A450 f 2/25, Rex vs. Chiwetha, May 28, 1939, interrogation addressed to Hahn by counsel for the accused.

37. NAN, Native Affairs Tsumeb, Vol. 22, f 31/2, April 8, 1940, Native Commissioner Ovamboland to Officer-in-Charge, Native Affairs, Tsumeb. Hahn was committed to his view of a "pure" matrilineal society where fathers played no significant role in their children's lives, despite the fact that he recognized that the society was patrilocal and that fathers named their children and received a part of bridewealth. By stating that maternal uncles had a right to claim children, he undermined his own policy of keeping Ovambo women and children in Ovamboland and out of the southern regions of the country at all costs; in this case, an Ovambo woman was seeking permission to bring her child south because her brother, the child's sole means of support other than herself, lived there.

38. Kambweshele and Shaanika interview; Ankumbo interview; Angala interview.

39. NAN, NAO, Vol. 48, file 46/1/1, Military Matters, Native Military Corps, personnel, Part 2.

40. This was the most common issue raised at the end of interviews, when I asked informants if they had anything they wanted to add.

REFERENCES

Andersson, Charles John. 1969. *Notes of Travel in South Africa.* 1875 reprint. Cape Town: C. Struik.

Berry, Sara S. 1985. *Fathers Work for Their Sons: Accumulation, Mobility, and Class Formation in an Extended Yoruba Community.* Berkeley: University of California Press.

Chanock, Martin. 1991. "A Peculiar Sharpness: An Essay on Property in the History of Customary Law in Colonial Africa." *Journal of African History* 32, 65–88.

Cornwall, Andrea and Nancy Lindisfarne. 1994. *Dislocating Masculinity: Comparative Ethnographies.* London: Routledge.

Estermann, Carlos. 1976. *The Ethnography of Southwestern Angola*, Vol. 1. New York: Africana Publishing Company.

Hahn, C.H.L., H. Vedder, and L. Fourie. 1928. *The Native Tribes of South West Africa.* Cape Town: Cape Times Ltd.

Hahn, Carl Hugo. 1984. *Tagebücher*, Vol. 2, B. Lau, ed. Windhoek: National Archives of Namibia.

Harries, Patrick. 1994. *Work, Culture and Identity: Migrant Laborers in Mozambique and South Africa, c. 1860–1910*. Portsmouth, NH: Heinemann.

Hayes, Patricia. 1998. "'The Famine of the Dams': Gender, Labour and Politics in Colonial Ovamboland, 1929–30." In *Namibia Under South African Rule: Mobility and Containment*. Athens, OH: Ohio University Press.

Kuusi, Matti. 1970. *Ovambo Riddles*. Helsinki: Suomalainen Tiedeakatemia.

Loeb, Edwin. 1962. *In Feudal Africa*. Bloomington, IN: Indiana University Press.

Louw, W. 1967. "Die Sosio' politieke Stelsel van die Ngandjera van Ovamboland." M.A. thesis, Port Elizabeth.

Lovett, Margot. 1994. "On Power and Powerlessness: Marriage and Political Metaphor in Colonial Western Tanzania." *International Journal of African Historical Studies* 27; 2: 273–301.

Mallory, Charles. 1971. "Some Aspects of the Mission Policy and Practice of the Church of the Province of South Africa in Ovamboland." Ph.D. dissertation, Rhodes University.

Mandala, Elias. 1990. *Work and Control in a Peasant Economy: A History of the Lower Tchiri Valley in Malawi, 1859–1960*. Madison, WI: University of Wisconsin Press.

McKittrick, Meredith. 1995. "Conflict and Social Change in Northern Namibia." Ph.D. dissertation, Stanford University.

——. 1996. "The 'Burden' of Young Men: Generational Conflict and Property Rights in Ovamboland." *African Economic History* 24: 115–29.

——. 1997. "Reinventing the Family: Kinship, Marriage and Famine in Northern Namibia, 1948–54." *Social Science History* 21, 3: 265–95.

Möller, P. 1974. *Journey Through Angola, Ovampoland and Damaraland*. Cape Town: C. Struik.

Moorsom, Richard. 1989. "The Formation of the Contract Labour System in Namibia, 1900–1926." In *Forced Labour and Migration: Patterns of Movement within Africa*, Abebe Zegeye and Shubi Ishemo, eds. London: Hans Zell.

Pelissier, Rene. 1977. *Les guerres grises: résistance et révoltes en Angola (1845–1941)*. Orgeval, France: Montamets.

Salokoski, Marta. 1992. "Symbolic Power of Kings in Precolonial Ovambo Societies." Unpublished licensiate thesis, University of Helsinki.

Schmidt, Elizabeth. 1992. *Peasants, Traders, and Wives: Shona Women in the History of Zimbabwe, 1870–1939*. Portsmouth, NH: Heinemann.

Tönjes, Hermann. 1911. *Ovamboland: Land, Leute, Mission*. Berlin: Martin Warneck.

Williams, Frieda-Nela. 1991. *Precolonial Communities of Soutwestern Africa*. Windhoek: National Archives of Namibia.

Interviews

All interviews were conducted by Meredith McKittrick and Fanuel Shingenge unless otherwise indicated.

Aipumbu, Rita and Mwahindange Benny Kafe. Omundjalala, Ombalantu. July 1997. Alugongo, Malakia. Ogongo, Uukwambi. July 1997.

Amadhila, Johannes. Eendombe, Ongandjera. July 1997.

Amupala, Tobias. Uutaapi, Ombalantu. July 1993.

Amutana, Selma. Ondando, Ondonga. July 1997.

Amutenya, Petrus. Okahao, Ongandjera. July 1997.

Amwaama, Albertina. Uukwandongo, Ongandjera. June 1996.

Andjengo, Aino. July 1997.

Andowa, Modestus. Anamulenge, Ombalantu. August 1993.

Angala, Tomas. Ombanda, Ongandjera. October 1993.

Angombe, Priskila. Ompemba, Ombalantu. July 1993.

Ankumbo, Max. Ombanda, Ongandjera. October 1993.

Augustus, Hilma. Oniipa, Ondonga. July 1997.

Elago, Rusia. Okalondo, Ongandjera. September 1993.

Iishitile, Gideon. Oshima, Ombalantu. August 1993.

Iitembu, Betuel. Oluteyi, Ongandjera. October 1993.

Kalenga, Johannes. Etilyasa, Ongandjera. September 1993.

Kambweshele, Wilbard and Bertha Shaanika. Interviewed by Fanuel Shingenge. Epangu, Ongandjera. August 1996.

Kamulunga, Titus. Okalili, Ongandjera. July 1997.

Mwatotele, Simon Kaupa. Ongwediva, Uukwanyama. July 1997.

Nangolo, Brasius. Okayile, Ombalantu. November 1993.

Negongo, Aune. Interviewed by Fanuel Shingenge. Uukwalumbe, Ongandjera. July 1996.

Pelema, Selma and Eliaser Kaanandunge. Ongozi, Ongandjera. August 1993.

Shihepo, Tomas. Interviewed by Fanuel Shingenge. Ombathi, Ombalantu. August 1996.

Shivute, Oiva. Uukwandongo, Ongandjera. June 1996.

3

"AND SHE BECAME A MAN": KING AHEBI UGBABE IN THE HISTORY OF ENUGU-EZIKE, NORTHERN IGBOLAND, 1880–1948

Nwando Achebe

INTRODUCTION

African women have been known to occupy a variety of leadership roles in their societies. In ancient Egypt, Hatshepsut ruled as Pharaoh. The Luena queen, NyaKarolo of Angola, was famed for her warrior instincts and for instituting a system of female chiefdoms in all of the countries she conquered; and the Lovedu rain-queens controlled the fertility of the crops. In some societies, a system of joint sovereignty existed whereby leadership responsibilities were shared between a king and a female counterpart. In these systems, women held power because of their relationship to the ruler in question, especially as mother, daughter, or sister. The mother of the *Fon* (male ruler) of the Kingdom of Kom, West Cameroon, advised him and watched over the children of the palace. The Asante had an office called the *Ohemaa*, which translates into the "chief's female counterpart." In the Mossi Kingdom, the eldest daughter of the Mossi king dressed in the king's attire and held royal power until the next ruler was installed.[1] Some small-scale African societies had a dual-sex political system, in which each sex managed its own affairs. Among the noncentralized Igbo, the region which is the focus of this chapter, a joint system of male (*ndi oha*) and female (*udele*) government typically obtained.

The tortoise, on setting out for a long journey, said to his people: if usual things happen, do not send for me; if the unheard-of happens, call me. This Igbo proverb serves as a warning to summon the public when extraordinary events occur. Popular wisdom has it that the Igbos have no kings. This chapter focuses on an area in Igboland where, contrary to this belief, Igbos not only have kings, but *female* kings. A 1930 government report on the social and political organization of Nsukka Division, northern Igboland, presents a short yet interesting example of female power and gender transformation. Enugu-Ezike is identified as a group that is distinguished by having a *female Eze* who is saluted as the *Agamega* or female leopard (Meek 1930). *Eze* is an Igbo word that means "king." This female king, Ahebi Ugbabe, is described by Assistant District Officer V.K. Johnson in a separate report as the "'chieftainess' . . . [who] . . . 'became a man,' and as such she has been regarded ever since" (Johnson 1934).

The account of Ahebi Ugbabe is eloquent yet perplexing. The challenge is to provide an explanation for this peculiarity. Two features of the foregoing commentary present an unusual opportunity to probe northern Igbo attitudes surrounding gender construction and negotiation. First, a woman is saluted as a leopard and is crowned King—qualities as well as structures that epitomize maleness and manhood—and second, we are informed that the same woman has effectively "become a man." Ifi Amadiume argues that sex and gender did not coincide in pre-colonial Igboland, but, instead, gender was flexible and fluid, allowing women to become men, thus creating unique Igbo categories such as female husband and female son[2] (Amadiume 1987). In this chapter, I adopt, reshape, and expand upon Amadiume's theoretical framework in my assessment of how "traditional" notions of manhood and masculinity were constructed, negotiated, and challenged by women and men in colonial Enugu-Ezike.[3]

While Amadiume's findings are useful to my discussion, her argument that colonialism undermined Igbo pre-colonial ideals of gender flexibility presents serious limitations that are challenged by Ahebi Ugbabe's life and consequently reexamined in this chapter. Instead, I propose that Nsukka Igbo gender transformations not only coexisted with British colonialism, but that colonialism created conditions that sometimes supported, reinforced, and extended the contours of acceptable gender transformations, allowing would-be female men to carry their quests for manhood further than would have been acceptable in the pre-colonial order. Conversely, I also argue that Nsukka society maintained the right to monitor, limit, and/or control the

extent to which gendered transformations could take root. This inquiry therefore assesses the sort of circumstance that would evoke society's resolve to
institute exclusionary rather than inclusionary clauses that would negate otherwise convivial gender transformations from woman to man and reveals
what would become of the (wo)men at the receiving end of this sanction.

Constituted primarily through oral history,[4] Ahebi Ugbabe's story illumi-
nates the changing foundations of gendered power under British indirect rule
and highlights the ways in which individual Igbo women and men negotiated
and shaped their colonial environment. During the course of her life, Ahebi
was able to remap the terrain of "traditional" and colonial gendered politics in
her district. Her story therefore contributes to scholarship that has sought to
deconstruct the category "man" by situating multiple gendered female masculinities such as female headman, female warrant chief, female king, female
husband, female masked spirit, as well as the biologically determined male
category of full man. It also reveals the retributions society imposes on individuals who carry gender transformations too far.

AHEBI UGBABE—BIRTH, CHILDHOOD, AND
DISAPPEARANCE

Ahebi Ugbabe was born sometime during the latter part of the nineteenth
century in Umuida, Enugu-Ezike. She was the daughter of Ugbabe Ayibi, a
farmer and palm wine tapper. Her mother, Anekwu Ameh, was a farmer and
trader from Unadu, at the outskirts of Enugu-Ezike. Ahebi Ugbabe had two
brothers and no sisters. When Ahebi was a young girl, she lived with her
mother's relatives in Unadu for a brief period. From every indication, she was
happy there. She later returned to her father's village, and, within the space of
a few years, she had escaped to Igalaland. Only after I had spent several
months asking questions and gaining the trust and confidence of individual
collaborators did I begin to get a sense of what really happened. Apparently,
when Ahebi Ugbabe was young (probably about thirteen or fourteen years
old), her family experienced a lot of misfortune. Their farms yielded little,
their trading did not flourish, and illness plagued various members of their
household. Ahebi's father, in an attempt to trace the origins of these ill fortunes, sought out the expertise of a diviner, *oje gba afa*. Diviners were
believed to be endowed with the skill to unearth secrets, perceive the
unknown—the present and the future—and discern the will of the gods. *Igba
afa* thus became a common and accepted way for individuals in society to
find out why certain misfortunes surrounded them and whether these could be
attributed to invisible powers.

Ani oma dibia, bu ani ojoo mmadu: a good time for the diviner is a bad
time for the people. After consulting his beads, the diviner delivered their rev-

elation. Ahebi's father had committed a grave crime against a kinsman, and, consequently, the goddess Ohe, whom he had offended, was exacting her punishment on his entire family. Ohe was the goddess of creation, fertility, and protection. She was known to punish individuals for inappropriate and offensive behavior, like murder, thievery, and adultery. Her *attama*, or chief priest, acted on her behalf by collecting the debts owed her, placing taboos on disagreeable behavior, and administering her oaths (Meek 1930).

One of the great injustices of history was unleashed when the seer revealed the mysteries of his divination: for things to get better, Ahebi would have to be offered as a living sacrifice to appease the great goddess, Ohe. The historical record remains clouded on what Ahebi's father's reaction to this news was. What we do know, however, is that in due course Ahebi was informed of this impending dedication. Her reaction to this news was anything but predictable. Ahebi Ugbabe—*nwatakili walu anya*, "the difficult and conceited girl who did not listen to reason"—did something that was extraordinary: she refused to be dedicated. Her actions were a symbolic expression of overt resistance. Her defiance was twofold: first, she was revolting against the domestic institution of "slavery" and all of its oppressions and subjugations; second, she was rejecting gerontocratic patriarchal authority and the tenets of her culture that allowed guiltless individuals, especially women, to become victimized by such dedications. Her actions pit her against her society, and, as a result, she was forced to bear the consequence of her decision—she could no longer live in Enugu-Ezike. Her only alternative was to remove herself from that community.

The young and confused Ahebi was thus driven into exile to Igalaland, just to the north of Nsukka. Once there, she was thrown into a harsh reality. She knew no one in Igalaland and therefore was forced to wander the unfamiliar environment. Few options were open to this young, unskilled, and uneducated girl. "Prostitution" therefore became a true reality—a means of survival—a means to an end.[5] Ahebi Ugbabe, resilient as always, became a "prostitute" and used this form of "work" to her advantage. She traveled widely and learnt to speak many languages, including Igala, Nupe, Igbo, and Pidgin English. She became an astute businesswoman, directing monies made from her sex work into trading. She first traded in *okanwu* (potash), then palm oil, and, within a short space of time, horses. In fact, at the height of her trading career, Ahebi Ugbabe would become one of the most affluent traders in the Igala-Igbo borderland area. Her meticulousness in trade allowed her to acquire economic power and political clout, hitherto inconceivable for individual women to attain. Her profession as a sex worker also put her in touch with a number of very prominent citizens, including some British colonialists and the Attah (King) of Igalaland, whose power extended into northern Igboland.

AHEBI UGBABE AND THE BRITISH: CHANCE MEETING OR COLLABORATION?

All of this mayhem was happening against the backdrop of an overwhelming colonial invasion. In January 1909 the British first patrolled the Enugu-Ezike area, which from that year until 1920 remained the scene of constant military and police attacks that were aimed at subjugating its peoples and bringing them under European rule (Johnson 1934). The British justified these actions under the guise of a noble motivation—the abolition of the domestic slave trade.[6] We know that Ahebi Ugbabe accompanied the British invaders into Umuida; however, what is not so clear is whether this was a chance meeting or possibly a calculated effort on Ahebi's part to punish her people and right a wrong done her many years before.

Perhaps the clearest confirmation of Ahebi's agency can be gleaned from archival evidence. In his eloquent report on the peoples of Enugu-Ezike, V.K. Johnson verifies that Ahebi Ugbabe did in fact collaborate with the British by revealing to them the routes to take to conquer her people (Johnson 1934). As for her motivation, Abraham O. Eya of Amufie, Enugu-Ezike, provides a plausible explanation for Ahebi's actions. He suggests that Ahebi accompanied the British back to Enugu-Ezike with the understanding and assurance that they would stamp out domestic slavery in her town. It is certainly conceivable that Ahebi Ugbabe, who herself was a candidate for cult dedication, would wish to see domestic slavery eradicated. Ahebi's act of betrayal could also be interpreted as a cold rejection of a culture that not only attempted to punish her for the crimes of her father, but also forced her into exile and a life of "prostitution."

AHEBI UGBABE'S TRANSFORMATION INTO A FEMALE HEADMAN AND WARRANT CHIEF

Whether Ahebi collaborated with the British to assist them in subjugating her people or for the more noble cause of suppressing the trade in slaves, by the mid-1910s, she had returned home to her people. Immediately following her return to Nsukka, Ahebi Ugbabe allied herself with the political elite. Her linguistic skills gave her access to the leading Igala and Nupe people, who dominated most parts of Nsukka, as well as the British colonial officers. Ahebi Ugbabe, who was versed in Pidgin English, was the only person in her village who could communicate with the British. She consequently wasted no time in cultivating a relationship with them and acted as an intermediary between her people and the new colonial masters.

Ever ambitious and talented, Ahebi recognized in the British new opportunities for political power as well as gendered transformations that had not previously existed in the pre-colonial Nsukka order. Within a few months of her return to Enugu-Ezike, Ahebi Ugbabe was able to expel Ugwu Okegwu, the aged and increasingly incompetent government-recognized headman who could not speak English, Pidgin English, or Igala and consequently had very limited political influence. This was the first in a series of gendered transformations that Ahebi Ugbabe realized in her ultimate quest to attain full manhood within the context of competing indigenous and alien (British and Igala) orders.

The government headman was a male elder appointed by the British to be the "head" of the community. In Nsukka political culture, the symbolic "heads" of the community were the *Onyishi Umunwoke* (i.e., the oldest man in the village) and the *Onyishi Umunwanyi* (i.e., the oldest woman in the village). However, British colonials often did not see eye to eye with the community-recognized *Onyishi Umunwoke* and as a general rule excluded Igbo women altogether from government matters and leadership positions (Van Allen 1972; Mba 1982). They consequently commonly appointed agreeable male elders whom they could not only mold into their stooges, but who would easily conform to their instruction. As a result, traditional Igbo ideals of respectability such as title taking and honor did not feature as factors in these government appointments. What was more, these so-called indigenous headmen would come to realize powers that were much too individualized and autocratic for indigenous sensibilities.

In October 1918, the Native Court of Enugu-Ezike was formed. The British chose four principal court members. As government headman, Ahebi Ugbabe had served the British well. It was therefore hardly surprising that Ahebi Ugbabe was to become the only woman in all of colonial Nigeria to be chosen to sit in the British Native Court as warrant chief (Meek 1930; Johnson 1934). She was described by V.K. Johnson in his intelligence report as "a female of strong Igala tendencies" who was allowed to sit as member of the council in recognition of her past services" (Johnson 1934).

THE ORIGINS OF A CONFLICT

Once Ahebi Ugbabe was made warrant chief a divide developed between her and the recognized leadership of male elders. A nodding acquaintance with the political system that was in place in Enugu-Ezike before Ahebi's return will help explain the root of these hostilities. The Enugu-Ezike group of Nsukka Division was made up of 33 villages. There was no central authority. Its system of government was rule by elders. Enugu-Ezike was divided into units, which included the biological family, the extended family, the kindred, and the quarter. The nucleus of the government was the male and female council, *ndi oha* and *udele*, which were composed of the male and female heads of kindreds or grades of titled officials who had executive powers. Political authority lay in the hands of the oldest person in each unit, namely the *Onyishi Umunwoke* and the *Onyishi Umunwanyi*, who were assisted by other elders and titled officials (Johnson 1934; Omeje 1978; Agbedo 1979).

This pre-colonial system was therefore a gerontocratic as well as community-based mandate, which recognized and upheld the views of the group, rather than the individual. The male ruling elite did not want to have any part in Ahebi's autocratic cross-gender political ascent. However, they found that they really did not have a choice in the matter because the British stood firmly behind Ahebi, and in so doing, excluded them from the day-to-day running and decision-making of the state.

THE CORONATION OF A FEMALE KING: PHASE THREE OF AHEBI'S GENDERED TRANSFORMATION

This European support, however, was not enough for the ambitious Ahebi Ugbabe. In the next year or so, she mounted a vigorous campaign to become *Eze* to further cement her position in government and society. It was only an exceptional person who could strive to become king. In fact, no other woman (or man, for that matter) before her in Enugu-Ezike had attempted this feat. Ahebi was therefore breaking new ground by introducing and imposing an autocratic form of individualized as well as masculinized authority—the office of king. What was more, Ahebi's title would be bestowed on her, not because of a relationship with a man (i.e., as queen, the wife of a king), but in her own right as a (wo)man, who had effectively transformed herself into a man. Astute as always, Ahebi was able to draw on her Igala connections, which inadvertently provided the basis and support for her third gendered transformation. She ingeniously engineered, redefined, and transformed the male political institution of *attah* (i.e., Igala paramount king) into a supreme female masculinized and Igbonized sovereign that espoused British and Igala ideals of rank and hierarchy, rather than Nsukka Igbo standards of gerontocracy, merit, and respectability.

In the early to mid-1920s Ahebi Ugbabe returned to Igalaland for her coronation as king. After her coronation, Ahebi came back from Idah, *okah* (the staff of male kingship) in hand, riding on horseback, accompanied by a huge entourage of musicians and dancers who played and sang songs that affirmed and celebrated her kingship. Great feasting and celebrating were said to have gone on for days.

The songs performed by her musicians were called *ikorodo*. In pre-colonial Nsukka, *ikorodo* music was only performed during sacred occasions to accompany masked spirits and their male initiates. The *ikorodo* songs performed to celebrate Ahebi's kingship situated her gendered transformation in extra-human and spiritual terms. One song proclaimed Ahebi to be *omeh oto nelue anyu!* ("a pit that swallowed the axe!") and further charged that *onyenye eyigi onwuruchi ma abugu Ahebi nwa Onu* ("No woman wears *owuruchi* except Ahebi, daughter of Onu"). These lyrics clearly situate Ahebi Ugbabe's power in non-human proportions, by claiming that she has been endowed with a physical strength that is greater than an axe—for only that which is greater than an axe can swallow the axe! Furthermore, the song's reference to *onwuruchi*—a beautiful and expensive Igala robe, which was patterned after the Igala *Ekwe* masquerade (an exclusive and secret male society) and worn exclusively by affluent men and men of distinction—introduces a spiritual element to her transformation.

Another song with the lyrics *Ahebi Ugbabe onu, Odo neji mmadu, onye neli mmadu, ologi ologi agboo*, ("Ahebi Ugbabe is a pit, an Odo masquerade[7] that catches men, a pit that swallows men, a pit that swallows men totally.") professed a symbolic gendered transformation into a female masquerade. It also defined Ahebi's female masculinity in spiritual terms, thereby setting her aside from mere male mortals, whom, we are told, she "catches and swallows totally." This lyric takes on added meaning when one understands that Nsukka men traditionally used the Odo masked spirit as an instrument to control female behavior. Therefore, Ahebi locates her gendered transformation in terms of a preexisting Igbo male institution, which she has effectively negotiated into a masculinized but uniquely biologically female mechanism and threatens to use it to control male behavior!

Not everyone in Enugu-Ezike was pleased by these events. The Igbo have a saying, *Idi otutu bu ugwu eze*—"A King has added strength and honor when his subjects are many." They also believe that *Ora nwe eze*—"The community owns the king." None of these sentiments were realized, however, as it became painfully obvious that a visible group of Ahebi detractors had surfaced. A song composed by one of Ahebi's official musicians confirmed this fact. The song *Onye si na Ahebi ama bu eze, nya bia ka o je jua ndi Idah*—a catchy tune with explicit lyrics—challenged, "Anyone who insist[ed] that Ahebi not be king to go and have it out with the Attah of Idah who made her king."

THE BIRTH OF A MYTHICAL AHEBI UGBABE

Ahebi Ugbabe went out of her way to acquire a reputation as an all-powerful, no-nonsense, and fearsome ruler. She did this to guarantee her place as warrant chief and king. She had medicine men concoct potions designed to keep her powerful and mysterious. Three times a year, a well-known medicine man from Igalaland would visit her, and he was said to prepare a bad medicine, which had the ability to seize people's souls. These were used to keep Ahebi supernaturally powerful and extend her fortunes.

The villagers also alleged that Ahebi had a live cock buried on her grounds. From time to time, they would hear haunted sounds of drumming followed immediately by the chilling sounds of a cock crowing from underneath the earth. Enough people claimed to have heard this terrible crowing to put fear into the hearts of her subjects. It was also rumored that Ahebi could have no lovers—that any man who spent a night with her would have to be killed. In fact, people claimed to know of an unfortunate man or two who had suffered this fate. Though probably exaggerated, Ahebi's sexual restriction raises questions of wider significance: what, if any kind of sexuality, would be appropriate for a female king such as herself? I can only hazard a guess here. It seems plausible that Ahebi's sexual restriction might have been imposed to guard against the possible birth of heirs who might be moved to attempt to usurp her position. A closer examination into the sexual ideologies of female kingship is needed to determine the validity of this thesis.

Ahebi's constructed mysticism worked ingeniously. She soon developed a reputation as a greatly feared ruler, the *Agamega*, the "female leopard." It is noteworthy that Ahebi Ugbabe chose *Agamega* as one of her titles and praise names. In its original Igala context, *Agamega* was a title confined to male kings and chieftains. What was more, an Igala king was believed to be transformed into a lion or leopard after he died (Meek 1930; Boston 1968).

DAY-TO-DAY GOVERNMENT: THE WORKINGS OF A FEMALE WARRANT CHIEF AND KING

Let us now turn our attention to the actual day-to-day operation of government under Ahebi. Ahebi Ugbabe, like the warrant chiefs of her time, turned her palace into a court (Afigbo 1972; Agbedo 1979). She settled cases between individuals and obtained money for these services. Ahebi's palace also served as a sanctuary for runaway women whose husbands abused them. King Ahebi Ugbabe married some of the women who decided to stay and consequently became their female husband. Another way that Ahebi would acquire wives was through the unscrupulous services of some of her servants—*ndi iboyi*—who were famed for harassing and kidnapping men's wives for themselves and their master.

The majority of the wives and concubines bore children for Ahebi, thus extending the Ahebi name to a new generation of descendants.[8] Some wives, especially the beautiful ones, were encouraged to service the physical needs of Ahebi's important male visitors like the Attah of Idah and the British colonial officers who were known to visit Ahebi's palace frequently. In addition to her numerous wives and concubines, King Ahebi Ugbabe had a host of female attendants, cooks, and bath maids. She also bought and kept "slaves." She did this in part as a prestige booster and to acquire workers for her fields and for heavy manual labor.

THE CULMINATION OF A VILLAGE CONFLICT

In 1930, roughly ten years after the British administration was instituted, the Roman Catholic Mission (RCM) arrived in Enugu-Ezike (Kalu 1996). Mr.

Helbert, the District Officer, a staunch Catholic himself, encouraged all of his warrant chiefs to embrace this denomination of Christianity and establish schools where reading, writing, and arithmetic would be taught (Agbedo 1979). In the beginning, mission schools were established in the homes of the warrant chiefs. Ahebi Ugbabe set up such a school in her palace. Jacob Elam from neighboring Aku was its first teacher.

School attendance was extremely poor. After a month of instruction, the teacher, in an attempt to boost enrollment, introduced himself to the elders of Umuida. The elders informed Jacob that if he came to teach the whole of Umuida his school should not be in Ahebi's palace, but at the house of the oldest man in Ogurte, Abugu Aina, according to tradition. The teacher, therefore, moved into Abugu Aina's house. A slighted Ahebi called in the police, who rounded up all the elders involved and threw them in the Nsukka prison for three days. She then sent word to the District Officer's interpreter, Ishmael, who found a replacement teacher, Samuel Nwume, for the palace school.

EKPE AHEBI MASQUERADE: THE FINAL INSULT

The underlying reason that the elders encouraged the first teacher, Jacob Elam, to move out of Ahebi's palace was that they had had enough of her antics and abuses. It was not simply that Ahebi had eroded the traditional leadership of the male elders by transforming herself first into a British-imposed headman, then warrant chief, and subsequently into an Igala-imposed king; she had also abused her political power. Particularly troubling to the traditional political elite were Ahebi Ugbabe's autocratic methods in which she committed unthinkable taboos against society, like refusing to consult with elders, utilizing forced labor to build her Ahebi Ugbabe Road, receiving bribes, and forcibly taking away men's wives.

The final straw was when the ambitious Ahebi, perhaps in her quest to achieve full manhood in Nsukka terms, pushed the limits of its gender system and invaded the last and ultimate sanctuary of Igbo full men: she created and brought out a masked spirit. This masquerade was called *Ekpe* Ahebi. It was the most beautiful masquerade the villagers had ever seen.

In his book, *The Dead Among the Living*, A.O. Onyeneke describes the significance of the masked spirit in Igboland: "The masquerade serves the special function of differentiating male[s] and female[s] in Igbo society. It is the exclusive function of the [full men], while the [women] are always excluded even where a female character is portrayed in the masking. . . . The social definition of [full] man therefore is the ability to control a masquerade" (Onyeneke 1987: 78).

The Igbo expectation about the relationship of women to masked spirits is clear. They distinguish, however, between categories of male associations

with masquerades as well. In Igbo sensibilities, the masquerade secret society
is the institution that separates full men (i.e., initiated biological men) from
uninitiated men and women. It is forbidden for any individual who is born
female (i.e., a biological woman) or a gender transformed/masculinized
(wo)man (including female husbands, female fathers, and female sons, etc.)
to control a masked spirit in Igboland. What is more, it is also forbidden for
uninitiated biological men to control masked spirits. Biological women
(again, including gender transformed (wo)men) and uninitiated biological
men were supposed to run away at the sight of a mask, for to claim knowledge of what is behind the mask would mean that a crime has been committed
against that mask. Therefore, while Ahebi Ugbabe had effectively transformed herself into a headman, warrant chief, and king (British and Igala
instituted female masculinities), as far as Igbo culture was concerned she
could neither create nor control a masked spirit, because she was biologically
female. Therefore, Ahebi's attempt to realize and humanize the aspiration of
her symbolic kinship praise song ("Ahebi Ugbabe is the Odo masquerade")
would meet with severe opposition from Nsukka full men. What was more,
her unspeakable actions caused the total desecration of her masked spirit,
since no woman nor uninitiated man could ever invoke an ancestral spirit.
This was in essence the gravity of Ahebi's crime.

ENUGU-EZIKE TAKES ACTION: THE CONFISCATION OF *EKPE* AHEBI

In Enugu-Ezike it was customary for a masked spirit to be "brought out."
This presentation epitomized the introduction of the masked spirit to the community and normally took place during a festive ceremony held at the *Onyishi
Umunwoke*'s *obu*, or house. The highlight of the ceremony was when each
masquerade in attendance paid tribute to the male *Onyishi* and his council of
elders, *ndi oha*. At this time Apeh Azegba, the same elder who orchestrated
the departure of Ahebi Ugbabe's first palace teacher, was the *Onyishi* and
therefore was the luminary who received the masquerades.

On the day in question, sometime in 1939, all of the masked spirits in
Ogurte congregated at the *Onyishi*'s *obu*. Separately, they rose and took center stage. Each masquerade first performed a short opening sequence, then
danced up to the *Onyishi* and bowed before him as a mark of respect. This
process was repeated many times over by each of the masked spirits in attendance, to the sheer delight of the people present. Soon it was the turn of
Ahebi's masked spirit, *Ekpe*, to pay tribute to Apeh Azegba. Amos Abugu
describes what happened next:

> Ahebi Ugbabe brought out kola nuts and offered them to Azegba, explain-
> ing that her masquerade had come to pay its respects. Azegba remained

silent for a time, shook his head, and then beseeched his ancestors to pre-
tend not to have heard the abomination that was uttered from Ahebi's lips—
after all, women were NEVER allowed to own masquerades in Igboland.
He then spoke directly to Ahebi. "Do you not know our culture?" He did
not even wait for her to respond, but instead asked his cronies to escort
Ahebi's *Ekpe* to the back yard—and there it remained, never to be seen
again. (Amos Abugu interview)[9]

The "traditional" leadership of male elders and full men had finally acted,
and the message was clear. Ahebi Ugbabe's impertinence and exaggerated
female masculinities would no longer be tolerated!

AHEBI UGBABE VERSUS OGURTE: THE COURT TRIAL AND BETRAYAL OF THE BRITISH

Ahebi Ugbabe, spoiling for a fight, immediately ordered Apeh Azegba and
his council of male elders to court. The case was so extraordinary and
unprecedented that it had to be taken to the Resident's Office in Onitsha.
After he heard the case, the resident pronounced his ruling: Ahebi Ugbabe did
not have the right to create or "bring out" a masquerade since she was a
woman. He then instructed the villagers to repay Ahebi whatever money she
had used to acquire the masked spirit, and then keep the masquerade. This
decision revealed the duplicity of the British colonials. They had used Ahebi's
knowledge of the geography of Enugu-Ezike to conquer and subjugate her
people and then patted her on the back by presenting her with a headman and
warrant chief position. They had also superficially supported her during
squabbles with individual members of her community. But when it really
counted, the British betrayed her in the worst possible way. For all intents and
purposes, the British no longer needed Ahebi's services and loyalty, as they
had already gained a foothold in Enugu-Ezike. In fact the action of the male
elders had shown that Ahebi was not as invincible as she once seemed. What
was more, she seemed to have lost the loyalty of a good fraction of her subjects, which could prove disastrous for the continued success of British indirect rule in Enugu-Ezike. Therefore, it could be argued that the British court
decision represented a superficial endorsement of "community values," in an
attempt to connect with a group of male elders whose influence they had previously underestimated. It also appears that the British resident viewed
Ahebi's action as overstepping her "native" authority as warrant chief, thus
alienating her subjects.

No sooner had the resident instructed that Ahebi relinquish her *Ekpe* masquerade to her community than her influence lessened, and her image as
superhuman and untouchable unraveled. Thus, after many years the community represented by the traditional leadership of male elders triumphed in their

battle against the autocratic rule of King Ahebi Ugbabe. Detractors immediately composed songs that were aimed at humiliating and ridiculing her. One such song, *"Ahebi akpogo ifu mma wolu obodo,"* submitted that "Ahebi Ugbabe [the gendered transformed (wo)man] had been initiated into the masquerade cult only to be stripped of all the rights and privileges due initiates, and had accordingly become an ordinary woman."

Although she remained powerful until she died in 1948, King Ahebi did not fully recover from the ruling. Moreover, her perceived abuse of power led the elders of Enugu-Ezike to vow that no single individual would ever rule them again. They were never going to allow another woman, female man, or man, for that matter, to assume the kind of absolute power that Ahebi had exercised. King Ahebi Ugbabe was indeed the first female and last king ever to rule in Enugu-Ezike.

CONCLUSION

Ahebi Ugbabe's story presents an unrivaled portrait of one (wo)man's power and agency in the face of a rapidly changing British colonial landscape, during an era when women were marginalized politically across Africa. It contributes much to our understanding of continuity and change in Nsukka gendered politics, as well as our knowledge about competing and overlapping definitions/constructions of female masculinities and manhood in colonial Nsukka Division.

In the course of her life, Ahebi Ugbabe asserted her fundamental right as a gendered Igbo actor to transform herself into a multiplicity of female masculinities. She was able to negotiate her life first within the historical context of British colonialism and subsequently, Igala ascendancy, so as to extend, alter and attempt to fundamentally challenge preexisting Nsukka gender ideals that governed the extent to which a woman could become a man. However, when this extraordinary woman attempted to achieve acceptance and full manhood in the ultimate sanctuary of full Igbo men, she was immediately reined in by indigenous gerontocratic male authority, revealing at once Igbo society's resolve to limit the extent to which female gendered transformations can materialize.

Let us examine in greater detail the historical conditions/context that unintentionally allowed Ahebi the space to alter and extend her gendered identity. In colonial Igbo country, the British invaders initially sought to create conditions that would recognize and celebrate the so-called native authority of Igbo male elders. They thus instituted the office of headman, superficially patterned after the indigenous *Onyishi Umunwoke*, so that the appointed Igbo elders soon became junior partners in the colonial political processes of their districts. However, by the 1920s, during a time when colonial rule was consolidating its hold in Igboland, the British switched their loyalties and began to give privileges to male youth. It is valuable to visualize this modification in broader terms. It would appear that the British sought out male youth whom they believed would be much more amenable and energetic than their aged predecessors and consequently be better suited to undertake their instruction. Once selected, the young Igbo men were empowered with warrants of office, which served to elevate and celebrate youth while pushing aside age and respectability, "traditional" Nsukka determinants of power and authority.

Although Ahebi Ugbabe was born a woman, she was able to tap into this British obsession with youth. She was young, beautiful, loyal, and dependable, and, most importantly, she had proved herself to be an invaluable asset to the consolidation of British rule in Enugu-Ezike. Evidence suggests that Ahebi not only worked to satisfy the sexual appetites of the British colonials, but she also revealed the routes by which to conquer her people. Her linguistic skills further cemented her connection with the British, since she was the only person in Umuida who could communicate with and relay British objectives to the colonized Enugu-Ezike citizens.

It could be argued that by embracing a highly masculinized form of colonial leadership (i.e., headman), Ahebi Ugbabe had sought to redefine a preexisting indigenous Nsukka female masculinity of *Onyishi Umunwanyi*—a dignitary who existed side by side with the *Onyishi Umunwoke* and who was already constructed as male in Nsukka consciousness. However, in this indigenous gendered system, age, respectability, and achievement were prerequisites for this type of gendered transformation into an "honorary man." Ahebi Ugbabe, who did not possess any of the determinants of Nsukka leadership, was nevertheless quick to tap into British colonial privileging of youth and transform herself into a young female headman. This ingenious gender and age negotiation would set the stage for Ahebi's supreme British-sustained transformation into a female warrant chief.

Ahebi's triumph in transforming herself into a warrant chief in 1918 revealed not only her extraordinary abilities, but also her exceptional ability to invent and reinvent herself within the new and viable context of British colonial rule. Like the headman position, which she had so ingeniously modified to fit her needs, Ahebi Ugbabe was again able to streamline British ideals of male youthfulness in leadership and assume the warrant chief office as an already transformed female man. In fact, Ahebi Ugbabe would become the only (wo)man to hold this office in all of colonial Nigeria. In becoming a female headman and warrant chief, Ahebi Ugbabe had therefore essentially redefined, expanded upon, and evolved a preexisting Nsukka female masculinity (*Onyishi Umunwanyi*) while adapting individualized and youth-based British masculinities within the context of indirect rule. She would subsequently turn to the Igala constitution to uphold her third in a series of supreme gendered transformations—a successful quest to become a female king.

When Ahebi created and brought out a masked spirit in her attempt to realize full manhood within the Nsukka indigenous context, full men as well as members of the Nsukka male gerontocratic elite immediately reined her in. They confiscated her *Ekpe* Ahebi masquerade, revealing at once that Ahebi had overextended the limits of acceptable female behavior. In confiscating Ahebi's *Ekpe* masked spirit, the male elders had in essence taken away Ahebi's spiritual-based masculinized powers, thus symbolically forcing her to retransform into a woman. Moreover, the British government decision to stand behind the Nsukka male elders established that they, too, were unwilling to defend such unprecedented behavior on the part of a (fe)male "junior partner" in "native" government.

Ultimately, Nsukka full men as well as its male gerontocratic elite had succeeded in stripping King Ahebi Ugbabe of most of her political clout. In the end, she was forced to perform her burial rites while she was still alive (*ikwa owe ya na ndu*) because she did not trust that her society would accord her a befitting burial. The *Omenani* (fixed laws that guide and order group relationships in Igbo society) had therefore proved victorious in their conflict against excessive and inordinate female ambition.

NOTES

1. In northern Igboland, after a man died, his first daughter "became" her father. She dressed in her father's attire, sat in his *obi* (traditional male residence in which only men congregated), and was saluted and addressed as her father by his close associates. She continued in this role until her father's true heir was identified. This practice of masculinizing oneself by donning male clothing is also a theme that presents itself in the life of Ahebi Ugbabe, who was known to have dressed in male garb during a number of public appearances.

2. Amadiume refers to this category as "male daughters." However, I have adopted the term "female son" for my own discussions, because I feel that this term captures more adequately the transformation from a daughter (i.e., female sex) to a son (i.e., male gender).

3. I use the concept of "man" in this essay to refer to the biological and physical characteristics that determine maleness; as well as the beliefs, attitudes, behavior, and actions that differentiate men from women. A " biological man" in this positioning has not been initiated into the masquerade cult (i.e., *ikpu ani,*) and therefore cannot create or control a masked spirit. Furthermore, a woman can transform herself into a "man," or, stated differently, a female man or (wo)man. I consequently use the terms "female man," and "(wo)man" interchangeably as the foregoing are in fact female masculinities. A "full man," on the other hand, must first be biologically male and, second, have undergone the Igbo ritual of *ikpu ani*. Therefore, the determinant of "full manhood" is not only biology, but also the ability to create and control a masked spirit.

4. This chapter represents months of archival and field research on Ahebi Ugbabe that I conducted during two separate research trips to Nigeria, a Ford Foundation Pre-Dissertation Fieldwork trip in 1996, and a Fulbright-Hays Dissertation Fieldwork trip in 1998. My vast fountain of information gathering was oral and provides the basis for the reconstruction of the history of this prominent female king and warrant chief. I conducted interviews pri-

marily in Igbo with numerous Nsukka and Igala collaborators who shared with me individual and group memories of this remarkable (wo)man. For want of space, I will not reference individual collaborator/s in the text, but rather provide a list of the collaborators interviewed in my bibliography.

5. Agbedo (1979: 65) and Agashi (1986: 17). I use the term "prostitution" advisedly and rather reluctantly, since this categorization is Eurocentric in its implication and does not, in my view, speak to the signification of the institution in northern Igboland. For more about this Nsukka institution, see Nwando Achebe (2000: Chap. VI).

6. It is interesting to note, however, that European initial concern centered on the amelioration of the treatment of "slaves," rather than an immediate eradication of slavery. In fact there is evidence to suggest that some missionaries purchased "slaves" to use as domestic servants, and others trained them as missionary workers and interpreters. See C. Ejizu (1986: 145–48) and Don Ohadike (1988: 443–50).

7. The Odo masquerade was the most powerful masked spirit and, by extension, indicator of manhood in Nsukka Division.

8. The biological "fathers" of Ahebi Ugbabe's children were not important; they did not pay the traditional brideprice and therefore had no rights to Ahebi's children. In a manner of speaking, they were simply sperm donors.

9. The events leading up to the seizure of *Ekpe* Ahebi were also corroborated by Boniface Abugu, Abodo Nwa Idoko, Wilfred Ogara, Samuel Ezeja, Fabian Azegba, and Uroke Nwa Iyida Oku (Raymond Iyida).

REFERENCES

Achebe, Nwando. 2000. "Farmers, Traders, Warriors and Kings: Female Power and Authority in Northern Igboland, 1900–1960." PhD dissertation, Department of History, University of California, Los Angeles.

Afigbo, A.E. 1972. *The Warrant Chiefs: Indirect Rule in Southeastern Nigeria 1891–1929*. London: Longman Group Limited.

Agashi, P.O. 1986. "Government at Nsukka 1929–1979." M.A. history project, Department of History, University of Nigeria, Nsukka.

Agbedo, Cyprian U. 1979. "Slavery and Slave Trade in Enugu-Ezike in the Pre-colonial Period." B.A. thesis, Department of History, University of Nigeria, Nsukka, June.

Amadiume, Ifi. 1987. *Male Daughters, Female Husbands: Gender and Sex in an African Society*. London: Zed Books.

Boston, J.S. 1968. *The Igala Kingdom*. Ibadan: Oxford University Press.

Ejizu, C. 1986. "Continuity and Discontinuity in Igbo Traditional Religion." In *The Gods in Retreat: Continuity and Change in African Religions*, Emefie Ikenga Metuh, ed. Enugu: Fourth Dimension Publishers.

Ezeh, Godwin Chukwuemeka. 1995. "A Political History of Nsukka, 1900–1960." M.A. thesis, Department of History, University of Nigeria, February.

Johnson, V.K. 1934. "Intelligence Report on Enugu-Ezike, Nsukka Division, Onitcha Province." OP.1071 ONDIST 12/1/709. Enugu: Nigerian National Archives, NAE.

Kalu, Ogbu U. 1996. *The Embattled Gods: Christianization of Igboland, 1841–1991*. Lagos: Minaj Publishers.

Mba, Nina. 1982. *Nigerian Women Mobilized: Women's Political Activity in Southern Nigeria, 1900–1965*. Berkeley: Institute of International Studies.

Meek, C.K. 1930. *Ethnographical Report on the Peoples of Nsukka Division, Onitsha Province*. Lagos: Government Printer.

Ohadike, Don. 1988. "The Decline of Slavery among the Igbo People." In *The End of Slavery in Africa*, Suzanne Miers and Richard Roberts, eds. Madison, WI: University of Wisconsin Press.

Omeje, Christopher Uchechukwu. 1978. "The Establishment of British Rule in the Old Nsukka Division." B.A. History and Archaeology Special Project, University of Nigeria, Nsukka, June.

Onyeneke, A.O. 1987. *The Dead among the Living: Masquerades in Igbo Society.* Nimo, Nigeria: Holy Ghost Congregation, Province of Nigeria and Asele Institute.

Van Allen, Judith. 1972. "'Sitting on a Man': Colonialism and the Lost Political Institutions of Igbo Women." *Canadian Journal of African Studies* 6: 165–82.

Interviews and Personal Communications

Unless otherwise noted, all interviews were conducted and tape recorded by the author and took place in Enugu-Ezike, Enugu State.

Abugu, Amos. Farmer. 4 October 1998.

Abugu, Boniface. Ex-councilor and retired headmaster, now farmer. 4 October 1998.

Abugu, Ignatius. Olu Oha Imufu Enugu-Ezike. 28 September 1998.

Abugwu, Chikere. Ahebi Ugbabe descendant. 29 September 1998.

Adibuah, Selina Ugwuoke. Parasitologist and medical scientist. Trans Ekulu, Enugu, Enugu State, 23 October 1996.

Agashi, Ogbu. Olu Oha. 26 September 1996.

Akogu, Alice (formally Ahebi). Stephen Ahebi's wife. Ofate, Kogi State, 5 October 1998.

Ameh, Bernard. Ahebi Ugbabe's great-great-grandson. 29 September 1998.

Asanya, Abugwu Eze Nwa. Ahebi Ugbabe descendant. 29 September 1998.

Asanya, Fidelis Eze Nwonu. Ahebi Ugbabe descendant. 29 September 1998.

Asanya, Jonathan Abugwu. Ahebi Ugbabe descendant. 29 September 1998.

Azegba, Fabian. Ex-councilor and headmaster. 2 October 1998.

Azegbo, Oshageri. Musician. 19 November 1998.

Eze, Erobike. Retired civil servant and farmer. Personal communication with author, Nsukka, Enugu State, 27 October 1998 and 13 September 1998.

Ezeja, Samuel. Schoolteacher. 25 November 1996.

Idoko, Chief Abodo Nwa. Herbalist. 26 September 1998.

Idoko, Chief Michael. Headmaster Ahebi Primary School. 25 November 1996.

Idoko, Pius. *Attama* Ohe. 23 November 1996 and 27 September 1998.

Nwaba, Enwo Odo Nweze. Ahebi Ugbabe descendant. 29 September 1998.

Nweke, Simeon. Ex-councilor. 26 November 1996.

Obeta, Barnabas. Ahebi Ugbabe biological nephew. 25 November 1996 and 2 October 1998.

Odum, Ayogu Onu. Ahebi Ugbabe descendant. 29 September 1998.

Ogara, Wilfred. Ahebi Ugbabe nonbiological son. 25 November 1996.

Oku, Uroke Nwa Iyida (Raymond Iyida). Former Igwe of Onitsha, Enugu-Ezike. 28 September 1998.

Omeke, Fabian. Ahebi Ugbabe descendant. 29 September 1998.

Onasanya, Michael Omeke. Ahebi Ugbabe Descendant. 29 September 1998.

Onu, Asanya. Ahebi Ugbabe descendent. 29 September 1998.

Onu, Ogbu Nwa Abugwu Asenya. Ahebi Ugbabe descendant. 29 September 1998.

Osogwu, Enwo Nwa Odo Nweze Nwaba. Ahebi Ugbabe descendant. 29 September 1998.

Ugbabe, Oyima Obeta Nwa. Ahebi Ugbabe biological niece. 2 October 1998.

Ugwuaku, David. Ahebi Ugbabe descendant. 29 September 1998.

4

OLD SOLDIERS, YOUNG MEN: MASCULINITY, ISLAM, AND MILITARY VETERANS IN LATE 1950s SOUDAN FRANÇAIS (MALI)[1]

Gregory Mann

INTRODUCTION

In 1950s Soudan Français, urban Muslim communities witnessed fierce battles over pedagogical traditions and rituals of prayer. The expanding political and social "space" accorded to what Launay and Soares have termed an "Islamic sphere" magnified the intensity of these conflicts. This sphere was "conceptually separate (though obviously not entirely autonomous) from 'particular' affiliations—ethnicity, kin group membership, 'caste' or slave origins, etc.—but also from the colonial (and later the post-colonial) state" (Launay and Soares 1999: 498). The space was a relatively open one, and it was a site of multiple conflicts over religious authority. Disputes that took their public form as disagreements about prayer rituals turned violent in several towns, including Sikasso and Bamako.[2]

Some of these battles are well known, while others have been overshadowed. Among the latter, a series of intense conflicts involved the followers and detractors of a certain Ousmane Sidibe, an itinerant *marabout*, or Muslim holy man. Sidibe preached in the Soudanese market town of San on several occasions in the mid-1950s, and each time his popularity, as well as his notoriety, mounted. According to one woman's recollection, he was never allowed to speak in the mosques; thus he taught in the streets, articulating his message in the most public of settings.[3] Although many women came to hear him, he was unpopular with many men, both among the Muslim elite and among the populace more broadly. In fact, he roused such rancor that he was repeatedly threatened and twice driven out of town.

On visits to San in December 1956 and again in May 1957, his opponents pelted Sidibe with stones, and the *gendarmerie* was forced to intervene.[4] When Sidibe returned in September of 1957, a crowd turned out to hear him speak. A larger crowd turned out to lynch him. They nearly succeeded. Only the protection of the *gendarmerie* saved Sidibe and his entourage from serious punishment, as the local French administrator, or *commandant de cercle*, described:

> In spite of all advice to abstention, Ousmane Sidibe (who leads the prayer with crossed arms)[5] arrived in San on the fourth of September from Koutiala, where, rumor has it, he had just burned copies of the Qur'an. . . . When he came to introduce himself at the offices of the *cercle*, I explained to him the critical situation in which he found himself, advised that he leave, and forbade all public meetings. The *cercle* offices were all but besieged by a menacing crowd whose delegates, in spite of my requests for tolerance, asked me to expel Ousmane Sidibe. The *gendarmerie* cleared the crowd from around the *cercle*, but could do no more than limit the damage of a brawl with the crowd chasing and molesting Ousmane and his followers, including the venerable *adjudant* [and president of the local veterans' association] Nianson Coulibaly, the primary organizer of Ousmane's return to San. Ousmane thus had to take refuge in the house of a friend [Nianson Coulibaly]. He sought shelter there but as the popular anger grew, he finally decided to follow the advice of the *gendarmerie*, and towards three o'clock he wisely took a truck for Segu.[6]

The administrator advised him sternly never to return to San. It is not clear that he ever did. However, his message continued to cause deep divisions within the town's Muslim community. A complaint to the local government early in 1960 accused Sidibe of sowing discord among Muslims:

> Completely transforming the sense of the Qur'an, [Sidibe] managed to get his disciples to change the manner of praying, of fasting, of making ablutions, of giving alms [*zakat*], etc. . . . It is his fault that the Muslims are divided into two camps that do not pray together, neither on Fridays nor on festivals ['*Ids*]; they perform neither funerals, nor naming ceremonies, nor marriages together. . . . Sidibe's teachings have been the cause of several divorces, separations of intimate friends, of brothers, of fathers and sons, mothers and daughters, etc.

In the town of San itself, his followers prayed in a separate mosque at least into the 1960s.[7]

The story of Ousmane Sidibe and his expulsion from San has many facets. Part of the history of the community's sexual mores and of its attitudes toward strangers, it is equally part of a larger wave of Islamic reform and Muslim conflict marked by a new scripturalism and a reconsideration of the relationship between charismatic spiritual leaders (*shaykhs*) and their adepts (*talibés*). In other towns, the ostensible roots of conflict lay in differences in ritual expression, most clearly indicated by whether or not one prayed with arms across the chest or at one's side. These differences seem to have been less controversial in San, where men following both variants had prayed together peacefully for years.[8] Some members of San's learned Muslim elite opposed Sidibe's message because they disagreed with his interpretation of the Qur'an, and this scholarly difference was made vivid among the populace by the rumor that he had burned copies of the Qur'an in a neighboring *cercle*.[9] The scholars and other Muslims objected to Sidibe's condemnation of those who consumed tobacco, kola nuts, or meat, which he considered impure (*haram*).

However, the violence of the reaction against Sidibe and the long-lasting rifts his message caused in the community stem from two aspects of that message (as it is remembered). Both struck at the core of senior Muslim masculinity. The first of these controversial aspects was his position on the role of women in Muslim families, of which more below. While his arguments about marital authority and domestic obligations could be seen as affecting all Muslim husbands and fathers, the second aspect had a greater effect on the town's scholars and *marabouts*. Sidibe deeply alienated local Muslim leaders when he condemned certain ritual practices. These included supererogatory prayers (Arabic, *wazifa*) and the esoteric sciences of Islam, that is to say, practices such as geomancy, divination, numerology, and the production of *gris-gris*, amulets meant to protect their bearers.[10] This production was not only economically lucrative, but was a trade in secrets or the powers based upon them. In attacking these practices, Sidibe attacked the *marabouts'* prestige and indeed their own version of senior masculine power, which was built on the spiritual and material value of their religious knowledge. Thus, "from the first day" Sidibe became "the *bête noire* of the local *marabouts*, in spite of his popularity [or notoriety] in the town," where he drew audiences as large as 2,000 people.[11]

Who among those 2,000 people supported Sidibe? On this point, administrative records and local memory agree: Sidibe's followers were, by and large, recent converts to Islam. Moreover, the commander of the *gendarmerie* reported that Sidibe's followers could be overheard insisting that "the old *marabouts* wanted to hide the truth from them, and that only Sidibe truly shed light on the Qur'an."[12] Among those followers were many women and an important contingent of military veterans, or *anciens combattants*, led by their president Nianson Coulibaly.

MASCULINITY AND MILITARY VETERANS

Religious riots are not the kind of social space in which one normally looks for veterans. Studies of African soldiers in the French colonial military (the *tirailleurs Sénégalais*) would not lead us to anticipate finding ex-servicemen in the midst of sectarian conflicts. Those studies have focused on soldiers and veterans as political subjects, even nascent nationalists, and they have often underemphasized the complexity of veterans' motivations and allegiances.[13] Thus, this chapter addresses two previously ignored aspects of the experiences of these soldiers and veterans. First, while most work on African soldiers ignores religious practice, here such practice is central to the analysis. Second, because most previous studies were blind to gender,[14] they missed the crucial fact that even in their absence, these soldiers were fathers, sons, husbands, and brothers (White this volume).

This essay examines veterans as gendered actors in their local communities and explores their role in the religious riot that swirled around Sidibe. It argues that, both within and outside of the "Islamic sphere" (Launay and Soares 1999), military veterans were crucial actors in the creation of the hybrid social and political world that characterized late colonial Soudan and independent Mali. While Muslim allegiances and disputes have long been crucial to political life in West Africa, in 1950s Soudan Français they marked a sharply disputed terrain in which both variations in (self-consciously) Islamic practice and the sources of senior masculine power were bitterly contested. This essay argues that in seeking recognition as senior men, San's veterans challenged the bases of the masculine power and authority of the town's Muslim elders. In doing so, they made religious practice a primary mode of gendered—and particularly masculine—politics. However, this dispute had its roots in material interests as well as social and ideological constructs. At issue were patterns of senior male patronage and the value of esoteric and religious knowledge which only certain men possessed, and which they exploited to the full.

SAN

The site of this conflict was the vibrant, dusty market town of San, along the Bani River in central Mali. From the sixteenth century, San played a prominent role in the regional and supraregional exchange of salt, kola, and slaves. In the second half of the nineteenth century, its leaders submitted peacefully to *al-hajj* 'Umar Tal and later to the French (Kamian 1959). By 1910, San was a *chef lieu de cercle*, the capital of a French administrative district, and its role in regional commerce grew. By the late 1950s, the town's

African population was estimated at 10,000 (Kamian 1959: 225). Under colonial rule, the *cercle* was also the object of intense recruitment for military service and forced labor.

Through all of these political changes, San continued to occupy a kind of cultural border zone; various ethnic groups lived in the town and its immediate hinterland. From the seventeenth century, Islam and, later, Christianity assumed powerful if distinct roles in the spiritual lives of the town and its environs. However, Islam remained largely a religion of the urban elite until after the Second World War, and local practices remained very strong, particularly in the surrounding villages. Thus as a crossroads and a node of linguistic, cultural, and religious diversity, San possessed an intrinsic hybridity which was enhanced in the 1950s by temporary and permanent immigration. The coexistence of multiple faiths and languages was not always peaceful. In 1956–57, Sidibe faced a community in transition, in which Islam had probably not yet become the majority religion.

Many of Sidibe's adepts were recent converts to Islam, and administrators attributed both their ignorance and their zeal to that fact.[15] Whatever local factors played into their allegiance to Sidibe, the *anciens combattants* who followed him were part of a larger social category which was significant to twentieth-century reform movements worldwide. Fundamentally, they were people with more faith than instruction who were immersed in a debate combining politics, theology, and practical concerns.

It was precisely this lack of Muslim education that led Moussa Doumbia, one of San's leading teachers of the Qur'an and a witness to the events, to argue that Sidibe's message appealed to the *anciens combattants* in particular because "They didn't know any better—these were people who didn't even pray." From his perspective as a learned man, an *'alim*, they had no instruction and therefore lacked the ability to think critically about Sidibe's message; he compared them to women in this regard.[16] However, the *anciens combattants'* purported ignorance was the result of a combination of factors different from those pertaining to women. These included their often low social class and their absences, which had deprived them of a local spiritual indoctrination or apprenticeship.

SOLDIERS, VETERANS, AND MUSLIMS

After years of travel, labor, and combat in Europe, North Africa, and Indochina, many former career *tirailleurs* found that homecoming was not easy. Both conscripts and volunteers were generally of low social status. Returning after years of absence, these men emerged into social and political contexts dramatically different from those they had left behind. Some had not been home for more than a decade. All had been absent during a crucial period in their lives and the lives of their peers.

While the *tirailleurs* were elsewhere, other men of their age had been investing in local life in a more immediate fashion than remittances, leave, and letters would allow. They were marrying, fathering children, increasing their holdings in land and livestock, and becoming more deeply immersed in the spiritual lives of their communities. While the soldiers were absent, their peers were improvising—with varying degrees of caution—on expectations of proper behavior for adult men in a gerontocratic society in which gender and age were intimately linked.

The soldiers had developed an alternative masculinity that combined local ideas with those derived from other African and French cultures, such as the command of linguistic and technological skills and access to consumer goods. While the demasculinization of men living under colonial rule has become a truism of colonial studies, whether as an effect of state power or as a method and a goal of its exercise,[17] the conflict analyzed below does not fit this paradigm. Indeed, European officers may have been challenged in their own gendered positions by the men they commanded.[18] While they were certainly influenced by other cultures, ex-soldiers experienced more immediate gendered conflicts within their communities than in the discursive spaces between colonizer and colonized.

Although a career soldier may have proved his masculinity as a young man, when he returned home he was no longer young. Moreover, while considered a masculine occupation, soldiering did not carry great prestige, and among older generations it was often connected to a heritage of slavery. Older idioms of the strength, courage, and bravery of men who went to war valorized the experiences of these men, but the shadow of servility hung over them. Thus while a certain status attached to having survived combat, the social meaning of that experience was highly debatable, particularly in the colonial context. Of course, veterans emphasized the value and singularity of their experiences, even as other members of the community dismissed them as slaves or the descendants of slaves.[19]

Veterans asserted their particular masculine identity in various ways, ranging from the quotidian, such as wearing old uniforms, to the exceptional, like marching in Bastille Day parades or turning out as a group to salute passing administrative dignitaries. Within their own circles, such as the association of *anciens combattants*, the veterans' shared experiences, military ranks, and decorations created a sense of community and suggested a hierarchy within it. Veterans' collective identity fully exploited the patronage of the colonial state and the individual's personal experiences—including combat, travel, and training—to maximize whatever privileges and prestige attached to being a veteran. The men also emphasized their differences from their civilian peers and often the distance from their own backgrounds.

With its aggressive programs of patronage, the colonial state fueled the process of creating this identity. Veterans had their own formal association and a *maison du combattant*, or veterans' lodge, constructed by the government. Other benefits were less tangible: the ability to converse in French, a familiarity with the French culture of command, and comparative ease of access to the apparatus of the state. In the rapidly changing political, social, and economic circumstances of post-war French Africa, these intangibles undoubtedly made the veteran a "special kind of a man" (Lindsay 1998: 449), but they did not necessarily ease reintegration. This same set of attributes reinforced the common perception of *anciens combattants* as eccentric, at best, or as asocial and mentally unstable, at worst.[20] In response to that discourse, material resources and patronage were the strongest retorts.

Material patronage, in the form of pensions, loans, and other cash payments, made it possible for the fortunate minority of veterans who received them to meet many of the expectations their households and extended families placed upon them. State resources also made it possible for Nianson Coulibaly, who succeeded his brother as president of the local veterans' association, to act as a patron to other men outside his immediate family. Such patronage was a crucial aspect of elder status.

In spite of such patronage, their military honors, and material resources, the veterans' collective identity remained in a variable tension with the ascendant masculinities of other men of higher social standing, such as African civil servants or political and religious elites. Some veterans, particularly those native to the town, were engaged in complex relationships of clientage, servitude, or dependence with these men. As clients and as patrons, all returning soldiers had to demonstrate their ability to live up to the expectations of an adult man. Active religious practice was a key component of these expectations, and it was crucial to reintegration. However, veterans' practices were not always in harmony with those of their communities.

Religious affiliations and practices were crucial components of senior masculine identity, and they both facilitated and troubled veterans' slow processes of homecoming and of becoming respectable men. After all, reintegration was a bid for respectability, and it entailed a claim of community membership. For veterans this meant some kind of—perhaps improvisational—variation on the type of behavior expected of an adult man who was no longer young. In local societies the cluster of traits that characterized senior masculine status was rarely enunciated. Senior status was essentially an unmarked category: any man with white hair would likely be addressed as *cékoroba*, but only certain of these men were true elders who held the respect of their peers and of significant members of the community. Like a younger man's masculinity, the elder's status could be gained and lost (see Miescher 1997: 490–1). It depended upon control of resources and juniors, family connections, domestic and public authority, and a shifting bundle of other characteristics, always including religious practice.

Any male elder demonstrated some kind of religious faith, which in San could have been Muslim, Christian, or strictly regional.[21] It was equally important that an elder possess or be able to call upon religious knowledge. In the practice of local religions and often of Islam, this frequently included specifically esoteric knowledge or religious secrets. The ability to deploy such knowledge—whether by oneself or through a third party[22]—was crucial to senior masculine status. Yet it was more than a matter of status. Such knowledge was, among other things, a powerful political tool, and the era of electoral politics only heightened its importance.

Crucially, knowledge of religious practices, including esoteric sciences and other secrets, was often curtailed among veterans. Their long absences had frequently denied them a local spiritual indoctrination, or apprenticeship, which they would normally have experienced over the course of many years. By choosing military careers, long-serving soldiers had foregone the acquisition of ritual knowledge and skills that were themselves undergoing rapid change. That particular consequence of their absences was of immeasurable importance. It limited their access to senior male status, and in some ways it marked them as followers rather than leaders. For those among them who were Muslims, including the many converts, it meant that their access to esoteric knowledge and to elder status could in some ways be mediated by the local Muslim leadership.

While their time away from home had deprived veterans of certain local experiences, it also exposed them to a variety of external influences. Religious life within the ranks remains obscure, but the diversity of soldiers' backgrounds and the novelty of their experiences probably accelerated the rate of exchange and the possibility of conversion.[23] Army camps and transit stations were rife with cultural exchange and creation, as soldiers talked about topics ranging from drum-making techniques to religion.[24] The tendency of some Sufis to pray with groups of others following the same spiritual paths (Ar., *turuq*) drew the attention of their officers throughout the Second World War (Blot 1946: 16). Returning from North Africa, some soldiers brought religious texts home with them, while others profited from their travels to visit the tomb of a Muslim "saint" (Ar., *wali*). A fortunate few *tirailleurs* made the *hajj* as they returned from Indochina,[25] and the government of French West Africa (AOF) sponsored prominent veterans to make the *hajj* as well. Although the title *al hajj* added to veterans' prestige, because they were recent converts and men of low status, their easy acquisition of the title may have rankled other Muslims, particularly scholars, *marabouts*, and elders who would never have the opportunity to make the trip.

Nevertheless, demonstration of religious faith and participation in the community's social events and religious ceremonies were key components in reintegration. Ex-soldiers remember the army as a secular institution, but when a soldier returned home he could not remain a "free-thinker."[26] Indeed, the veteran Odiouma Bagayogo claimed that "Most, I could say the majority, of the *anciens combattants* embraced Islam." His friend Naenzo Dao, known as Souleymane, concurred: "You must be either Muslim or Christian," as a veteran. "Why?" I asked. "The milieu influences the veterans." Bagayogo patiently explained,

[E]veryone is Muslim or Christian. You can not remain isolated. Because in the Muslim milieu, he who is not a Muslim is seriously inconvenienced. . . . When he dies, no one will come [to the funeral ceremonies] other than his own relatives. If he is Christian, the Christians attend, and the Muslims do too, but they don't pray.[27]

These men were speaking of religious events, public occasions in which one's community participated, such as naming ceremonies, marriages, or funerals. For men recently returned to or entering a community these events were all the more important, as they allowed a person to build a social network and demonstrate goodwill. Among Muslims, they served as the most visible evidence of the community's unity or, as in the case of San, its rupture. Thus veterans were all but obliged to participate, even if, like Nianson Coulibaly, they did not slip easily into the social aspects of religious life.

After the soldiers returned home, their religious practices often manifested themselves as controversial elements in an already tumultuous social climate. In a post-war crisis of authority, local chiefs and elders were fighting off attacks from younger generations and new elites empowered by electoral politics. More to the point, the Muslim communities of the Soudan Français were experiencing a wave of reform and rejuvenation. To some extent this wave was composed of ripples from abroad, such as those created by reformist movements with roots in the eighteenth-century Arabian peninsula. Other elements of the reform were decidedly internal to the West African Muslim community. In the spiritual realm, the 1940s and 1950s marked a generational "changing of the guard," as some Muslim leaders passed away, the authority of others declined, and a new generation of reformers and *'ulema*, or scholars, rose to prominence (Robinson and Triaud 1997). In San, at least, the key issue in the Muslim community in this period seems to have been that of authority—who would interpret texts, and who would set standards for observance and prayer? Who would lead and who would follow?

Ousmane Sidibe brought such questions to the fore. His critiques of spiritual (and domestic) authority were deeply gender-inflected, and the contest for the allegiances of recent converts to Islam and of junior men became a contest for the preservation or reconfiguration of senior male authority. This was the question at the root of Moussa Doumbia's critique of the veterans (cited above), that they participated because, like women, "They didn't know any better." In making this comparison, Doumbia implied an alternative and in his view inferior masculinity, characterized by the ignorance of men who lacked certain knowledge and skills valuable to him.

MARRIAGE, MUSLIMS, AND A *MARABOUT*

In addition to the veterans, many of San's Muslim women supported Sidibe and his message, as both oral and administrative accounts recall.[28] If prayer rituals, modes of education, and practices such as the fabrication of amulets were at the core of the Muslim conflicts in 1950s West Africa—as indeed they continue to be—how and why did women become central to this particular religious dispute, and to a discourse in which they had long been marginalized? Sidibe asserted that God had given women certain "rights" that good Muslims must respect, that husbands were obligated to support their families, and that extramarital sex was wrong. Most seriously, he argued that many marriages were fraudulent and should be annulled, as the couple had lived together or had had sex before being married. He vehemently condemned adultery.

Embedded in this set of prescriptions for relations between the sexes was a message to which many women readily subscribed. Couched in a language of moral virtue and religious law, Sidibe's streetside preaching gave women an opportunity to demonstrate publicly their expectations of how a good Muslim man ought to behave. When he addressed questions of sexuality and promiscuity, Sidibe offered a message to which many women were sympathetic, in that he argued that men's sexual activities and demands should be limited to marriage.

Many men objected to their wives hearing this message. Oumou Sidibe, the wife of a former gendarme, remembers that her husband told her to stay at home, as Ousmane's teachings were not an affair (literally, "the path") for women.[29] Outside San itself, one *chef de canton* is reported to have told his wives that if they went to hear Sidibe preach, they should never return to his household.[30]

Sidibe delivered his message at a time when such issues were particularly sensitive, a fact that surely exacerbated the community's reactions. Conflicts over marriages and dowries had multiplied in recent years, and Sidibe was preaching only shortly after the implementation of a pair of decrees that extended new legal protections to women. These were the decree of 15 June 1939, known as the decree Mandel, and that of 14 September 1951, known as the decree Jacquinot. The first declared invalid any marriage to which the bride did not consent and forbade the marriage of prepubescent girls. The second declared that single women over 21 years old were free to marry as they chose, without regard for the practice of the dowry. Both decrees weakened the power of patriarchs.

Many Muslims deeply opposed these measures, which they saw as contrary to the *shari'a*. Indeed, one French authority on Islam in West Africa asserted that "among the symptoms of the social evolution, women's increasing aspirations to emancipation worry the Muslim men of the AOF more than any other, and those aspirations generate the sharpest criticisms against us."

He added, "The emotion provoked by the application of the decrees is not simply a manifestation of masculine egoism or of a spirit of gain," referring to dowries; rather he considered that emotion to be based on religious principles.[31]

While such "aspirations" were particularly threatening to elder men (and women) whose daughters were near the age of marriage, their effect on veterans was quite the opposite. A message concerning the sanctity of marriage had great resonance among men who had been absent from home for many years: many of them had lost their fiancées or wives to other men during their absence.[32] Nevertheless, it is impossible to say how deeply the *anciens combattants* were invested in this particular aspect of Sidibe's message. They may have been more attracted by other aspects of his teachings. However, since the issue of women's rights and responsibilities is the one most closely associated with Sidibe, it is likely that those who followed him agreed with his opinions on the subject. At the very least, they were not strongly opposed to them; had they been, they would also have been reluctant to identify with him publicly.

POLITICS AND RELIGIOUS REFORM

Along with the tensions surrounding marriage and the reciprocal obligations of spouses, the community violence Sidibe incited cannot be analyzed in isolation from the intense political struggles that characterized the 1950s. In San, electoral and political violence between supporters of the "radical" US-RDA and the conservative *Parti Progressiste Soudanais* (abbreviated as PSP) flared periodically throughout the decade. The struggle between the parties was so bitter that in one village that voted US-RDA, the pro-PSP chief closed off a well used by his political opponents.[33] Elsewhere in the territory, Muslim politicians who left the US-RDA for its rival party were accused of a betrayal tantamount to apostasy. A poem in the US-RDA's party paper claimed that "for them, no more God, as God counsels good . . . they have renounced the *fatia* [sic, the opening *sura* of the Qur'an] . . . because they had sworn . . . to serve and to struggle for the RDA."[34]

At the time of the riots in San, many of Sidibe's primary supporters in town were PSP militants, and this long-standing conflict between the parties can only have enhanced the sectarian violence that broke out. However, Sidibe himself had fluid allegiances, and he was not deeply invested in electoral politics. It was the parties that alternately courted and lambasted him, not the other way around. In the mid-1950s, he was considered a supporter of the PSP, until its militants in Koutiala disavowed him. He appears to have taken up the banner of the US-RDA in 1958, just as that party was becoming dominant and seeking the support of Muslim leaders.[35] However, that alliance was fragile; the US-RDA leadership appreciated the numerical weight Sidibe's supporters lent them, but many of the party's local militants disapproved of the party's association with him.[36] In sum, nationalist politics merely fanned the flames of a conflict whose roots lay in the convergence of religious and gendered disputes.

CONCLUSION

As veterans were seeking to become respectable adult men, it may at first appear paradoxical that some chose to ally themselves with a man who aroused *dis*respect. Little respect is apparent in the *'alim*'s remark that the *anciens combattants* followed him because "they didn't know any better."[37] Nor was the respect due an aged man evident in the beating of Nianson Coulibaly. But the manifestation of certain kinds of religious practice was both a bid for respectability and an act of rebellion as veterans attempted to participate in social life on their own terms. In the case of Ousmane Sidibe, they put themselves at the epicenter of a fierce contest over what the Muslim community was, who could participate in it, and how.

San's *anciens combattants* challenged gendered expectations even as they responded to them. Along with other men, these veterans recognized the significance of religious practice for community standing, but their distinct experiences and their relative marginality predisposed them to adopt a critical approach to local practices. The issue for them was the acquisition of relative seniority, yet it was more than the difference between being junior or senior men. Without an understanding of the mobilizing force of differing articulations of masculinities, it is difficult to appreciate just what veterans had at stake in the Sidibe controversy.

To do so requires moving the analysis of masculinity out of the domestic realm and into a particular sphere—the Islamic—that was becoming increasingly crucial to the social and political life of AOF. To some extent the conflict in San did reflect a public dispute about household obligation and authority, like those that troubled Nigeria's railway community (Lindsay 1998, 1999). However, the riot and the acrimony that followed in its wake developed because the spiritual—not solely the material—bases of the authority of prominent elder Muslims were called into question.

While social conventions often present both gender and religion as timeless and immutable—and they are deeply embedded in the lives of communities, often across long time frames (Bourdieu 1998)—they are also subject to both gradual and abrupt changes. In late 1950s San, the catalysts behind those changes were simultaneously local and supraregional. In this moment of rapid political and social change, ex-soldiers and an itinerant *marabout* drew upon ideas emanating from multiple metropoles to articulate, however incompletely, their own conceptions of what kind of actions and resources merited senior male status.[38] These disruptive ideas did not come from France, but from centers of Islamic reform like Bamako and Kankan, or indirectly from the *hijaz*. Colonial and Muslim ideas shared an emphasis on the value of different kinds of knowledge. The combination of the more iconoclastic of these new ideas with the multiple and unsettled discourses of power, status, and gender already at work in San was explosive. With their emphasis on self-consciously "universal" and rational interpretations of Islam, reformist ideas appealed greatly to some of San's veterans and set them on a collision course with the town's elder Muslim men, who were deeply invested in the power and legitimacy of their particular knowledge.

At their core, these ideas were supra-ethnic, and this was a crucial component of their "universality." Sidibe was probably Fulbe, Coulibaly was Bamana, and the town's Muslim elders and ruling families were Fulbe, Bamana, and Marka(-Dialan). Although in other contexts and at other historical moments, concepts of masculine comportment and ethnic identity may have been tightly linked (see Hodgson this volume), in late colonial Soudan Français they were not. Rather, they were exceedingly porous. Religious affiliations began to supersede other community ties and understandings of membership. At the same time, the relative importance of "local" origins began to decline in the face of increasing mobility and urbanization. Both military veterans and Muslim reformers sought to demonstrate their affinities with global communities and their escape from such restrictive aspects of local society as the complicated hierarchies and slavery-inflected relationships that characterized much of the social life in the region.

Veterans clearly did not see their status as inherently subordinate to those of their peers and age-mates, and they refused to be marginalized. However, in this conflict between Sidibe's (male) followers and detractors, some of the older ideas about masculinity were "hegemonic" (Connell, 1995; Carrigan et al., 1985), in so far as the logic of ascendant senior masculinity continued to contain the argument within itself. Disputes over religious practice did not imagine alternatives to such fundamental concepts as the idea that religious practice was germane (even crucial) to senior masculine status, or that elder men should wield symbolic and ritual power over women and juniors. These ideas were pervasive, and the former in particular has if anything become more pronounced in contemporary Mali (Brenner 1993a, b). That particular logic marked the boundaries of the dispute, which began as a discussion over who was a good Muslim, but became an argument over who was a good man.

NOTES

1. Thanks to the Malian interlocutors named below, the editors, Ben Soares, Mamadou Diawara, and Luise White, and Northwestern University's Africanist community for help with this essay. All faults are mine. Interviews conducted in and around San were carried out with the assistance of Goumba Coulibaly, whom I thank. Research was funded by the Fulbright-IIE and the AED-NSEP.

2. See Kaba (1974) and Amselle (1985). Both focus on southern Malian reformist networks, linked to such Muslim metropoles as Kankan and al-Azhar in Cairo. However, these were not the sole networks in operation. On twentieth-century vernacular proselytization see Tamari (1996), Soares (1997a), Manley (1997), Niezen (1990), and Niezen and Bankson (1995).

3. Interview, Oumou Sidibe, San, 3 and 5 Feb. 1998. Sidibe is a common family name. Oumou is not this elderly woman's real name, which she preferred not to enter into print.

4. Commandant DuChamp, monthly report, April–May 1957, 26 May 1957; ANM IE38FR.

5. Praying with one's arms crossed was and is often considered a sign of adherence to 'reformist' ideas. An eyewitness account contradicts the statement that Sidibe prayed with crossed arms; interview, Moussa Doumbia, San, 23 March 1999.

6. DuChamp, monthly report, Aug.–Sept. 1957, 25 Sept. 1957; ANM IE38FR. Also, Gendarmerie Nationale, Groupe du Soudan, Renseignements sur la situation du territoire du Soudan au cours du 3ème trimestre 1957; ANS 17G585 v152.

7. Manuscript written by Baba Cissé, titled "Troubles causées par les conférences à San du marabout Ousmane Sidibe," dated 2 May 1960, San *cercle* archives. Information on the mosque is drawn from papers of Father Bernard de Rasilly, parish offices, San.

8. DuChamp, monthly report, May–June 1957, 25 June 1957; ANM IE38FR.

9. DuChamp, monthly report, Aug.–Sept. 1957, 25 Sept. 1957; ANM IE38FR. Also, Extrait du Compte-rendu mensuel des évènements politiques, Koutiala, 30 Aug. 1957; San *cercle* archives. A returning soldier had brought the books from Casablanca.

10. The term "esoteric sciences" is taken from Brenner (1985a). See also Brenner (1985b) and Soares (1997b).

11. DuChamp, monthly report, Dec. 1956, 29 Jan. 1957; ANM IE38FR.

12. Rapport du Maréchal des Logis Chef Lambert, Commandant la Brigade, sur les conséquences de l'activité du Marabout Sidibe Ousmane, actuellement à San. 7 Jan. 1957, No. . . . 2/4 (sic). San *cercle* archives.

13. For the post-1940 period, Echenberg (1991) and Lawler (1992) have written the most useful studies of the *tirailleurs*.

14. Exceptions are Parsons (1999) and Killingray (1999).

15. Commandant Beauvais (Koutiala), extract from monthly report, Sept.–Oct. 1956, 19 Oct. 1956; San *cercle* archives. See also Soares (1997b: 350–1).

16. Interview, Moussa Doumbia, San, 9 July 1998.

17. Luhrmann (1996), Sinha (1995), Nandy (1983), and Fanon (1967).

18. Interview, Commandant Louis Baron, Aix-en-Provence, 9 Oct. 1998. On European (mostly British) ideas of masculinity and representations of European men in the colonies, see, notably, Sinha (1995) and Roper and Tosh (1991).

19. See, for example, le Président des Anciens Combattants, Section Locale de San, to M. l'Administrateur en chef de la France d'Outre-Mer, Commandant de Cercle, San, 17-3-52; ANM 2D39FR. Also, Diabaté (1979).

20. See Diabaté (1979) and Mann (2000: Chap. 2).

21. Although San's ruling elite was historically Muslim, in the 1950s Muslims were no more than a plurality in the town, which had (and has) large minorities of Christians and practitioners of local religions. Islam became the majority faith within a few years of independence (1960).

22. Soares (1997b) notes that even well-known religious leaders often "subcontract" such interventions to third parties who are considered to be particularly skilled. He also

emphasizes that any "boundaries" between Islamic and other practices are exceedingly porous. There exist shared repertoires of skills, knowledge, and practices.

23. Compare Michel (1995), who examines administrative concerns about proselytization in the ranks during the First World War.

24. Séché (1919); Coulibaly (1983). See also various ENFOM *mémoires*.

25. Gén. Salan, Commandant en Chef, Indochine, to Général Commandant les Forces Armées de l'AOF et Togo, Saigon, 17-7-52. #251 EMIFT/I/Aff/Af; ANS 4D76v100.

26. This was the term used by veterans, who attest that their immediate superiors were indifferent to their religion. A former officer confirmed this (interview, Commandant Baron). However, concerns about religious allegiances were more pronounced in the higher echelons of command.

27. Interview, Odiouma Bagayogo and Naenezo (dit Souleymane) Dao, Bamako, 23 Jan. 1998. The fact that neither Dao nor Bagayogo nor Nianson Coulibaly was given a Muslim name at birth suggests that their parents were not Muslims.

28. Interviews, Oumou Sidibe; "Dioula" Moussa Coulibaly, Diabougou, 31 July 1998; Moussa Doumbia, San, 9 July 1998.

29. In Bamanankan, *a ko, "i sigi so kono. Musow ka sira te."* Interview, Oumou Sidibe, 3 Feb. 1998.

30. Interview, "Dioula" Moussa Coulibaly.

31. J. Beyries, "Rapport de Mission sur la Situation de l'Islam en AOF (1952)," pp. 123–4 and *infra;* ANSOM 1 affpol 2158.

32. See, for example, Governor of Côte d'Ivoire to Haut Commissaire AOF, #615/BM, 13 Dec. 1948; ANS 4D76v100.

33. DuChamp, monthly report, May–June 1957, 25 June 1957; ANM IE38FR.

34. *l'Essor*, 17 March 1958, quoted in Chailley (1962: 21).

35. Moussa Doumbia states that Sidibe was pro-RDA but does not date this allegiance more precisely; interview, San, 9 Sept. 1998. Administrative reports refer to his support of the PSP: DuChamp, monthly report, Jan.–Feb. 1957, 27 Feb. 1957; ANM IE38FR.

36. Interview, Gaoussou Konaté, San, 24 March 1999; and Moussa Doumbia, San, 23 March 1999.

37. Interview, Moussa Doumbia, San, 9 July 1998.

38. On "multiple metropoles," see Hunt (1996).

REFERENCES

Archival Sources

ANM: Archives Nationales du Mali (Bamako)
ANS: Archives Nationales du Sénégal (Dakar)
ANSOM: Archives Nationales, Section Outre-Mer (Aix-en-Provence, France)
ENFOM: Ecole Nationale de la France d'Outre-Mer (housed with ANSOM)
San *cercle* archives

Works Cited

Amselle, Jean-Loup. 1985. "Le Wahabisme à Bamako." *Canadian Journal of African Studies* 19, 2: 345–57.
Blot, Lucien. 1946. *La Sécurité en AOF*. Mémoire. Aix-en-Provence: Ecole Nationale de la France d'Outre-Mer.

Bourdieu, Pierre. 1998. *La Domination masculine*. Paris: Seuil.

Brenner, Louis. 1985a. "The 'Esoteric Sciences' in West African Islam." In *African Healing Strategies*, Brian M. du Toit and Ismail H. Abdalla, eds. New York: Trado-Medic Books.

———. 1985b. *Réflexions sur le savoir islamique en Afrique de l'Ouest*. Bordeaux: Centre d'Etude d'Afrique Noire.

———. 1993a. "Constructing Muslim Identities in Mali." In *Muslim Identity and Social Change in sub-Saharan Africa*, Louis Brenner, ed. Bloomington, IN: Indiana University Press.

———. 1993b. "La Culture arabo-islamique au Mali." In *Le Radicalisme islamique au sud du Sahara. Da'wa, arabisation et critique de l'Occident*, René Otayek, ed. Paris: Karthala and MSHA.

Carrigan, Tom, Bob Connell, and John Lee. 1985. "Towards a New Sociology of Masculinity." *Theory and Society* 14, 5: 551–603.

Chailley, M. 1962. "Aspects de l'Islam au Mali." In *Notes et Etudes sur l'Islam en Afrique noire*, M. Chailley et al., eds. Paris: Peyronnet.

Connell, R. W. 1995. *Masculinities*. Berkeley: University of California Press.

Coulibaly, Bourama Lamine. 1983. *le Soudan Français dans les guerres coloniales: Indochine, Algérie*. Mémoire, Bamako: Ecole Normale Supérieure.

Diabaté, Massa M. 1979. *le Lieutenant de Kouta*. Paris: Hatier.

Echenberg, Myron. 1991. *Colonial Conscripts: The Tirailleurs Sénégalais in French West Africa, 1857–1960*. Portsmouth, NH: Heinemann.

Fanon, Frantz. 1967. *Black Skin, White Masks*, Charles Lam Markmann, trans. New York: Grove Press.

Hunt, Nancy Rose. 1996. "Introduction, Special Issue: Gendered Colonialism in African History." *Gender & History* 8, 3: 323–37.

Kaba, Lansine. 1974. *The Wahhabiyya: Islamic Reform and Politics in French West Africa*. Evanston, IL: Northwestern University Press.

Kamian, Bakari. 1959. "Une Ville de la république du Soudan: San." *Les Cahiers d'outremer* 12, 47: 225–50.

Killingray, David. 1999. "Gender Issues and African Colonial Armies." In *Guardians of Empire: The Armed Forces of the Colonial Powers, c. 1700–1964*, David Killingray and David Omissi, eds. Manchester, UK: Manchester University Press.

Launay, Robert and Benjamin F. Soares. 1999. "The Formation of an 'Islamic Sphere' in French Colonial West Africa." *Economy and Society* 28, 4: 497–519.

Lawler, Nancy Ellen. 1992. *Soldiers of Misfortune: Ivoirien Tirailleurs of World War II*. Athens, OH: Ohio University Press.

Lindsay, Lisa. 1998. " 'No Need . . . to Think of Home'? Masculinity and Domestic Life on the Nigerian Railway, c. 1940–1961." *Journal of African History* 39: 439–66.

———. 1999. "Domesticity and Difference: Male Breadwinners, Working Women, and Colonial Citizenship in the 1945 Nigerian General Strike." *American Historical Review* 104, 3: 783–812.

Luhrmann, Tanya. 1996. *The Good Parsi: The Fate of a Colonial Elite in a Postcolonial Society*. Cambridge, MA: Harvard University Press.

Manley, Andrew. 1997. "The Sosso and the Haidara: Two Muslim Lineages in Soudan Français, 1890–1960." In *Le Temps des marabouts. Itinéraires et stratégies islamiques en Afrique Occidentale Française, v. 1880–1960*, David Robinson and Jean-Louis Triaud, eds. Paris: Karthala.

Mann, Gregory. 2000. The *Tirailleur* Elsewhere: Military Veterans in Colonial and Post-colonial Mali, 1918–1968." Ph.D. dissertation, Northwestern University.

Michel, Marc. 1995. "Pouvoirs religieux et pouvoirs d'état dans les troupes noires pendant la première guerre mondiale." *Economica* 295–308.

Miescher, Stephan F. 1997. "Becoming a Man in Kwawu: Gender, Law, Personhood, and the Construction of Masculinities in Colonial Ghana, 1875–1957." Ph.D. dissertation, Northwestern University.

Nandy, Ashis. 1983. *The Intimate Enemy: Loss and Recovery of Self under Colonialism.* Delhi: Oxford.

Niezen, R. W. 1990. " 'Community of Helpers of the Sunna': Islamic reform among the Songhay of Gao (Mali)." *Africa* 60, 3: 399–424.

Niezen, R. W. and Barbro Bankson. 1995. "Women of the Jama'a Ansar al-Sunna: Female Participation in a West African Islamic Reform Movement." *Canadian Journal of African Studies* 29, 3: 403–28.

Parsons, Timothy. 1999. "All *askaris* Are Family Men: Sex, Domesticity, and Discipline in the King's African Rifles." In *Guardians of Empire: The Armed Forces of the Colonial Powers, c. 1700–1964*, David Killingray and David Omissi, eds. Manchester, UK: Manchester University Press.

Robinson, David and Jean-Louis Triaud, eds. 1997. *Le Temps des marabouts. Itinéraires et stratégies islamiques en Afrique Occidentale Française, v. 1880–1960.* Paris: Karthala.

Roper, Michael and John Tosh, eds. 1991. *Manful Assertions: Masculinities in Britain since 1800.* London: Routledge.

Séché, Alphonse. 1919. *Les Noirs, d'après des documents officiels.* Paris: Payot.

Sinha, Mrinalini. 1995. *Colonial Masculinity: The "Manly Englishman" and the "Effeminate Bengali" in the Late Nineteenth Century.* Manchester: Manchester University Press.

Soares, Benjamin F. 1997a. "The Fulbe *shaykh* and the Bambara 'Pagans': Contemporary Campaigns to Spread Islam in Mali." In *Peuls et Mandingues. Dialectique des constructions identitaires*, Mirjam de Bruijn and Han van Dijk, eds. Paris: Karthala.

———. 1997b. "The Spiritual Economy of Nioro du Sahel: Islamic Discourses and Practices in a Malian religious center." Ph.D. dissertation, Northwestern University.

Tamari, Tal. 1996. "L'exégèse coranique (*tafsir*) en milieu mandingue: rapport préliminaire sur une recherche en cours." *Islam et sociétés au sud du Sahara* 10: 43–80.

PART II

(RE)MAKING MEN
IN COLONIAL AFRICA

5

THE MAKING OF PRESBYTERIAN TEACHERS: MASCULINITIES AND PROGRAMS OF EDUCATION IN COLONIAL GHANA

Stephan F. Miescher

In one of the few cross-cultural surveys on masculinity, David Gilmore (1990) has argued that there is *one* approved way of being an adult male in any given society. Gilmore, however, avoided the possibility that there might be different notions of masculinity and that they might be contested. This chapter refutes Gilmore's finding by documenting the coexistence of various forms of masculinity for twentieth-century Ghana. R.W. Connell (1995) suggests an alternative approach. Recognizing different forms of masculinity in Western societies, he examines a hierarchy and relations of power among these masculinities: one "hegemonic masculinity" with "subordinate" or "subversive" variants. This chapter critiques this model as well, since it fails to recognize historical and cultural situations within which several hegemonic forms of masculinity may coexist (cf. Cornwall and Lindisfarne 1994). It is not always obvious whether notions of masculinity are dominant, since understandings of masculinity depend on specific contexts and on different subject positions that may educe contrary readings of hegemony.

Ghana has a long history of contested masculinity and femininity (cf. Akyeampong and Obeng 1995). In the colonial period, there were multiple notions of masculinity. Diverse institutions, local and foreign, promoted contradictory images of proper male behavior. In the Akan areas of southern Ghana, not unlike southwestern Nigeria (Lindsay this volume), there were at least three ideal notions of masculinity in the early twentieth century: adult masculinity signified by marriage; senior masculinity reflected in the figure of an elder (ɔpaynin); and the status of the big man (ɔbirɛmpɔn). Concerning adult masculinity, Kwawu elders expected a man to "look after the health of his wife, to clothe and feed her and to farm for her and house her." As a father, he should "rear [his children] till they come of age" and find them suitable marriage partners; he could demand that they work for him, even after divorcing their mother.[1] A man's responsibilities extended to the well-being of his own abusua (matrilineage), since he would be succeeded by a nephew (or niece). Reaching senior masculinity, the position of an ɔpanyin did not depend on a specific age, wealth, or number of followers and wives, but rather on a person's comportment, reputation, and ability to speak well, mediating conflicts and providing advice. The status of a big man was reserved for successful traders and cocoa farmers, some occupying chiefly office, who fulfilled the expectation of sharing wealth and behaved like the pre-colonial ɔbirɛmpɔn (cf. McCaskie 1995: 42ff.).

Since the nineteenth century, mission societies have complicated these understandings of masculinity. Basel missionaries founded schools to shape young boys into a different kind of men: monogamous husbands who showed primary allegiance to wife and children and secondarily to their abusua. New colonial institutions like scouting, police, and civil service established additional male arenas with distinct behavioral codes. Understandings of masculinity were defined, promoted, and negotiated in these homosocial settings in which men engaged with other males across generations. Moreover, mothers, daughters, sisters, and spouses expressed their expectations of men. In the twentieth century, none of these institutions or settings occupied a privileged position of fabricating a single hegemonic masculinity. Rather, different social contexts created expectations of specific notions of masculine behavior.[2] The colonial state issued guidelines about personal comportment of male civil servants. But these ideals were no longer as valid when a clerk employed in Accra operated as a member of his matrilineage within his hometown. Unlike Jean and John Comaroff's (1991, 1997) analysis of the Tswana and missionary encounter in colonial South Africa, my main concern is not with attempts at making hegemony. Rather, I seek to foreground experiences of men exposed to mission education, negotiating between competing notions of masculinity.

Based on an exploration of life histories, this chapter examines how a group of male teachers selectively engaged with masculine ideals, such as those promoted by the Presbyterian Church, educational reformers, and those dominant in their hometowns. These teachers did not perceive some of these notions as hegemonic and others as subordinate. Rather, they created their own synthesis of different cultural practices that were determined by specific contexts. Arranging their lives around contested expectations about their responsibilities and obligations, they engaged with and complicated ideas about gender, authority, seniority, and Christian education, while redefining themselves as men.

LIFE HISTORIES

The five teachers whose life histories are featured here were educated in schools established by the Basel Mission, continued by the Presbyterian Church under the guidance of the United Free Church of Scotland (Scottish Mission). These teachers come from Akan-speaking towns in Akuapem and Kwawu in Ghana's Eastern Region. Born close to, and trained within, the missionary centers of Akuropon and Abetifi, these men present prime accounts for exploring the Presbyterian agenda and examining how the missionary project evolved from the 1920s through the 1950s. Unlike elsewhere in colonial Africa, in 1918 this mission church became "self-governing," with power-sharing between senior African pastors and European missionaries (Smith 1966: 160).

Two teachers, L.M. Date-Ba (born 1904) and Benjamin E. Ofori (born 1909), are from Mamfe and Akuropon in Akuapem, which consists of Akan and Guan people. The latter, as the original inhabitants, practice patrilineal, the former, matrilineal, descent. Akuapem, which became part of the British Gold Coast Colony in 1850, is the Basel Mission's oldest educational hub. Its industrious farmers played an instrumental role in launching Ghana's cocoa industry (Middleton 1983; Hill 1963). The other three teachers come from Kwawu: Kofi Boakye Yiadom (born 1910) and the Rev. E.K.O. Asante (born 1911) are from Abetifi; Emmanuel Frempong Opusuo (c. 1923) is from Pepease. After breaking with their Asante overlord in 1875, Kwawu chiefs invited the Basel Mission to open a church and school in Abetifi. The missionaries were instrumental in negotiating the 1888 protectorate treaty, gradually incorporating Kwawu into the Gold Coast Colony (Miescher 1997a, b). The matrilineal Kwawu people have been well known for their trading activities (Garlick 1967). Since 1900, economic and educational opportunities have led to increased social differentiation in Kwawu and Akuapem.

To explore these teachers' life histories, I conducted several interviews with each of them; some also shared with me their personal papers, including letters and autobiographies.[3] Although these accounts represent singular experiences, they also describe spaces and institutions that have been instrumental and formative for a larger group of scholars, *akrakyefoɔ*, in twentieth-century Ghana. The narratives presented here do not reveal all layers of their subjectivity. Rather, speaking to me as a European, an outsider who reminded them of college principals and supervisors, these teachers tended to disclose versions of their lives that resembled Presbyterian masculinity. The ruptures and silences in their accounts, combined with a reading of autobiographical texts, allowed me to explore additional contours of their subjectivities and reveal encounters with competing masculinities.

PRESBYTERIAN MASCULINITY: *AKRAKYEFOƆ*

There is a consensus in gender studies about the importance of missionary activities in reconstructing notions of femininity and masculinity across colonial Africa. Schools have been identified as sites where gender values were "produced and disseminated" (Morrell 1994: 56). By focusing on missionaries, scholars have often ignored the contributions of African teachers and evangelists.[4] In colonial Ghana, formal education was dominated by mission societies like those of the Presbyterian Church, which grew out of the Basel Mission. Since the nineteenth century, Basel missionaries separated their followers by acquiring land outside existing towns. In these Christian Quarters, converts were expected to live according to missionary rules that intervened in everyday life and reorganized gender relations.[5] Contrary to Akan ideals, husband and wife were expected to live together with their children, share meals, worship together, and plan their children's education. For sons, schooling was compulsory, while for daughters it was optional. A select group of girls received training in domesticity by living with and serving European missionaries and learning about cooking, needlework, hygiene, and motherhood. Inheritance among Basel Misson followers was no longer organized along matrilineal lines, as practiced by Akan people, instead favoring wife and children at the expense of the *abusua* (Miescher 1997b).

The Basel Mission established an education system for boys and girls: primary schools (to Standard III) and a few middle boys' boarding schools (to Standard VII), followed by a seminary training teacher-catechists, some of whom were later ordained. As a Swiss and German organization, the Basel Mission was expelled by the British government during World War I. Still, its educational legacy of vocational *and* academic training had a lasting impact. Students who passed Standard VII were called *krakye* (pl. *akrakyefoɔ*) in the Akan-Twi language, derived from English "clerk."[6] *Akrakyefoɔ* were trained to work as clerks, accountants, storekeepers, pupil teachers, and, if they pursued their education, certified teachers and pastors. They were "true medial figures" (Beidelman 1982: 212) who stood "educationally, economically, and culturally betwixt-and-between modern European and traditional native culture" (5); or, in Nancy Hunt's (1999: 12) more sophisticated analysis, they were "hybrid middle figures"—crucial players in the intricacies and translations of colonial encounters. Becoming part of a new social group, while remaining members of their local communities and extended families, *akrakyefoɔ* were subjected to different and conflicting expectations as men.

SEPARATION THROUGH FORMAL EDUCATION

Teacher L.M. Date-Ba was born into a Christian milieu: his father was a primary school teacher; his mother belonged to the small cohort of literate women. Date-Ba's childhood was marked by a distinction between the teacher's home and the "un-educated village people." The father hoped to see his son climb the social ladder by becoming a pastor. In 1910, like many teachers, the father quit the mission to farm cocoa, by now Ghana's most important export (Kay 1972: 6). This enabled him to provide his children with higher education.[7]

The other four men lived as children outside Christian congregations. Reflecting on their childhood, they identified elders toward whom they developed a strong sense of deference. B.E. Ofori (1993a) had a father who acted as *ɔpanyin* for the Okuapemhene (paramount chief) of Akuapem. The young Ofori accompanied him to the palace, carrying his stool. E.K.O. Asante served his great-uncle Nana Adaakwa. Observing him as *abusua* head, assisting in trading and cocoa farming, Asante learned about expectations of senior men. Kofi Boakye Yiadom helped his grandfather, Nana Amponsah, the ruler of Akwasihu, a powerful man with many wives and children. E.F. Opusuo worked with his father at the cocoa village of Adonso.[8] None of these role models were literate or joined a mission church. Embodying a different notion of masculinity, these elders symbolized an alternative reference point of male comportment and accomplishment. Although the teachers did not follow their occupations, the latter's status and expression of senior masculinity never lost significance. Especially when the teachers advanced in years, they reconnected with the role models of their youth. They sought to embrace their elders' dignity and prestige without jeopardizing their own positions as *akrakyefoɔ*.

Although the Presbyterian Church went through a phase of growth in the interwar period, the original Basel Mission settlements maintained their character. Having replaced missionaries, pastors and presbyters (church elders) supervised relations among and conduct of church members.[9] Presbyterian schools exposed those not born into Christian families to this world. Becoming a pupil brought many changes: teachers examined homework and personal hygiene. If pupils failed to attend Sunday church, or their clothes were considered dirty, teachers used the cane or dismissed them. Wearing khaki school uniforms and exempted from farm work, pupils were reminded of their new, minority status.[10]

Following primary school, the more successful students entered the boys' boarding schools of Abetifi and Akuropon. Such institutions, guaranteeing pupils' isolation from unwanted influences, had been a principal strategy of the Basel Mission in reshaping personhood (cf. Agyemang 1967). "Harsh discipline and strong religious indoctrination" (Boateng 1975: 83) dominated the curriculum. A rigid schedule introduced pupils to a modern concept of time. They were taught to compete against classmates in academic subjects, sports, and garden work. Pupils acquired practical skills in carpentry and masonry (Asante 1993a). Those from non-Christian backgrounds joined the church at the boarding school, with baptism and confirmation often performed the same day.[11] Becoming full church members not only indicated the new faith, but showed the "heathen town" that they had broken away from their parental worlds. Widely adopted in mission schools across colonial Africa, Christian names became an outward sign of personal transformation (Comaroff and Comaroff 1991: 219).

Date-Ba, Ofori, Asante, and Opusuo pursued their education at the Presbyterian Training College, Akuropon. During the 1920s, the college's organization went through reforms stimulated by the government's increased commitment to education (Foster 1965: 155ff.). The college introduced team sports to complement academic courses, renewed an interest in African languages, and expanded teachers' training from three to four years, with an optional fifth year for instruction in catechism. While the Scottish Mission continued the Basel Mission practice of training teachers as church agents, a more practical and less dogmatic theology was adopted.[12] Parading woollen suits, students emphasized their social position as *akrakyefoɔ*. Date-Ba (1993a) was "dressed to school," wearing "good shoes" and "a tie." He used his attire not only to demonstrate his status but to challenge teachers; his choice of clothing became a form of resistance (see Prein 1994). Following complaints about overdressing students, the college introduced uniforms in 1929, causing an uproar (Yeboa-Dankwa 1973: 55; cf. Packard 1989).

The college was formative in constructing professional identities. The interviewed men developed a sense of belonging that altered their self-understanding or subjectivity. Although students remained in contact with their hometowns, they considered themselves above their age-mates. Even other *akrakyefoɔ* like former boarding school colleagues were now beneath them. The college, with its high value on "character training," had turned them into teachers who became self-proclaimed "disciplinarians" (Date-Ba 1993a). The notion of a "German discipline"—identified by Opusuo (1992b) as physical work, strict rules, close supervision, and severe corporal punishment—is crucial in their recollections. Evaluating the work of younger colleagues, they lamented the disappearance of this discipline.[13]

Photo 5.1. The Rev. E.K.O. Asante, seated second from the right, with classmates at the Presbyterian Training College, Akuropon, c. 1933.

WORKING AS TEACHERS

As part of the 1925 Education Ordinance, a central register and improved salaries strengthened teachers' professionalization (Kimble 1963: 119). Although the number of trained teachers expanded during the 1930s, still only a minority were certified college graduates.[14] *Akrakyefoɔ* with Standard VII certificates could seek employment as pupil teachers, especially if they had attended prestigious boys boarding schools. Leaving training college, graduates like Asante, Date-Ba, Ofori, and Opusuo were posted to small villages. Based on "good performance" (Date-Ba 1993a), they hoped for promotion to teach in larger towns or at a middle school. Uncertified teachers like Boakye Yiadom did not have these options.

Within rural communities, teachers were in an ambivalent position. Because of their literacy, they enjoyed status while being scrutinized by villagers. Remaining outsiders, they represented church authorities and often acted as mediators, "enabling traditional community leaders to communicate with or gain access to external sources of wealth and power," as Sara Berry (1985: 112) noted for southwestern Nigeria. The Colonial Office identified teachers as the "chief agency through which new ideas" reached villagers (Great Britain 1935: 2). The *Gold Coast Teachers' Journal*, published by the Education Department, featured articles on water purification, village mobilization, and cocoa farming. In the waning years of colonial rule, education officer

Francis Austin (1956) reflected on relations between teacher and villagers. He noted that the latter considered the former as somebody "raised above them," expecting "inspiration and guidance." A teacher became the "center of attraction"; his comings and goings were "closely watched" and "private comments [we]re passed on him." Austin urged readers to renovate dwellings, clean their compounds daily, and plant "flowers and shrubs." Teachers should induce "young men" to form sports clubs and influence chiefs to improve hygiene (19f.). Their unique status is reflected in the village practice of calling them "teacher" in lieu of proper names (Roberts 1975: 254).

Relating their experiences, the interviewed men reflected on pressures and expectations they felt from colonial and missionary authorities. While inspectors showed up occasionally, local opinion was always present. Opusuo remembered:

> When people saw you drinking, going about drinking, becoming intoxicated, going in bad company, in fact drinking outside, they would not respect you. So if you make friends, you have to make friends who are well behaved, friends whose characters are not questionable. (1992b)

According to Opusuo an unblemished reputation had financial benefits, since villagers provided teachers with food.

Having a good character, *ɔwɔ suban papa*, is an important concept in Akan culture. The Ghanaian philosopher, Kwame Gyekye (1987: 128ff.), argues that *suban* (character) is expressed in a person's habits and conduct; "deeds and actions" signify his or her status. Teachers, fearing loss of respect, maintained their distance from villagers. As headmaster in the 1930s, Date-Ba (1993a) "hardly had any friends who were not teachers." When Opusuo (1992a) taught in a Methodist school, he felt lonely. Engaging with colleagues, preferably from the same church, reaffirmed group identity, re-created bonding experiences of boarding school and training college, and helped form a teachers' union. Such collective representation was needed to be heard by church officials and education inspectors, the latter almost exclusively Europeans until the 1950s.

The Colonial Office emphasized "outside help" from missionaries and government officers to uplift rural communities (Great Britain 1935: 12). Teachers, however, recalled with bitterness how overpaid European inspectors ignored them and declined to pay respect. As college graduates they did not consider themselves inferior to such officials. Clashes with superiors resulted in transfers, hindering promotions. Date-Ba's sense of justice brought him into conflict. In 1934, after an argument about his teaching style, he was transferred from the Akuropon Boys' Boarding School to a "bush school." He not only served as president of the Presbyterian Teachers' Union for ten years, but is remembered as "a strong man" who "could fight" (Opusuo 1994). As a union leader, Date-Ba (1993a) acted as a "bold man," speaking for his and other teachers' interests. The narrator in Kofi Awonoor's novel, *This Earth, My Brother*, adeptly observes, "The history of colonial education is one long war between the young and arrogant white school inspectors and the teachers" (1971: 48).

While education officers enforced a dress code, teachers themselves regarded their clothing as crucial for their professional identity. During the week, teachers wore the obligatory "nickers"; on Sundays they wore suit and tie, prepared to assist in church service. Professional dress demanded economizing salaries. Opusuo (1993b) ordered his first tailor-made suit from London "for 75 shillings" after several years of teaching. Dress standards were intensively debated in the Gold Coast as elsewhere in colonial Africa (cf. Martin 1994; Comaroff and Comaroff 1997: 242ff.). In the early 1930s, when Ephraim Amu, music master and teacher-catechist at the Presbyterian Training College, preached in "native cloth" (dress of Akan male elders) he created a scandal. Church elders saw his appearance as an act of the "devil" and suspended him from preaching (Agyemang 1988: 75). Amu had a broader agenda: he encouraged his students to exchange their European dress for cloth, hence reorienting their masculine selves in alignment with their "African past." Church leaders considered Amu's choice of "African attire" as backsliding into "heathen practices." He was sacked from the college (Agyemang 1988: 89ff.). The Amu episode and the interviewed teacher's recollections exemplify Hilde Hendrickson's (1996: 8) argument about clothing being "critical in the representation and reproduction of society"; clothing differences serve as "critical link between social groups across space and through time."

Becoming a teacher meant consuming certain goods (cf. Burke 1996). All teachers mentioned the importance of furniture in surrounding themselves with material objects according to their status. Opusuo (1993c) recalled his inadequacy when his room contained only his trunk and one mat with sheets on the floor. Hearing someone's steps, he ran to the door to prevent the visitor from seeing his room. Only upon buying his first set of furniture—chairs, table, writing desk, cupboard, and bedstead–did he feel secure enough to have girlfriends. His identity as a man and teacher had a close correlation with the arrangement of his domestic space (see Comaroff and Comaroff 1997: 303f.).

SEXUALITY AND MARRIAGE

In Akan societies, men reached adult masculinity by entering marriage, taking "the role of material providers and proctector of families" (Akyeam-

Photo 5.2. E.F. Opusuo, wearing his first tailor-made woolen suit, purchased from London, Winneba, 1950.

pong 1996: 153). During the colonial era, marriage was "not a state of being but a series of multiple, often overlapping, processes" (Allman and Tashjian 2000: 54) that involved different forms: customary marriage, some blessed in a church; partially formalized concubinage; and Ordinance marriage. Several institutions—the colonial state, chiefs, lineage elders, and mission churches—regulated marriage.[15] According to Presbyterian rules, the only accepted place for sexuality was a monogamous marriage; pre- and extramarital sexual relations were frowned upon and could lead to suspension or exclusion.[16] Within Akan societies, there was more flexibility. Although premarital sex was not encouraged, a man who had fathered a child acted properly as long as he supported the mother during pregnancy. After delivery, he should either marry or compensate her, and pacify her father or guardian.[17] Akan customary marriages, to the dismay of the Presbyterian Church, could easily be dissolved. Although a father was expected to name and look after his children and their mothers, men often failed to provide for all children. Instead they focused on nephews and nieces who would inherit from and succeed them.[18]

Living with different concepts about marriage and sexuality was problematic for men in Presbyterian congregations. Discussing contemporary teenage pregnancy, Date-Ba (1993a) insisted that in his youth "it was not like that." He and his age-mates did not have sex with women before completing school. Opusuo experienced the same rigid situation during the 1940s. If a college student was seen "with a girlfriend" and reported to the principal, he "might be sacked" (1992b). Fearing the consequences, he became "afraid of women."[19] Teachers were pressured to marry since single Akan men had not reached full personhood. Catechists in particular were expected to represent Christian families. Colonial officials also preferred married teachers who needed their wives' support to create a "modern" household that exemplified "health" and "hygiene" to be emulated by villagers (Great Britain 1935: 12). Date-Ba (1993a) was only permitted to take the post of head teacher if he agreed to marry.

In Presbyerian congregations, teachers were popular spouses. Elizabeth Ntim (1993) recalled her "ambition of marrying a teacher" who would look after her children and guarantee her support, including house servants for fetching water and firewood. In 1937, Asante married Felicia Animaa, who had been selected by his mother. Felicia had attended the Agogo girls boarding school, established by the Basel Mission in 1931 to train "brides of young teachers" (Hartenstein 1932: 107) with domestic skills essential for Christian motherhood.[20] These experiences confirm Carol Summers's argument (1999: 80) for southern Rhodesia, where teachers pursued "strategic" marriages with educated Christian women to achieve "adulthood, parenthood, and success within African communities" and to manage "missionaries' fundamental discomfort with the autonomy of individual African educated men." Yet in colonial Ghana, decisions about ideal marriage partners did not lie solely with teachers; frequently mothers played crucial roles. Furthermore, Presbyterian marriage ideals were formulated by missionaries *and* senior African pastors.

Not all teachers conformed to Presbyterian expectations. The records of the Abetifi Native Tribunal contain numerous cases of fathers complaining about their daughters being seduced by teachers.[21] Opusuo (1993b) talked about his strategies of hiding "many girlfriends" from church superiors. This was not without risk, since an unwanted pregnancy could jeopardize a teacher's career. Opusuo (1994) learned from his teacher friends about "contraceptives." Still, in 1955 two of his girlfriends became pregnant while he was already engaged to another woman. Opusuo (1993c) settled with their families to provide support until his children were born and offered "a few pounds" as compensation. Disregarding Presbyterian rules, Opusuo considered his decision adequate as long as he educated his children.

Boakye Yiadom also struggled to accommodate conflicting expectations.[22] Since he spoke freely about his involvement with sixteen women who gave birth to his twenty-seven children and shared his autobiographical writings, we can reconstruct how he negotiated between different notions of masculinity. According to Presbyterian rules, he usually lived with one woman with whom he had performed customary marriage rites—with five of them, sequentially—and their union was consecrated by the church. He sought to prevent church officials from learning about former wives and "concubines." This arrangement was for him neither problematic nor contradictory to his aim of leading a life as a devout Presbyterian teacher-catechist, since he claimed to have compensated the extramarital mothers of his children and provided for his offspring. Yet there are discrepancies in Boakye Yiadom's representation of his marriages. In one autobiography (n.d.b.), addressed to the Presbyterian congregation, Boakye Yiadom mentioned only two of his Christian wives. In another, more intimate autobiography (n.d.a), written like a diary, as well as in our interviews (1994a, b), he revealed different layers of experience about organizing his sexual relationships by navigating through and around church regulations. He encountered accusations of sexual misconduct and was once forced to leave Presbyerian schools. Eager to enhance his qualifications, he returned and enrolled at the Presbyterian Training College in 1950. Seeking to conform to the college's expectations, he presented himself as a single man without children (1994b).

Fatherhood is for Boakye Yiadom an important part of his conception as a man. His numerous children demonstrate his accomplishment at having fulfilled a central aspect of adult masculinity. He noted, "When you beget, you become a man yourself. I have become a man" (1993). This father identity is reflected in his self-presentations. During our interviews, he spoke at length about his children. In *My Own Life* (n.d.a), he recorded their names, commented on their births, and tracked some of his sons' and daughters' expenses. His position as father was acknowledged among his non-Christian relatives, as long as he had and named his children. This recognition applied whether he had actually entered customary marriages with their mothers, or only compensated them. Needless to say, Boakye Yiadom was expected to provide for all of his children. If he failed to do so, this must have caused serious tensions. Considering his moderate salary, he struggled to pay school fees, which became a father's obligation in the twentieth century (cf. Fortes 1950: 268). Jean Allman (1997: 308), documenting a shift from reciprocal obligations to paternal rights over children in colonial Asante, suggests that school fees became "a never ending source of conflict between mothers and fathers." Since the interwar years fathers increasingly resisted paying the rising costs of rearing their children. Boakye Yiadom's case supports this assessment.

In the 1950s, the beginning of self-rule under Kwame Nkrumah's Convention People's Party (CPP) brought many changes. The Accelerated Development Plan in Education promoted a rapid expansion of primary schools and gradually removed differences between government and non-government teachers (Gold Coast 1951). These policies "inexorably altered" (Smith 1966: 173) the relationship between churches, schools, and government. Although churches nominally retained their own discipline codes, these became difficult to enforce. Presbyterian teachers ceased to be church agents; they became government employees. This shift is ingrained in the memories of the interviewed men. Opusuo (1993c) recalled how suspension for "immoral behavior" was reduced. Boakye Yiadom (1994b) emphasized that an education officer was more interested in classroom performance than marital activities, now considered "private matters."

SENIOR MASCULINITY

Seeking senior masculinity, this cohort of educated men profited from the decolonization process initiated by the CPP government. The Africanization of the civil service and mission churches, as well as opening of schools, created employment opportunities for those with an advanced education, like Date-Ba, Ofori, Asante, and Opusuo.[23] Ofori (1993a, b) became an assistant education officer in 1952. Stationed outside his hometown, Ofori climbed the Education Department's ladder until his retirement in 1970. Date-Ba supported the oppositional, Asante-based National Liberation Movement and ran unsuccessfully as their candidate for the Legislative Council in 1956 (cf. Allman 1993). Serving as education officer, his outspokenness kept him in trouble. Date-Ba's career took a steep upward turn in the post-CPP period when he was appointed district magistrate in Winneba. In 1970, he retired and returned to Mamfe in grand style, followed by "a long trek, containing all my luggage, my sheep and goat, fowls and eggs" (1993a). At least in memory, this homecoming echoed the public appearance of the pre-colonial ɔbirɛmpɔn displaying his riches (cf. McCaskie 1995: 44). Asante (1993d) attended Trinity College, the theological seminary of the Presbyterian and Methodist Churches. In 1948, he volunteered as the first African missionary to work in Ghana's least developed Northern Region. Basel Mission representatives lauded Asante's service on behalf of an increasingly independent Presbyerian Church.[24] Returning south, Asante continued a successful career as pastor. While Opusuo also served as education officer, Boakye Yiadom lacked the credentials to move beyond the position of a primary school head teacher.

How did these career paths reflect senior masculinity? For Date-Ba, Ofori, Asante, and Opusuo, their improved salaries and status symbols, like government cars, enabled them to invest socially in their hometowns. Like most migrant men from Kwawu and Akuapem, they sought to build a house. This should not only provide a suitable home for old age, but mark their economic success and status of senior masculinity, commemorating them beyond their lives (cf. van der Geest 1998). Asante and Opusuo chose sites in Christian Quarters of Abetifi and Pepease, indicating their moves from the old "heathen town." Upon retirement, teachers took up responsibilities of an *ɔpanyin*. Still, they saw themselves as modern *akrakyefoɔ*. They attended to furnishing their European-style sitting rooms, displaying a book cabinet, a radio, and possibly a television set. There they received visitors *within* the enclosed building, and not *outside,* sitting on the slightly raised, three-walled platform of their enclosed courtyard, as had been common for Akan *mpanyinfoɔ* (elders). The spatial organization of their houses represented their accomplishments and marked belonging to the *akrakyefoɔ*.

Their identities and status of senior masculinity were challenged by conflicting expectations. As salaried men, these teachers had been under pressure from less fortunate *abusua* members to provide assistance. Were they modern men who mainly looked after the well-being of their wives and children according to the Presbyterian model, who invested their savings in a house or cocoa farm for their own use? Or did their solidarity belong to *abusua* members who expected them to provide for their sisters' children and help in lineage enterprises? These men attempted both. They were determined to give their children the best education *and* prove themselves as a caring *wɔfa* (maternal uncle) for selected nephews and nieces. They assisted in renovating lineage houses. Opusuo served as *abusuapanyin* (lineage head), while Asante acted as advisor in lineage affairs and for the Presbyterian Church. Although Boakye Yiadom lacked the means for such generosity, he still claimed senior masculinity for himself.

CONCLUSION

The narratives presented here have not provided a full account of these men's lives. They only expose aspects, partially guided by my questions and interests, partially steered by my interview partners' memories and intentions—not always a conscious process—to reveal specific events and recollections. Thereby they disclosed sections of their subjectivity while guarding others. At times, different accounts, formulated for separate audiences, provide insights into contradictory subjectivities, as in Boakye Yiadom's representations of his relationships with women, or the discrepancies between Asante's presentation of his life in the interviews and that in his autobiographical portrait (n.d.). During the former, Asante reflected on his childhood, education, and responsibilities toward children and *abusua*. In the latter, written like a eulogy for his funeral service, he focused on his accomplishments as teacher and pastor, highlighting building projects and explaining his hometown contributions. Asante revealed little about relations with his *abusua* or his sixty years of marriage; he omitted his experience as the father of ten children.

The accounts of these men exemplify life experiences common to many teachers in twentieth-century Ghana. Having gone through mission education, they were exposed to cultural values and social patterns that created new opportunities but proved problematic, especially in their understanding of proper behavior and expectations about being a man. In their life histories, we can recognize a process of negotiating between competing masculinities. Although these men's sense of self was deeply affected by their prolonged education, neither a Presbyterian form of masculinity nor Akan ideals around senior masculinity and *ɔbirɛmpɔn* (big man) status became fully dominant and hegemonic. Similar to lawyers in post-colonial Kenya—though from a different class (Cohen and Odhiambo 1992: 80ff.)—these teachers seemed to have embraced a multiplicity of masculine identities that fit different and changing life contexts: as *akrakyefoɔ*, claiming a certain status; as teachers at their work stations; as catechists, spreading the gospel; as husbands and fathers within their marriages; and as members of their lineages and elders within their hometowns. None of them fully belonged to the new educated African elite with national aspirations, international contacts, and broader financial possibilites (see Ranger 1995). Instead, because they were situated as middle figures within the social stratification—lay-magistrate Date-Ba occupying the upper realm, teacher-catechist Boakye Yiadom the lower—their wealth was limited and their ambitions remained local, focused on hometown and *abusua* affairs.

Elsewhere in colonial Ghana, farmers, traders, migrant workers, attendants to chiefs, and diviners were less exposed to the missionary project and yet were also faced with competing notions of masculinity and perceived differences among each other in diverse social contexts subject to historical change. Examining processes of negotiation of such expectations and complex programs of identity definitions among various audiences within changing settings expands the investigation of gender in colonial Africa and contributes to the emerging literature on men and masculinities in African studies and beyond. Negotiations over identity and expectations did not mitigate men's capacities to act with authority in a gendered manner toward others. Rather, these middle figures, playing a pivotal role within colonial Africa, found ways to articulate their life experiences and maintain their reputations within the midst of substantial conflicts over gendered behavior, transforming the geometries of multiple and conflicting masculinities into working and productive capacity. These teachers succeeded in creating for themselves spaces in which they, and others who followed, addressed and resolved tensions over the meanings of masculinity while constructing identities that enabled them to act in a gendered fashion as men.

ACKNOWLEDGMENTS

Financial support for research in Ghana and Switzerland (1992–1994) was provided by the Wenner-Gren Foundation (Gr. 5561), the John D. and Catherine T. McArthur Foundation, the Janggen-Pöhn Stiftung, and Northwestern

University. Bryn Mawr College enabled me to return to Ghana in July 1997, UCSB in August 2000. For comments on earlier drafts I am grateful to Emmanuel Akyeampong, David William Cohen, Nancy Rose Hunt, Keith Shear, Luise White, and the participants of a faculty seminar at the UCSB History Department in June 2000. Special thanks go to Lisa Lindsay for suggestions concerning the final revisions.

NOTES

1. Eugene Addow, "Notes on Kwawu," an ethnographic account prepared for colonial anthropologist R.S. Rattray, c. 1927, in R.S. Rattray Papers, ms. 102: 1. London: Royal Anthropological Institute, Museum of Mankind, hereafter "Notes on Kwawu."

2. Jeater (1993: 266) makes a smilar argument concerning moral discourse on marriage and sexuality for southern Rhodesia.

3. Interviews were conducted in English; informal conversations took place in Twi. I am very grateful to my interview partners. For a discussion of life history research, see Miescher (2001).

4. Schmidt (1992); Jeater (1993); Allman and Tashjian (2000). The Comaroffs' (1991) first volume neglects African mediators, but the second (1997: 65, 78ff.) is more attentive. But see Landau's (1995: 133ff.) discussion of African Christian agents in nineteenth-century Botswana, Ranger's (1995) biography of the extraordinary Samkange family, Summers's (1998) discussion of African teachers' contested authority, and Hunt's (1999) presentation of local nurses in the history of medicalized birthing in the Belgian Congo.

5. Basel Mission Archives, hereafter BMA, D-9. 1c, 11a and 13b, *Ordnung für die evangelischen Gemeinden in Ostindien und Westafrika*, 1865, revised 1902.

6. Allman (1993: 28–36) suggests a historicized definition for Asante school leavers, evoking a continuity with the pre-colonial social group of *nkwankaa* (commoners) or "youngmen," deprived of access to chiefly office and wealth. Here, like that of Arhin (1983), the focus is on the impact of colonial education.

7. Date-Ba (1993a, b). For the impact of cocoa on schools, see BMA, *Jahresbericht der Evangelischen Missionsgesellschaft* (hereafter *Jahresbericht*), 1912, 55ff., and 1913, 98ff.

8. Asante (1993b, e, 1994), Boakye Yiadom (1994a, n.d.b.), Opusuo (1992a, 1993c).

9. BMA, D-9.1c, 13d, *Regulations, Practice and Procedure of the Presbyterian Church of the Gold Coast* (1929) (hereafter *Regulations*). Cf. Smith (1966: 207ff.).

10. Date-Ba (1993a), Ofori (1993b), Asante (1993a), Boakye Yiadom (1994a). In 1931, 4% of Abetifi's population had received at least a Standard IV education. In 1948, this figure had climbed to 13%; cf. Gold Coast (1932: 105; 1950: 124).

11. Asante (1993f), Opusuo (1993c), Boakye Yiadom (n.d.b.).

12. Yeboa-Dankwa (1973: 46ff.), Smith (1966: 178ff., 192). The Basel Mission critiqued the changes; *Jahresbericht* 1929, 33–7.

13. Date-Ba (1993a, b); Ofori (1993a, b); Opusuo (1993a, c).

14. In 1930, there were 1,184 trained teachers, 1,162 men and 22 women; by 1940, these numbers had increased to 2,189 trained teachers, 1,911 men and 278 women (Gold Coast 1942: 29, 31).

15. For state interventions, see Roberts (1987), Allman and Tashjian (2000: 151ff., 170ff.). Kwawu marriages are discussed in Bleek (1975: 139ff.).

16. The Presbyterian Church recognized two marriage forms: customary ones blessed by the church and those under the 1884 Marriage Ordinance; see *Regulations*, 17ff.

17. Customary court cases from the Abetifi Native Tribunal support this norm (e.g., Kwawu Traditional Council (hereafter KTC), Vol. 1: 192–208, *Alfred Mensa vs. Francis Kofi*, November 18, 1930); cf. Asante (1993c), Boakye Yiadom (1994b).

18. For conjugal expectations in Kwawu, see Addo's "Notes on Kwawu"; for neighboring Asante, see Fortes (1950), Allman and Tashjian (2000: Chaps. 2–3).

19. Asked about homosexual relations in all-male institutions, Opusuo responded that he never heard of it, but doubted if there was much "opportunity to do that, unless perhaps in the holidays" (1993c).

20. Asante (1993f), F. Asante (2000); cf. Ofori (1993b).

21. KTC, Vol. 1: 329, 343–59, *J.D. Ofori vs. S.W. Antwi*, October 1932. Cf. pastor D.E. Akwa's report about "fornication between a teacher and a schoolgirl" in Abetifi, BMA, D-3, 7, February 22, 1917.

22. This section is based on Miescher (2001).

23. Compare reports by Basel missionaries administering Presbyterian schools: Wilhelm Stamm, BMA, D-11, 12, Abetifi, April 15, 1950, and Elizabeth Debrunner, BMA, D-11, 9, Akuropon, December 28, 1954.

24. Inspector Witschi, BMA, D-4.7, 4, Abetifi, January 18, 1950, and Inspector Raaflaub, BMA, D-4.7, 5, Tamale, March 3, 1954.

REFERENCES

Agyemang, Fred M. 1967. *A Century with Boys: The Story of the Middle Boarding School in Ghana, 1867–1967*. Accra: Waterville House.

———. 1988. *Amu—The African: A Study in Vision and Courage*. Accra: Asempa Publishers.

Akyeampong, Emmanuel K. 1996. *Drink, Power, and Cultural Change: A Social History of Alcohol in Ghana, c. 1800 to Recent Times*. Portsmouth, NH: Heinemann.

Akyeampong, Emmanuel and Pashington Obeng. 1995. "Spirituality, Gender and Power in Asante History." *International Journal of African Historical Studies* 28, 3: 481–508.

Allman, Jean Marie. 1993. *The Quills of the Porcupine: Asante Nationalism in an Emergent Ghana*. Madison, WI: University of Wisconsin Press.

———. 1997. "Fathering, Mothering and Making Sense of *Ntamoba*: Reflections on the Economy of Child-Rearing in Colonial Asante." *Africa* 67, 2: 296–321.

Allman, Jean and Victoria Tashjian. 2000. *"I Will Not Eat Stone": A Women's History of Colonial Asante*. Portsmouth, NH: Heinemann.

Arhin, Kwame. 1983. "Rank and Class among the Asante and Fante." *Africa* 53, 1: 2–22.

Asante, E.K.O. 1993a. Interview with the author. Abetifi, January 26.

———. 1993b. Interview with the author. Abetifi, February 2.

———. 1993c. Interview with the author. Abetifi, March 30.

———. 1993d. Interview with the author. Abetifi, May 18.

———. 1993e. Interview with the author. Abetifi, June 7.

———. 1993f. Interview with the author. Abetifi, August 16.

———. 1994. Interview with the author. Abetifi, September 27.

———. n.d. [after 1981, rev. 1994]. *Rev. E.K.O. Asante—a Profile*.

Asante, Felicia. 2000. Interview with the author and Pearl Ofosu. Abetifi, August 22.

Austin, Francis A. 1956. "The Village School Teacher." *Gold Coast Teachers' Journal* 28, 1: 19–25.

Awonoor, Kofi. 1971. *This Earth, My Brother*. Garden City, NY: Doubleday.

Beidelman, T.O. 1982. *Colonial Evangelism: A Socio-Historical Study of an East African Mission at the Grassroots*. Bloomington, IN: Indiana University Press.

Berry, Sara. 1985. *Fathers Work for Their Sons: Accumulation, Mobility and Class Formation in an Extended Yoruba Community*. Berkeley: University of California Press.

Bleek, Wolf. 1975. *Marriage, Inheritance, Witchcraft: A Case Study of a Rural Ghanaian Family*. Leiden: Afrika-Studiecentrum.

Boakye Yiadom, Kofi. 1993. Interview with the author. Abetifi, June 27.

————. 1994a. Interview with the author. Abetifi, August 28.

————. 1994b. Interview with the author. Abetifi, November 15.

————. n.d.a. [1946–81]. *Autobiography: My Own Life*. 2 Vols.

————. n.d.b. [after 1978]. *My Life History: The Autobiography of Akasease Kofi Boakye Yiadom*.

Boateng, F. Yao. 1975. "The Catechism and the Rod: Presbyterian Education in Ghana." In *African Reactions to Missionary Education*, Edward H. Berman, ed., pp. 75–91. New York: Teachers' College Press, Columbia University.

Burke, Timothy. 1996. *Lifebuoy Men, Lux Women: Commodification, Consumption, & Cleanliness in Modern Zimbabwe*. Durham, NC: Duke University Press.

Cohen, David William and E.S. Atieno Odhiambo. 1992. *Burying SM: The Politics of Knowledge and the Sociology of Power in Africa*. Portsmouth, NH: Heinemann.

Comaroff, Jean and John Comaroff. 1991. *Of Revelation and Revolution: Christianity, Colonialism, and Consciousness in South Africa*, Vol. 1. Chicago: University of Chicago Press.

Comaroff, John L. and Jean Comaroff. 1997. *Of Revelation and Revolution: The Dialectics of Modernity on a South African Frontier*, Vol. 2. Chicago: University of Chicago Press.

Connell, R.W. 1995. *Masculinities*. Berkeley: University of California Press.

Cornwall, Andrea and Nancy Lindisfarne. 1994. "Dislocating Masculinities: Gender, Power and Anthropology." In *Dislocating Masculinity: Comparative Ethnographies*, Andrea Cornwall and Nancy Lindisfarne, eds., pp. 11–47. London and New York: Routledge.

Date-Ba, L.M. 1993a. Interview with the author. Mamfe, January 20.

————. 1993b. Interview with the author. Mamfe, September 19.

Fortes, Meyer. 1950. "Kinship and Marriage among the Ashanti." In *African Systems of Kinship and Marriage*, A.R. Radcliffe-Brown and Daryll Forde, eds. London: Oxford University Press.

Foster, Philip J. 1965. *Education and Social Change in Ghana*. Chicago: University of Chicago Press.

Garlick, Peter. 1967. "The Development of Kwahu Business Enterprise in Ghana since 1874: An Essay in Recent Oral Tradition." *Journal of African History* 8, 3: 463–80.

Gilmore, David. 1990. *Manhood in the Making: Cultural Concepts of Masculinity*. New Haven, CT: Yale University Press.

Gold Coast. 1932. *1931 Census*. Accra: Government Printer.

————. 1942. *Report of the Education Committee, 1937–1941*. Accra: Government Printer.

————. 1950. *Census of Population, 1948*. London: Crown Agent.

————. 1951. *Accelerated Development Plan for Education, 1951*. Accra: Government Printer.

Great Britain. Colonial Office. 1935. *Memorandum on the Education of African Communities*. London: HMSO.

Gyekye, Kwame. 1987. *An Essay on African Philosophical Thought: The Akan Conceptual Scheme*. Cambridge: Cambridge University Press.

Hartenstein, Karl. 1932. *Anibue: Die "Neue Zeit" auf der Goldküste und unsere Missionsarbeit*. Stuttgart and Basel: Evangelischer Missionsverlag.

Hendrickson, Hilde, ed. 1996. *Clothing and Difference: Embodied Identities in Colonial and Post-Colonial Africa*. Durham, NC: Duke University Press.

Hill, Polly. 1963. *Migrant Cocoa Farmers of Southern Ghana*. Cambridge: Cambridge University Press.

Hunt, Nancy Rose. 1999. *A Colonial Lexicon of Birth Ritual, Medicalization, and Mobility in the Congo*. Durham, NC, and London: Duke University Press.

Jeater, Diana. 1993. *Marriage, Perversion, and Power: The Social Construction of Moral Discourse in Southern Rhodesia, 1894–1930*. Oxford: Clarendon.

Kay, Geoffrey. 1972. *The Political Economy of Colonialism in Ghana: A Collection of Documents and Statistics, 1900–1960*. Cambridge: Cambridge University Press.

Kimble, David. 1963. *A Political History of Ghana: The Rise of Gold Coast Nationalism, 1850–1928*. London: Clarendon.

Landau, Paul Stuart. 1995. *The Realm of the World: Language, Gender, and Christianity in a Southern African Kingdom*. Portsmouth, NH: Heinemann.

Martin, Phyllis M. 1994. "Contesting Clothes in Colonial Brazzaville." *Journal of African History* 35, 3: 401–26.

McCaskie, T.C. 1995. *State and Society in Pre-Colonial Asante*. Cambridge: Cambridge University Press.

Middleton, John. 1983. "One Hundred and Fifty Years of Christianity in a Ghanaian Town." *Africa* 53, 3: 2–29.

Miescher, Stephan F. 1997a. "Becoming a Man in Kwawu: Gender, Law, Personhood, and the Constructions of Masculinities in Colonial Ghana, 1874–1957." Ph.D. dissertation, Northwestern University.

———. 1997b. "Of Documents and Litigants: Disputes on Inheritance in Abetifi—a Town of Colonial Ghana." *Journal of Legal Pluralism* 39: 81–119.

———. 2001. "The Life Histories of Boakye Yiadom (Akasease Kofi of Abetifi, Kwawu): Exploring the Subjectivity and 'Voices' of a Teacher-Catechist in Colonial Ghana." In *African Words, African Voices: Critical Practices in Oral History*, Luise White, Stephan F. Miescher, and David William Cohen, eds., pp. 162–93. Bloomington, IN: Indiana University Press.

Morrell, Robert. 1994. "Boys, Gangs, and the Making of the Masculinity in the White Secondary Schools of Natal, 1880–1930." *Masculinities* 2, 2: 56–82.

Ntim, Elizabeth. 1993. Interview with the author and Pearl Ofosu. Abetifi, August 26.

Ofori. B.E. 1993a. Interview with the author. Akuropon, January 5.

———. 1993b. Interview with author. Akuropon, October 31.

Opusuo, Emmanuel Frempong. 1992a. Interview with the author. Pepease, December 19.

———. 1992b. Interview with the author. Pepease, December 21.

———. 1993a. Interview with the author. Pepease, March 24.

———. 1993b. Interview with the author. Pepease, April 2.

———. 1993c. Interview with the author. Pepease, August 22.

———. 1994. Interview with the author. Pepease, August 27.

Packard, Randall M. 1989. "The 'Healthy Reserve' and the 'Dressed Native': Discourses on Black Health and the Language of Legitimation in South Africa." *American Ethnologist* 16, 4: 686–703.

Prein, Philipp. 1994. "Top Hats: African Resistance in German South West Africa, 1907–1915." *Journal of Southern African Studies* 20, 1: 99–120.

Ranger, Terence. 1995. *Are We Not Also Men? The Samkange Family & African Politics in Zimbabwe, 1920–1964*. Portsmouth, NH: Heinemann.

Roberts, Penelope. 1975. "The Village Schoolteacher in Ghana." In *Changing Social Structure in Ghana*, Jack Goody, ed., pp. 245–60. London: International Africa Institute.

———. 1987. "The State and the Regulation of Marriage in Sefwi Wiaso (Ghana), 1900–1940." In *Women, State and Ideology: Studies from Africa and Asia*, Haleh Afshar, ed., pp. 48–69. London: Macmillan.

Schmidt, Elizabeth. 1992. *Peasants, Traders, and Wives: Shona Women in the History of Zimbabwe, 1870–1939*. Portsmouth, NH: Heinemann.

Smith, Noel. 1966. *The Presbyterian Church of Ghana, 1835–1960*. London: Oxford University Press.

Summers, Carol. 1998. "Giving Orders in Rural Southern Rhodesia: Controversies over Africans' Authority in Development Programs, 1928–1934." *International Journal of African Historical Studies* 31, 2: 279–300.

———. 1999. "Mission Boys, Civilized Men, and Marriage: Educated Men in the Missions of Southern Rhodesia, 1920–1945." *Journal of Religious History* 23, 1: 75–91.

van der Geest, Sjaak. 1998. "*Yebisa Wo Fie*: Growing Old and Building a House in the Akan Culture of Ghana." *Journal of Cross-Cultural Gerontology* 13: 333–59.

Yeboa-Dankwa, J. 1973. *Presbyterian Training College, Akropong-Akwapim (Founded 1948): 125th Anniversary Celebrations*. Accra: Waterville Publishing House.

6

"TAKEN AS BOYS": THE POLITICS OF BLACK POLICE EMPLOYMENT AND EXPERIENCE IN EARLY TWENTIETH-CENTURY SOUTH AFRICA

Keith Shear

An enduring issue in colonial African studies concerns the dependence of European power on African intermediaries and the scope that this dependence afforded Africans to shape the social order (Fields 1985). Usually considered in relation to non-settler territories, the issue is also pertinent to settler colonies, including South Africa. Indeed, South Africa's rulers experienced perhaps more keenly than their counterparts elsewhere the contradictions of upholding a racially exclusive monopoly of power, while depending on ever more black intermediaries to provide the control and specialized knowledge of Africans that a vast settler project entailed.

South African officials well understood these contradictory imperatives. About the first—that reliance on black police qualified white power—one administrator wrote bluntly: "If Swaziland is to remain a native State like Basutoland, then European police may not be essential but ... if we are to prepare it for incorporation into the Transvaal the less we have of native authority the better."[1] With over 90 percent of the land in settler hands, South African governments were loath to challenge the principle that whites and their property should be policed by their own kind. Unlike elsewhere in colonial Africa, most rank-and-file police as well as all officers were white: between 1910 and 1939 there were 6,000 to 8,000 white and 3,000 to 4,000 black police (Table 6.1). Officials also clearly perceived the second governmental imperative: since black intermediaries were indispensable in the surveillance of the African majority, white power was limited without them. Settler efforts to translate formal title into real possession of the land, and of the labor of its occupants, intensified colonial intrusion into Africans' lives and tended to enlarge the number of black police on whom rulers relied.

South African administrators' responses to their concerns about the reliability of African police revealed their ambivalence toward a more systematic engagement with the internal dynamics of African communities. The measures they adopted to quiet their anxieties about "native authority" emasculated black policemen institutionally and socially, thus impairing official knowledge about, and weakening the state's interventionist capacities in, African communities. This chapter considers these measures together with African policemen's own experiences and how other Africans perceived them. Enlistees' subjectivity, which bore upon the success of strategies to contain the contradictions arising from Africans' employment as policemen, cannot simply be read off from officials' belief that they had secured the type of African police force they desired. The concerns of white administrators exhausted neither the meaning of African policemen's actions nor how African civilians understood these actions. Social and ideological cleavages within black communities lent significantly greater ambiguity to black policemen's position than a binary collaboration and resistance model suggests (e.g., van Onselen 1973). These cleavages were grounded in gendered popular idioms that articulated conceptions of African masculinity very different from those entertained by white administrators.

THE RACIAL CALCULUS OF POLICING

The principle of predominantly white policing had significant implications for colonial control. That few white policemen knew African languages undoubtedly frustrated government. Magistrates attributed lax pursuit of tax defaulters to the "difficulty . . . that the majority of European Police cannot speak the Native language." In 1927 there were 40 police stations in Natal, where the Post Commander was "entirely dependent on his Native Police" for interpretation.[2] Such dependence broadened that "native authority" that had been deemed inappropriate for a "white" state. Unlike whites, African police in rural districts were recruited nearby, knew the terrain well, and thus were drawn into local politics. In 1937 the Transkei's Chief Magistrate, describing relations between African police and civilians as sometimes "too smooth," suspected "collusion" was "unavoidable." White policemen themselves, worrying that they did "not get true information" from black constables, protested against being "the glorified clerk of [the] Native constable." African policemen, of course, did not always exploit such situations and could experience them as oppressive and discriminatory. They complained of white police taking "shelter under" them, sending them into dangerous crime scenes, and later taking the credit.[3] Nonetheless, significant potential existed to qualify state power, for as the expressions of white concern testify, officials' appropriation of African work and skills simultaneously involved an incorporation of African voices and perspectives that bureaucratic language and conventions could never entirely redescribe and neutralize. Official information originating with and purveyed by intermediaries answering to concerns very different from those animating administrators had an epistemological status potentially incompatible with the entrenchment of a modern regime of power.

What was done to address anxieties about the status of information mediated by Africans? Officials contemplated circumventing their dependence on Africans by recruiting or equipping white police with African language skills. But the South African Police (SAP) pursued these options unenthusiastically, for its managers associated African language fluency in whites with lower-class status and untrustworthiness.[4] The SAP's queasiness about white linguists only emphasized the indispensability of black intermediaries. Prevented in the 1920s from significantly increasing black recruitment, district officers resorted to subterfuges to secure more African police—for example, hiring supposedly temporary "Special Detectives" on day's pay, sometimes for years at a stretch.[5]

The administration adopted a more determined white labor preference stance during the depression, dismissing 1,000 black police in 1931 to make way for 286 white recruits. The Commissioner, I.P. de Villiers, reasoned strangely that this would "not affect the police position, since one European mounted constable is obviously of more value to the State from a police point of view, than three Native constables who perform their duties on foot."[6] De Villiers had little confidence in Africans, who he claimed could "not think logically at all," and declared himself "very loath to give the native police greater power." Experienced officers and detectives disagreed. A retired Deputy Commissioner believed black constables "did about 80% of the Police work." A city detective obtained his "best evidence" from "qualified native detectives."[7] However management justified it, the dismissal of African police from the late 1920s impeded the state's surveillance and control of African communities.

The reduction coincided with the limits that the state encountered in using the courts to suppress perceived political threats. The contradictions were clearest in Durban, where Detective Sergeant Reginald Arnold had day-today charge of the central government's monitoring of black politics. Arnold, who spoke Zulu fluently, boasted of his ability to "gain all information first-hand," supposedly without depending on hired African intermediaries. Arnold's exploits excited headquarters' suspicions of white police linguists, and he was reproved for his "friendliness with political agitators." And indeed, Arnold's informants in African politics, particularly Industrial and Commercial Workers' Union (ICU) Yase Natal leader A.W.G. Champion, could manipulate him. As the ICU divided in late 1928 over the role of national leader Clements Kadalie's politically moderate "European Adviser" William Ballinger, Arnold, coached by Champion, was telling his superiors that Ballinger's "tendencies" were secretly "Communist," an accusation Champion knew would subject his adversary the "Adviser" to uncomfortable state scrutiny.[8]

By mid-1930, the Criminal Investigation Department (CID) in Durban was struggling "to obtain reliable information owing to the Detectives and inform-ers becoming known." In late April, Arnold's informers and "Native Staff" had been threatened with violence at an ICU Yase Natal meeting and evicted. Arnold could do little but observe, for, as he noted, his record of speeches was drawn from memory, "and should anything grave and seditious be uttered I stand alone unsupported in any statement I may be called on to make." The ICU Yase Natal had successfully intimidated the state's black intermediaries in Durban. An out-of-town detective concluded that the Durban CID, having no "reliable system of obtaining information," needed entirely new surveil-lance networks. Now the 1930 Riotous Assemblies (Amendment) Act—which removed the courts, with their more exacting standards of corroboration, from suppression of political agitation—substituted for the extensive commitment of fresh resources. The state sought a shortcut through its difficulties in Durban in using the new legislation to banish Champion from the city.[9]

The reduction in African police numbers from the late 1920s was thus of a piece with the state's departure from a court-centered approach to political policing and significantly stalled the post-Union trend of employing more African police. Table 6.1 shows that the depression alone cannot account for the reversal, for black numbers rose only slowly with the return of prosperity and by 1939 had barely recovered their 1920 level.

It would be stretching the evidence to claim that this reversal represented a definitive retreat from more ambitious schemes of surveillance and control of African communities, for the absolute number of black police remained con-siderable. The post-1935 increase, indeed, was a deliberate modification of the policy of dismissing black intermediaries. In late September 1937, de Vil-liers sought approval to recruit 250 more African constables, ostensibly to combat an increase in urban criminality. De Villiers now professed to believe "that the prevention of crime by Natives, and the policing of Native Locations

Table 6.1 White and Black Police Strengths for Selected Years 1910–39[10]

Year	White	Black
1911/12	6,244	3,177
1920	6,352	3,678
1924	6,415	3,879
1925	6,354	3,865
1926	6,481	3,960
1927	6,525	3,997
1928	6,597	4,046
1929	6,603	3,941
1930	6,667	3,919
1931	6,671	2,895
1932	6,947	2,964
1933	6,975	2,988
1934	7,068	3,011
1935	7,278	3,025
1936	7,184	3,163
1937	7,181	3,372
1938	7,230	3,437
1939	7,754	3,676

can more efficiently be dealt with by Native Police."[11] This was standard segregationist rhetoric, but it was surprising in one who had been so "loath to give the native police greater power." Only days before, however, two white constables had been killed in an uprising against a police raid at Vereeniging in the southern Transvaal. If the late-1930s increase in African police augured a return to more vigorous state intervention, then this was a circumspect activism, which in hiding behind the cloak of "native authority" continued to reflect the contradictions that had long simultaneously promoted and restrained the state's reliance on black police.

INSTITUTIONALIZING THE CONTRADICTIONS

Unable to dispense with African police, officials' strategies for managing the contradictions focused on black policemen's recruitment, training, and service conditions. Policy in all of these areas was thoroughly institutionalized by 1939. Consider, first, recruitment. Officers sought qualities they stereotypically believed Africans inherently possessed rather than any they might acquire. "The better native is the kraal native," argued W.E. Earle of the Natal CID in 1912. "You cannot teach that class of man to read and write." Earle was typical in rejecting educated Africans as "failures and untrustworthy." De Villiers, who admitted to "a prejudice [against] employing natives who . . . were born in towns," opined in 1937 that "the one boy who one generally does not want to employ is the Lovedale boy," who supposedly was prone to corruption and insubordination.[12] White officers desired servility coupled with rudimentary English and literacy—an ideal they did not expect in urban African enlistees, who often were better educated than many white rank-and-file police.[13]

There were some dissonant voices. De Villiers's predecessor as commissioner, Colonel Truter, stated in 1912 that it "would be a very excellent thing" to have well-paid, depot-trained, educated African police. But the Cabinet negatived his recommendation.[14] Subsequently most white officers emphatically opposed educated African recruits, and the SAP progressively entrenched wages and recruitment patterns that excluded them. Police pay discouraged educated Africans aspiring to a "respectable" urban middle-class family lifestyle. In 1930, when African constables' annual starting pay was £48, a study put the minimum annual subsistence income for an African family in Johannesburg at £84.[15] Black policemen's pay was geared to a migrant work force, while their enforced residence in barracks, like the compounding of mineworkers, provided an "encapsulated" environment bearable only to men oriented to sustaining rural patrimonies (Moodie 1994). From officials' perspective, barracks prevented fraternization with local African communities that might have frustrated the state's policies or discredited its authority.[16] But city Africans found police barracks life intolerable. They feared that the police's unpopularity made their families vulnerable to retaliatory attacks during nighttime absences. Meanwhile, African policemen were denied family medical benefits on the grounds that their polygynous households would place an unreasonable burden on the state—an argument that presupposed the nonrecruitment of urban educated elite Africans.[17]

The African police force's migrant character was emphasized in the complaints of white liberals and long-term black urban residents that "native policemen" were "uneducated, uncivilised, . . . unchristian," and unscrupulous. Ethnic stereotyping powerfully informed such rhetoric, with Zulu-speaking police—who in many predominantly Setswana- or Sesotho-speaking Transvaal and Free State communities constituted at least half of all African police—being particularly resented.[18] White police consistently fostered this ethnic sentiment with their favoritism. "You can always get a desirable class of Zulu policeman, but it is difficult to get the right stamp from the other tribes," Pretoria's Superintendent Betts said in 1912. "I find," commented Pretoria's Sergeant Niemoller in 1936, "the Zulu is the much more reliable man than the man from what I might call the local population."[19]

From the first this favoritism was reflected in deliberate recruitment patterns. During the South African War, Pretoria's African community petitioned the authorities "against the employment of illiterate Zulus as Policemen." The Military Governor, although acknowledging the "Zulu Police" were "sometimes a little violent under provocation," defended them as "trustworthy obedient and efficient Police." Captain Peters, the town's Police Commissioner, praised his "Zulu" sergeants as veterans of the British-led campaign against Sekhukhune's Pedi in 1879. "It should require something more therefore than . . . irresponsible assertions," he held, "to rule these men as inefficient policemen." Ironically, the complaints were endorsed by T.G. Truter, later the first SAP Commissioner, but then an Assistant Resident Magistrate. Truter described Pretoria's African police as "raw Zulu[s]"—brutal, arrogant, "foreign and inimical to the natives of this Colony"—whose actions would cause "serious native disaffection in the future." Truter's warning was prescient. On Christmas Eve 1901, the "whole location," several thousand residents, charged the tents in which Pretoria's 150 "Zulu" policemen were encamped, and "simply knocked [the Zulus] to pieces." The uprising forced the town to diversify the ethnic composition of its African police, but the new policy was short-lived and was not emulated elsewhere. A 1913 commission reported complaints that "nearly all" the Witwatersrand's black police were "Zulus" who did "not treat other natives with reasonable sympathy." Over the decades, the proverbial figure of the illiterate "Zulu" constable, unable to tell whether a pass was in order or not, but who would arrest its holder nonetheless, exemplified for city Africans the oppressive arbitrariness of the social order.[20]

Official favoritism toward "Zulus" originated in perceptions of South Africa's nineteenth-century military and missionary history. Ethnic ranking was commonplace in turn-of-the-century Africa, as imperial armies sought allies in conquering colonial territories (Kirk-Greene 1980). In South Africa, colonial military expansion began earlier, but as Peters's comment shows, the wars of the 1870s and 1880s against independent African polities were of sufficiently recent memory to influence turn-of-the-century ideas and to dispose officials to prefer Natal Africans. Meanwhile, the nineteenth-century regimentation of northern Nguni-speakers, under and in opposition to the Zulu kings, continued to shape relations of power and authority in Natal into the twentieth century. Later, rural male youth socialization rituals reproduced patterns of social militarism (Morrell 1998). Such rituals, however, were not unique to Zulu speakers and in themselves did not prepare "Zulus" to be more violent than others. But institutionally situated in the police, and structurally relocated in ethnically segmented migrant labor markets and rural–urban/

traditionalist–Christian antagonisms, this prior rural preparation could produce the peculiar brutality associated with the "Zulu" police. White officers, admiring regimental discipline and obedience, and inserting themselves into these hierarchies and cleavages, found Zulu speakers "easier to handle" than other recruits. This employers' convenience, and the military class prejudices leading them to sympathize with "Zulus" as "Nature's gentlemen," made plausible to them stereotypes about Natal Africans' suitability for police work. As a Rand magistrate put it, Zulus were "brought up under discipline from birth, and the one who understands discipline is the best one to administer it." By contrast, the exposure to schooling and Christianity of many Xhosa speakers—earlier nineteenth-century allies discarded after the defeat of independent African power—rendered them unreliably ambitious in settler eyes. By the time of the Union, this contrast was common sense to most officers. Truter, asked why Xhosa speakers' reputation stood "lowest," professed ignorance. "The Xhosa is generally reckoned to be a questionable person, a thief, a liar, and a cheat." But "Zulus" he knew to be "very good boys."[21]

Natal chiefdoms became recruiting grounds for several police divisions. Natal officers competed in recruiting Africans from chiefdoms like Sibindi's that had assisted in suppressing the 1906 Bambatha rebellion. Transvaal officers established long-term alliances with Natal chiefs who provided migrant recruits and used their powers of rural resource allocation to discipline their followers in the police.[22] The 1937 Police Inquiry Commission's call for better educated African police, and the pay increase that followed, did little to disturb these alliances. Although de Villiers instructed officers not to hire illiterate candidates in urban areas, a proviso permitted exceptions if "insufficient [educated] recruits . . . [were] obtainable." A senior Rand officer soon invoked the saving clause "to introduce new blood." Requiring 70 African policemen, and claiming that despite "numerous applicants very few [were] suitable," he sent a subordinate to rural Natal to recruit 50 Zulu constables, who, while "hav[ing] little education," would be of "a good stamp."[23] The pattern persisted after World War II. In 1945, Pretoria approved a scheme to have Pika kaSiteku Zulu—a Zulu royal, and, as *induna* for three decades under successive managers of Durban's Native Administration Department, the nemesis of radical politicians—seconded to the SAP to tour Zululand and use his "prestige amongst the natives" to recruit men "of the type the Force requires." Pika would be given an African constable as a servant to emphasize his status. Only a sudden increase in volunteers aborted the plan, which epitomized the possibilities for distributing largesse and patronage that the police had afforded Natal chiefs for a half-century.[24]

The entrenchment of expectations geared to reproducing a force of uneducated migrants was accompanied by other policies that infantilized black police, marginalized their institutional status, curtailed their authority, and contributed to their own consciousness of their roles as highly contradictory intermediaries. Training was one such area of policy: the only instruction most black recruits received before being placed on duty was a warning not to arrest whites, even when provoked or assaulted.[25] Officials did periodically consider systematic training for black policemen, but the idea was repeatedly dismissed. Truter, we know, submitted a proposal soon after Union, but the mere sight of "native constables being drilled at the depot [caused] such an outcry [from the white public] that the Government had to stop them being drilled at all."[26] Nothing more plainly connoted the dangers of "native authority." In 1923, responding to deputy commissioners' requests, Truter authorized the creation of divisional "training schools for Native Police" as long as the schemes required no additional expenditure or staff—a limitation that guaranteed failure. "[N]othing much came of it. . . . [T]here was no real training," Truter recalled later.[27] In the late 1920s, some deputy commissioners again called for a "proper method of training Native Recruits." But their new chief, de Villiers, was even less sympathetic than Truter. Denying that Africans could "absorb . . . theoretical instruction," de Villiers insisted they need be taught only "saluting, turning and simple marching movements."[28]

While some black police regretted not receiving training, many were more emphatic about their uniform, which was uncomfortable and conveyed little of the prestige that has been claimed for uniforms elsewhere in colonial Africa (van Onselen 1973: 408–9). In 1914, Transkeian magistrates, discussing proposals to prescribe shorts for African policemen, noted that the "fashion [was] quite unknown in the Territories and would be the object of ridicule."[29] It is unclear whether the uniform was insisted upon following this complaint, but by the inter-war years shorts certainly differentiated black from white police, while khaki, a 1930s innovation, further contrasted with the blue worn by whites, and as such seemed to many a calculated slight. African police were compelled to wear the shorts with puttees, which caused circulatory problems and rashes. The uniform was cold in winter and soiled rapidly, leading to a succession of demoralizing reprimands.[30]

But the chief objection, as the magistrates suggested, was to the symbolism of the shorts, which to many African civilians signaled incomplete adulthood. One former African constable testified in 1937 that, since African male adults never wore shorts, the uniform detracted "from the dignity of the police, especially the native constables; they are taken as boys and not as men." A serving black policeman agreed that the uniform was "very very disgraceful to the Union Government," and brought the state into contempt among Africans.[31] "[E]very respectable person, or any adult person," *Bunga* Councillor Sangoni insisted, "considers it a disgrace to wear short trousers. . . . People . . . look upon [an African policeman] as though he were a boy." Transkeian magistrates reiterated in 1939 that African policemen felt "ridiculous in the eyes of the Native people" and were "often laughed at and referred to as boys" for wearing shorts, which was not "in the interest" of government. Senior SAP officers, in rejecting these complaints, offered the competing, but locally irrelevant, masculine image of the "finest soldiers" in many of the world's armies, who did "not think it any disgrace" to wear shorts (United Transkeian Territories General Council 1939: 160–1). Interestingly, in other circumstances that did not challenge their own masculine ideals, white officers could be more sensitive to the generational status of African police within black communities. When headquarters limited the age of new African recruits to 35, Natal's Deputy Commissioner Fulford considered this too low since "Natives under 30 are looked on as children by the rural native."[32]

The constriction of promotion opportunities also suggested to Africans a diminution in the status of black policemen and elicited further gendered observations. African policemen in the inter-war decades contended that the number of noncommissioned officer positions open to them had declined visibly. As *Bunga* Councillor Samuel Pantshwa put it in 1935, "In the magistrates' offices we do not see any more sergeants. . . . Only cows are being kept in the small offices—there are no bulls." As with the perception of their degrading uniform, the denial of higher rank to African policemen was depicted as a deliberate emasculation discrediting to the state. Pantshwa's taunt apparently had some effect, for when the *Bunga* next met, in 1936, the SAP had appointed at least one African corporal in each Transkeian district. But higher rank seldom drew additional respect from white policemen, who continued to treat African NCOs "just as any ordinary constable."[33]

Possession of firearms was another issue on which black policemen lost ground in the early twentieth century. Although colonial governments had always strictly regulated black policemen's access to firearms, the restrictions were less severe before 1910, especially in the Cape Colony, where black police were issued revolvers to protect themselves and were kept in practice in case they had to fire them. Following Union, it became government policy to limit firearms to whites. The first Union Cabinet singled out the Cape policy for revision, ordering that African policemen's revolvers be replaced by *assegais* and sticks. In 1914 the Transkeian Magistrates' Conference strongly objected, arguing that this development had already been taken advantage of to defy African policemen's authority. The government heeded the magistrates on this occasion and returned the revolvers. But in February 1917, SAP headquarters instructed divisional police chiefs in Cape Town, Grahamstown, and Umtata to repossess black policemen's revolvers. Thenceforth, no "coloured or native police" would be allowed to use firearms except in extraordinary, individually approved instances.[34]

Black police were as vocal about the firearms policy as they were about their training, uniform, and limited promotion prospects. In the Transkei— which until the early 1920s the authorities treated as a military "frontier" territory requiring "pacification"—African policemen protested when, unlike white constables, they were forced to patrol unarmed.[35] In fact, the state was disarming black policemen in the Transkei at precisely the time that its enforcement of dipping regulations and restrictions on the movement of cattle was provoking determined and even violent resistance (Beinart and Bundy 1980: 280–5). Even in the 1930s, after the Transkei supposedly had been under "ordinary police control" for years, African police feared moving about the countryside unarmed; some carried sticks or *sjamboks* but confessed they would feel safer with revolvers.[36] The Deputy Commissioner claimed in 1930 that instances of African mounted policemen being "driven out of" rural locations were increasing and suggested that they all be given revolvers, but Pretoria demurred. In the cities, too, African constables considered their work highly dangerous. African police at Korsten in Port Elizabeth petitioned their station commander in 1932 to allow them to carry kerries to exact greater respect from the settlement's defiant residents. Police management, drawing on stereotypical ideas about African men's "natural" weapons, greeted petitions for knobkerries more sympathetically than requests for revolvers. It was "a well known fact," a senior officer asserted, "that to deprive a Native of his Kerrie is to take away a portion of his manhood." Unlike African policemen's objection, on similar grounds, to wearing shorts, the question of kerries did not challenge white colonial men's own notion of the appropriate markers of masculinity.[37]

Bureaucratic routine further curtailed black policemen's authority. Since education was considered undesirable in African police, they were not expected to produce written reports. They usually reported orally to the white station commander, who took down a verbatim written statement, which the African constable then thumbprinted. This ritual was followed even with educated black policemen who were capable of writing their own reports in one of the official languages. A Natal lance sergeant observed in 1937 that he had "never heard of a native taking a statement. . . . [W]e have the men who can read and write, but I have never yet dared a native to take a statement. It would lead to trouble."[38] This observation reveals yet again the pervasive anxiety about "native authority." Hofmeyr (1993: chap. 3) shows how the subordination of supposedly "oral" Africans to "literate" whites constructed and reproduced authority and bureaucratic credibility in racially exclusive terms. Reporting procedures in the police daily enacted this subordination, although constraints on communication could complicate, and even subvert, the white supremacist ritual of appropriating African work and skills.

African constables' relations with their white counterparts, who insultingly called them "kaffirs," were a source of grievance in other ways too. That both the SAP and its predecessors issued strict regulations proscribing white members from treating African policemen as domestic servants suggests that this practice was endemic. Another order, however, insisted on black policemen's different and inferior status. "No familiarity or joking," it ran, "is ever to be allowed between men of the Force and native constables; such behaviour

invariably leads to lack of discipline which is seldom the fault of the natives."
Thus in management's eyes only white police ideally were fully members of
the force: adult, male, and responsible for their behavior.[39]

Some black policemen unsurprisingly opposed the SAP's treatment of
African civilians. Ezekiel Mafule, a policeman in Pretoria in the 1920s,
keenly resented unequal racial policing. And even after 24 years' service,
Johannesburg Detective Corporal Mashaba's diction betrayed a fundamental
resistance to identifying with his employer. "The reason we do not agree with
the police," he told the Police Inquiry Commission in 1937, "is that the police
always raid the locations and make searches." Rural African policemen
sought to transfer to headmen unpopular duties like arresting tax defaulters
and impounding livestock.[40] Others convinced themselves that, as Russel
Gxumisa (1994) put it, "a policeman is never . . . wrong." At Flagstaff in Pondoland from the late 1930s, Gxumisa monitored resistance to taxation and
cattle dipping. Gxumisa, while conceding that the protesters sometimes "were
right," reconciled himself to his role by observing organizational mottoes
such as "Arrest [only] where necessary," which he believed licensed him to
let people off with a warning.

"SATANS AFTER PEOPLE"

Despite some black policemen's scruples and lived contradictions, African
civilians tended not to differentiate black from white policemen. "The public
with whom we deal," acknowledged one African constable, "are much
against us." Black policemen's reputation for violence was largely unquali-
fied. City residents countrywide told of African police assaulting them with
sjamboks and sticks. African children, raised in milieux where such assaults
abounded, incorporated a revealing figure of the policeman into their play. In
1937 an East Rand clergyman recalled seeing boys "together at a game in
which one got hold of another and with a flexible wire bound his hands round
and started shamboking him. I asked them what they were doing and the reply
was 'We are playing policemen.'"[41]

Police management denied the abuses by claiming that black policemen
had no discretion to act independently of a white policeman's orders. Both the
claim and the denial were improbable. The claim was untrue because to be
effective African police necessarily "exercise[d] authority of [their] own
motion" much more frequently than their officers cared to admit and received
powers of arrest for precisely this reason (Union of South Africa 1937a:
18–19, para. 67). This was one of the contradictory imperatives of rule we
have noted all along. The denial of abuse was hardly more credible, given the
number and consistency of complaints. Senior officers, indeed, wanted ordinary Africans to have "a very healthy fear" of black police.[42] Russel Gxumisa
(1994) certainly believed "the majority were quite afraid" of him. Black

policemen's harsh treatment of African civilians was a structured function of the police institution, and, even in egregious cases that could not be denied, dismissal seldom ensued. Gxumisa was disciplined but not dismissed after he and another policeman assaulted a civilian who had taunted them by saying "SAP" stood for "Satans After People"—a phrase that identified African police as purveyors of evil in the community.

African constables were in any case no less violent or venal in the presence of white policemen, whose reputation was no better. Transvaal Native Congress leader S.M. Makgatho, in a 1917 speech criticizing Prime Minister Botha's appeal to blacks to join the Native Labour Contingent in France, offered almost interchangeable descriptions of white and black policemen:

> We are loyal but many of these European Police who kick us and shove us about are to our knowledge ignorant men. . . . Their native assistants are great strapping Zulus, . . . cowards, who are content to walk round the streets worrying our women. In the day they demand from us passes which they hold up-side-down and, because they cannot read, interrogate us as to their contents. . . . When we speak of joining the contingent our very women curse us and ask whether the Government for whom we risk our lives is not the same that allows the Police to enter our homes at night to pull us out of bed and trample on our children.[43]

Two decades later, residents of Pretoria's locations complained that white police winked at black constables' appropriation of confiscated home brew for their own consumption or sale. Residents were particularly incensed when the liquor was taken to nearby homes where the African policemen had "women friends" who would host them or "sell the beer for the police."[44]

This evidence suggests how gender concerns hardened such resentments into perceptions of ethnic and status difference as the enforcement of segregationist controls quickened. Male members of established urban African Christian communities feared that black policemen would take sexual advantage if their wives and daughters were subjected to the pass laws. Already black women were being intercepted on suspicion of conveying liquor.[45] "Respectable" men's concerns about the usurpation of their patriarchal privileges by other African men (especially migrant illiterate non-Christians, which most black constables were) thus reinforced worries about the extinction of officials' recognition of their middle-class "exempted" status. The questioning of black policemen's masculinity and adulthood resulting from the state's institutional strategies to contain "native authority" can only have intensified the educated elite's status concerns about the repercussions of sexual assault. The consequent hardening of perceptions of difference in the inter-war years facilitated a prevalent public ridiculing of African police, who retaliated with increasing violence. We need not subscribe to white officials' essentialist beliefs about Africans' "natural" cruelty to acknowledge that black policemen may have had reasons of their own to exploit their authority.[46]

Nighttime raids in which policemen forcibly entered homes, overturning belongings and uncovering people in their beds, ostensibly to search for liquor and tax evaders, provided ready occasions for sexual assault and other forms of violence. Senior officers conceded that nocturnal raids created "a general upheaval" in which "all kinds of things [might] happen," and undoubtedly African policemen used these situations to settle scores. The opportunities only increased with the escalation of raiding in the 1920s and 1930s, which targeted women disproportionately, and made little allowance for class distinction. In Vereeniging's Top Location, for example, in the eleven months preceding the September 1937 riots, nearly 80 percent of the 361 Africans warned or arrested were women.[47]

Evidence that long-term city residents challenged black policemen dates to the early 1900s. In Pretoria during the South African War, Zulu-speaking constables demanding passes endured prevarication, argument, and jeers about their illiteracy, while those on nighttime beat duty were frequent targets of flying stones and bottles.[48] These individual skirmishes, typical of challenges in later decades too, escalated into the mass armed attack on the "Zulu Police" on Christmas Eve, 1901. Such dramatic resistance was rare, however, with subsequent collective targeting of black police tending to be orchestrated by politicians at public meetings. Makgatho's 1917 speech is one example. Another is the April 1930 ICU Yase Natal meeting in Durban from which Detective Sergeant Arnold's "Native Staff" were evicted. Women, leading a beerhall boycott, were especially militant in denouncing black policemen at this meeting. From the platform, Mrs. Montombela "warned those dogs of persons who called themselves Natives who were selling their manhood in working for the Police that their day was at hand, she advicated [*sic*] that these persons should be driven away."[49] No comment better illustrates how African policemen's masculinity, and even their humanity, were socially compromised.

Not only "dogs," but "snakes," "satans," and "baboons" were terms of abuse commonly directed at black police. An African detective sensitively observed "that whenever a policeman effects an arrest he is not wanted—he is doing something which is like a disgrace."[50] It is not only to black policemen's role as agents of an oppressive colonial order, however, that the virulence of civilians' feelings toward them should be attributed. Community resentments were grounded in complex local cleavages shaped by gender and status issues, the production and consumption of liquor, and the ethnicizing dynamics of the labor market. In particular, elite African men felt both their domestic identities as patriarchs, and their public status of entitlement to official favors, threatened by "uneducated, uncivilised, and unchristian police" who, precisely because they did exercise state powers, seemed to exemplify the challenges to their subjectivity that urban Christians perceived in the male migrant workforce more generally.

CONCLUSION

Early twentieth-century South African governments confronted the contradictory imperative of extending their surveillance and control of African communities while minimizing the potential of indispensable African intermediaries to qualify the racially exclusive monopoly of power. This conundrum of rule, familiar to European administrators throughout Africa, shaped the South African state's policies, structures, and personnel. The authorities knew that in governing Africans they would "always" need to operate "through the medium of" African police, who alone could "gather information regarding the natives which it [was] essential for Government to know" (Transvaal Colony 1904: Part II, A.4). But officials also feared that their reliance on African police involved concessions to "native authority" that could endanger white supremacy. Black policemen's dependability could never be taken for granted, for the effectiveness of their employment was inseparable from their insertion in the hierarchies and idioms of local black politics. Administrators hoped, through selective recruitment and institutional discipline, to determine the mode of black policemen's insertion in African communities. But the complex dynamics of seniority and gender in African community politics remained largely beyond the comprehension or conscious influence of white officials, whose precautions, in compromising their intermediaries' local reputations as adult men, limited black policemen's usefulness and thus reproduced the conundrum of rule. The consequences were that the state moderated its surveillance ambitions, continued to rely on a predominantly white police force, and in doing so allowed greater than intended scope for that "native authority" that policy was so anxious to keep in check.

ACKNOWLEDGMENTS

My research was assisted by a grant from the Joint Committee on African Studies of the SSRC and ACLS with funds provided by the Ford, Mellon, and Rockefeller Foundations. For their encouragement and criticism I thank David Cohen, Jonathon Glassman, Lisa Lindsay, Stephan Miescher, James Oakes, Christina Smith, and Lynn Thomas.

NOTES

1. FK 1175, Lord Milner, South African Papers, J. Smuts to Milner, 6 April 1901.

2. SAP 15/128/27, Commissioner for Inland Revenue to Commissioner of Police (Compol), 21 October 1921, enclosing Resident Magistrate, Bizana, to Commissioner for Inland Revenue, 12 October 1921; JUS 1/240/30/1, Acting Compol to Secretary for Justice

(SJ), 3 November 1927; SAP 20/10/45, Acting Deputy Commissioner (Decompol), Pietermaritzburg, to Compol, 17 May 1929.

3. K80, Vol. 54, 4 March 1937, Fyfe-King, 4029, Taylor, 4039, and Poswayo, 4079–80; Vol. 56, 8 March 1937, Botha, 4217; Vol. 57, 9 March 1937, Johnston, 4257; Vol. 89, 28 April 1937, Mkise, 7650.

4. JUS 1/240/30/1, Acting Compol to SJ, 3 November 1927.

5. SAP 31/68/25, Decompol, Bloemfontein, to Decompol, CID, Pretoria, 7 December 1925, enclosing Divisional CI Officer to Decompol, 4 December 1925.

6. MFN, M10/15, Private Secretary, Minister of Justice, to Private Secretary, Minister of Finance, 14 September 1933, enclosing Compol to Minister of Justice, 13 September 1933.

7. K80, Vol. 34, 1 February 1937, de Villiers, 2422; Vol. 54, 4 March 1937, Taylor, 4039; Vol. 94, 4 May 1937, Martell, 8129.

8. JUS 1/18/26, Part 22, Acting Compol to SJ, 4 December 1928, enclosing Arnold to Sub Inspector, CID, Durban, 27 November 1928; Part 23, Compol to SJ, 7 January 1929, enclosing Arnold to Officer in Charge, CID, Durban, 31 December 1928.

9. GNLB 55/1, Arnold to Officer in Charge, CID, Durban, 27 April and 19 May 1930; JUS 1/18/26, Part 27: Compol to SJ, 13 June 1930, enclosing District Commandant (DC), Durban, to Decompol, Pietermaritzburg, 9 June 1930, and Kruger to DC, Durban, 3 June 1930; Compol to SJ, 16 June 1930, enclosing Decompol, Natal, to Compol, 10 June 1930.

10. Union of South Africa (1926: 83, Annexure 7; 1932: 294; 1941: 391).

11. SAP 9/4/37, Compol to Minister of Justice, 28 September 1937.

12. K373, No. 109, 2 September 1912, Earle, 20–1, 28; K80, Vol. 34, 1 February 1937, de Villiers, 2420–1, and Vol. 101, 17 May 1937, de Villiers, 8719, 8722. Lovedale, a famous mission school, connoted to whites the subversive consequences of educating Africans.

13. K80, Vol. 14, 4 December 1936, Long, 973; Vol. 45, 19 February 1937, Harvey, 3475; Vol. 46, 20 February 1937, Tyamzashe, 3507. Russel Gxumisa (1994) recalled his contempt for an Afrikaner policeman whose English was so weak that he hid while Gxumisa went to English-speaking farmers to have the patrol book signed.

14. K373, No. 162, 23 October 1912, Truter, 30–1.

15. K80, Vol. 13, 2 December 1936, Molako, 868–70; SAP 3/8/34, Enclosure in Compol to Government Secretary, Mafeking, 15 November 1934; Phillips (1930: 62–3).

16. SAP 15/33/29, Decompol, Transvaal, to Compol, 9 November 1929.

17. K80, Vol. 72, 3 April 1937, Sebotse, 5976–7; Vol. 89, 28 April 1937, Molise, 7627–8, and Judas, 7655–6.

18. K80, Vol. 6, 24 November 1936, Junod, Stowell, and Lefe, 311, 324, 350–1; Vol. 13, 2 December 1936, Motou, 884.

19. K373, No. 161, 29 October 1912, Betts, 26; K80, Vol. 8, 26 November 1936, Niemoller, 467.

20. LD, AG 1815A/02, J.G. Maxwell to Richard Solomon, 21 January 1902, enclosing Compol to Military Governor, and Truter's Report on the Native Police (both undated); K373, No. 161, 29 October 1912, Betts, 25–6; Union of South Africa (1913: paras. 142–3).

21. K373, No. 214, 14 November 1912, Taberer, 32; No. 109, 2 September 1912, Earle, 28; No. 254, 27 November 1912, Britten, W53; No. 162, 23 October 1912, Truter, 32, 35.

22. K373, No. 109, 2 September 1912, Earle, 28, and No. 162, 23 October 1912, Truter, 35; K80, Vol. 59, 12 March 1937, Fulford, 4449.

23. SAP 39/5/28, Circular to Decompols, 22 October 1937; Decompol, Witwatersrand, to Compol, 21 December 1937; Compol to Decompol, Johannesburg, 24 December 1937.

24. SAP 39/5/28, Decompol, Pietermaritzburg, to Compol, 13 November 1945, enclosing DC, Durban, to Decompol, 5 November 1945, and Manager, Municipal Native Administration Department, to DC, Durban, 1 November 1945; Compol to Secretary to the Treasury, 1 December 1945; Decompol, Natal, to Compol, 24 January 1946.

25. K80, Vol. 73, 5 April 1937, Zim, 6003.

26. K373, No. 162, 23 October 1912, Truter, 31.

27. SAP 20/10/45, Extract from Proceedings of Fifth Annual SAP Conference, 1923; K80, Vol. 109, 28 May 1937, Truter, 9096.

28. SAP 20/10/45, Decompol, Transvaal, to Compol, 11 April 1928; Acting Decompol, Pietermaritzburg, to Compol, 17 May 1929; Acting Compol to Decompol, Pietermaritzburg, 14 November 1930; K80, Vol. 101, 17 May 1937, de Villiers, 8722.

29. NA 5231/1914/F607, Acting Chief Magistrate, Umtata, to Secretary for Native Affairs (SNA), 8 May 1914.

30. Union of South Africa (1937a: para. 56(e)); K80, Vol. 13, 2 December 1936, Molako, 870; Vol. 54, 4 March 1937, Betheldana, 4082; Vol. 47, 22 February 1937, Stinga, 3537.

31. K80, Vol. 39, 11 February 1937, Jantjes, 2931–2; Vol. 47, 22 February 1937, Stinga, 3537.

32. SAP 20/10/45, Acting Decompol, Pietermaritzburg, to Compol, 17 May 1929.

33. United Transkeian Territories General Council (1935: 184; 1936: 287); K80, Vol. 54, 4 March 1937, Betheldana, 4081; Vol. 73, 5 April 1937, Zim, 6004–5.

34. NA 5231/1914/F607, Acting Chief Magistrate, Umtata, to SNA, 8 May 1914, and Under-SNA to Chief Magistrate, Umtata, 24 July 1914; SAP 24/5/31, Memorandum, 17 May 1951.

35. Union of South Africa (1919: para. 511). On policing arrangements for "frontier districts," see Union of South Africa (1912: 8).

36. K80, Vol. 57, 9 March 1937, Mlingwa, 4357. For "ordinary police control," CGS, Group 1, Box 7, File Secret 10, Confidential Memorandum, 6 February 1930.

37. SAP 24/5/31: Decompol, Transkei, to Compol, 2 April 1930; Compol to Decompol, Umtata, 16 August 1930; Decompol, Grahamstown, to Compol, 2 June 1932.

38. K80, Vol. 8, 26 November 1936, Niemoller, 468; Vol. 69, 30 March 1937, Green, 5599; Gxumisa (1994).

39. K80, Vol. 89, 28 April 1937, Mkise, 7650; SNA 2168/02, Assistant SNA to SNA, 8 November 1902, enclosing extract from Natal Police Force, Revised Rules and Regulations, para. 326; SNA 1490/07, Chief Staff Officer, South African Constabulary (SAC), to SNA, 18 January 1906, enclosing Extract from General Regulations, para. 280; Transvaal Colony (1908: para. 107).

40. K80, Vol. 5, 23 November 1936, Mafule, 297–8; Vol. 96, 7 May 1937, Mashaba, 8369–71; Vol. 54, 4 March 1937, Poswayo, 4080.

41. K80, Vol. 47, 22 February 1937, Ngcaba, 3545; Vol. 46, 20 February 1937, Godlo and others, 3497; Vol. 96, 7 May 1937, Khabo, 8367–67a ; Vol. 91, 30 April 1937, Clark, 7781.

42. K373, No. 168, 25 October 1912, Mavrogordato, 54–5.

43. JUS 1/399/13, E. Barrett to SNA, 26 June 1917, enclosed in Barrett to SJ, 4 July 1917.

44. K80, Vol. 5, 23 November 1936, Komane, 256–7.

45. Union of South Africa (1913: para. 142); K357, No. 129, 2 March 1920, Beer, 18.

46. K80, Vol. 4, 20 November 1936, Woon, 222.

47. Union of South Africa (1937a: 70, para. 279; 1937b: 16); K80, Vol. 8, 26 November 1936, Kruger, 514.

48. LD, AG 1815A/02, J.G. Maxwell to Richard Solomon, 21 January 1902, enclosing Compol to Military Governor [undated].
49. GNLB 55/1, Arnold to Officer in Charge, CID, Durban, 27 April 1930.
50. K80, Vol. 47, 22 February 1937, Loni, 3544.

SOURCES

Archival

National Archives, Pretoria

JUS Department of Justice

K80 Police Inquiry Commission, 1936–37

K357 Inter-Departmental Committee on Native Pass Laws, 1920

K373 Commission to Enquire into Assaults on Women, 1912–13

MFN Private Secretary, Minister of Finance

NA Native Affairs

SAP South African Police

Defence Archives, Pretoria

CGS Chief of the General Staff

Transvaal Archives, Pretoria

FK Facsimile Volumes

GNLB Government Native Labour Bureau

LD Law Department

SNA Secretary for Native Affairs

Oral

Gxumisa, Russel. 1994. Interviewed by Keith Shear.

REFERENCES

Beinart, William and Colin Bundy. 1980. "State Intervention and Rural Resistance: The Transkei, 1900–1965." In *Peasants in Africa: Historical and Contemporary Perspectives*, Martin A. Klein, ed., pp. 271–315. Beverly Hills, CA: Sage Publications.

Fields, Karen E. 1985. *Revival and Rebellion in Colonial Central Africa*. Princeton, NJ: Princeton University Press.

Hofmeyr, Isabel. 1993. *"We Spend Our Years as a Tale That Is Told": Oral Historical Narrative in a South African Chiefdom*. Portsmouth, NH: Heinemann.

Kirk-Greene, Anthony H. M. 1980. "'Damnosa Hereditas': Ethnic Ranking and the Martial Races Imperative in Africa." *Ethnic and Racial Studies* 3, 4: 393–414.

Moodie, T. Dunbar, with Vivienne Ndatshe. 1994. *Going for Gold: Men, Mines, and Migration*. Berkeley: University of California Press.

Morrell, Robert. 1998. "Of Boys and Men: Masculinity and Gender in Southern African Studies." *Journal of Southern African Studies* 24, 4: 605–30.

Phillips, Ray E. 1930. *The Bantu are Coming: Phases of South Africa's Race Problem*. London: Student Christian Movement Press.

Transvaal Colony. 1904. *Transvaal Administration Reports for 1903*. Pretoria: Government Printing and Stationery Office.

———. 1908. *Transvaal Police Act, 1908, with Regulations Framed Thereunder and Standing Orders for the Transvaal Police*. Pretoria: Government Printing and Stationery Office.

Union of South Africa. 1912. *Memorandum Explanatory of the South African Defence Bill*. Cape Town: Government Printer.

———. 1913. *Report of the Commission Appointed to Enquire into Assaults on Women*. Cape Town: Government Printer.

———. 1919. *Third Report of the Public Service Commission of Enquiry*. Cape Town: Government Printer.

———. 1926. *Report of the Commission of Enquiry to Enquire into the Organisation of the South African Police Force Established under Act No. 14 of 1912*. Cape Town: Government Printer.

———. 1932. *Official Year Book, No. 13 (1930–1931)*. Pretoria: Government Printing and Stationery Office.

———. 1937a. *Interim and Final Reports of the Commission of Enquiry to Enquire into Certain Matters Concerning the South African Police and the South African Railways and Harbours Police*. Pretoria: Government Printer.

———. 1937b. *Report of the Vereeniging Native Riots Commission of Enquiry*. Mimeographed typescript.

———. 1941. *Official Year Book, No. 22 (1941)*. Pretoria: Government Printer.

United Transkeian Territories General Council. 1935. *Proceedings and Reports of Select Committees at the Session of 1935*. King William's Town: King Printing Company.

———. 1936. *Proceedings and Reports of Select Committees at the Session of 1936*. King William's Town: King Printing Company.

———. 1939. *Proceedings and Reports of Select Committees at the Session of 1939*. Umtata: Territorial Printers.

van Onselen, Charles. 1973. "The Role of Collaborators in the Rhodesian Mining Industry, 1900–1935." *African Affairs* 72, 289: 401–18.

7

INDUSTRIAL MAN GOES TO AFRICA

Frederick Cooper

Travelers' reports of the late nineteenth century are replete with tales of male laziness.[1] African men, European readers were often told, either sat around drinking and gossiping or else ran around enslaving or killing each other, while women took care of the daily tasks on farms and in households. Men's role in pastoralism and hunting was usually acknowledged, and some travelers avoided this stereotyping altogether, yet on the whole European readers learned that their idea of useful work did not apply to the African man, and that steady, regular work was what African men tried hardest to avoid.

In the 1950s, when primacy of place in European writing about Africa had been given to bureaucrats and, increasingly, to social scientists, the connection of gender and work had changed. The writers were now beginning to see—or at least to hope and to advocate—that Africans would work in railways, mines, ports, commercial enterprises, and factories, as well as in modern agricultural enterprises, in a manner comparable to that of Europeans. The workers in question, in virtually all analyses of the subject, were male. Industrial man had come to Africa.

Industrial man had a wife. In fact, women were—in colonial debates—absolutely central to determining the future of industrial men. Colonial officials in the 1940s and early 1950s were not satisfied with the actual African men they saw in places of work; they believed that their vision of African men socialized and acculturated to the demands, rhythms, and values of industrial labor was an attainable one, but that it had yet to be achieved. Culture, not race, was the basic problem. The making of industrial men had to begin at birth and go through the critical years of childhood. African woman would create African industrial man.

Hence the critical focus of British Labour Officers and French Inspecteurs du Travail in the post-war decade was on what they called the "stabilization" of workers' families. We would now call this a question of social reproduction. The socialization of a young man could not be left to the backward family structures and environments—let alone the dubious nutritional practices—of villages, but had to take place in or near places of work, where a new culture was being defined and where surveillance could be exercised. The key new feature of labor policies after the war concerned women: they had to be brought to the place of work to raise the next generation of workers. Yet women were the backward ones. It was they who had to be transformed, and their vital duty of raising industrial men had to be conducted under colonial supervision.[2]

The labor question in post-war Africa was thus debated in gendered terms. Whether the initial bias in the development of wage labor toward hiring males in mines, railways, and often even in domestic service was shaped by colonial prejudices or Africans' supposed belief that men were more dispensable is another question. The majority of workers who received wages in 1945 were male, and as officials thought about work in the ensuing years, they tended to define ever more explicitly the kinds of things that men did as "work" and the kind of things that women did as something else. Sometimes this was called "customary labor" and—as in the French Code du Travail of 1952—defined out of the domain of labor regulators, but what concerned officials the most about women's economic and social roles was what they did to reproduce a male labor force.

My concern in this chapter is with the colonial discourse about work and reproduction, not with the changing social patterns in African cities and mine towns, which, not surprisingly, rarely fit into the dualistic reasoning of officials. I will illustrate with French and British examples the stress on the cultural construction of the proper worker in the early post-war years and go on to an examination of the most explicit case of official coding of gender roles in reproducing a working class, the French program of family allowances implemented in 1956.

TOWARD STABILIZATION AND FAMILY WAGES: THE CASE OF KENYA

At the end of World War II, two problems with the system of cheap, migratory labor commanded official attention: worries about the low and allegedly declining productivity of African workers and fear that workers and other urbanites had become a dangerous class. Work stoppages in Kenya's port of Mombasa in 1934, 1939, and 1942, as well as a threatened port and railway strike in 1945, had shaken the government. It was in official investigations into the 1939 and 1945 incidents that new ways of thinking about the labor question were first articulated. The 1947 general strike in Mombasa, in which some 15,000 Africans helped to shut down the port for twelve days, made clear that African men, moving into and out of jobs, sharing residential space with hawkers and criminals, constituted a dangerous mass. Breaking that mass into its component parts—each of which could be led to aspire to follow its own occupational interests and alleviate its grievances through industrial relations machinery on the British model—became an imperative of labor policy. The problem of order gave an immediate focus to longer range concerns with the quality of the labor force being formed in Kenya, and, as wages in key occupations rose, so too did concern with productivity. In Mombasa, the issue of decasualizing dock labor had provided a focus ever since the 1939 strike; in Kenya more generally—as in the British copperbelt—the issue of stabilizing the work force and reducing migrancy was debated at length between 1945 and 1954.

The committee that investigated the barely averted general strike in 1945 went a long way toward putting the issue in new terms. It stressed the dangers of a situation in which the long-term, married worker—now a significant portion of the Mombasa labor force—received similar wages and had no higher career expectations than the casual laborer. This meant that the "'sanction of the Sack' is largely inoperative," that productivity was sapped by the poor health and bad attitudes of migrant laborers, and that—among the labor force as a whole—order was threatened by "the beginnings of class-consciousness, complicated by race-consciousness" (Kenya 1945: 43, 56–7).

The committee believed that these problems could only be resolved by paying African men wages sufficient to support families, by building increments and incentives into the wage structure, and by providing workers and their families the "opportunity for a civilized life." It concluded, "There seems to be no escaping the fact that the evils which are commonly attributed to 'detribalisation' can only be cured by more complete detribalisation (Kenya, 1945: 50, 97).

The top officials concerned with labor were by then articulating their concern with the issue of reproduction. The absence of increments in the standard pay scales on the railway "will condemn its unskilled staff to a completely celibate life," wrote the Acting Labour Commissioner in early 1945.[3] The opposite side of this anxiety with the conditions of a womanless working life was the fear that rural life might prove too attractive to the African man:

> [T]he tribesman gradually builds up a household for himself on the modest native scale until, after a limited number of absences at work, he is established in what are, for him, comfortable conditions. . . . [T]he idea of continuous employment as his main support is entirely strange, and in fact repellent, to his mentality. (Orde Browne 1946: 5–6)

The African Labour Efficiency Survey, conducted among Kenyan railway workers in 1947 by a team of British specialists in industrial labor, strongly made the connection between reproduction and culture on the one hand and performance in the workplace on the other. The survey actually did little surveying, but it articulated an ideology. It insisted that Africans could be efficient workers, but only if a cultural and physical transformation were effected. The industrial sociologists used their report to condemn African culture as incompatible with industrial society and values. The African came out of his village too malnourished to work hard and too undisciplined to work well: "He is ineffective in many industrial techniques by the very nature of his birth, his upbringing, and his native culture" (Northcott 1949: 12–13). The connection with the nineteenth-century view of gender and labor was made explicitly:

> The East African has not been bent under the discipline of organized work. In his primitive economy, the steady, continuous labour is carried out by women. . . . Though the tasks he performed were prescribed by tribal law and custom, he could do them in his own way and at his own speed, for to him time had no economic value. . . . To work steadily and continuously at the will and direction of another was one of the hard lessons he had to learn when he began to work for Europeans. (Northcott 1949: 7)

The significance of this argument was clear: the lessons of industrial civilization would only be learned if new generations of workers were brought up in the proper situation: "To enable him [the African] to become efficient in this modern age the resources of the environing industrial civilization must be placed in his hands and he must be taught to use them" (Northcott 1949: 12–13).

The Labour Commissioner, Hyde-Clarke, was willing to face the implications of this: male workers had to be paid enough so that their families could be brought up at their places of work. He insisted that under the status quo, labor only appeared to be cheap, but it required "large uneconomic labour forces . . . a very great deal more in housing, supervision, accommodation, and feeding than is really necessary."[4] This was where the issue became difficult. As Hyde-Clarke later put it, "[E]veryone was in favour of a stabilised African work force but no one wanted to pay for it" (quoted in Amsden 1971: 49). A long legislative debate ensued, culminating eventually in an accommodation with the settlers, who protected themselves from paying the costs of reproduction by limiting the new wage—intended, however implausibly, to cover the cost of supporting a family—to urban and industrial workers.

The two-tiered minimum wage, enacted in 1954, was more of an ideological triumph than a practical one. In some of the most vulnerable industries, the initiatives of African workers did force wages well above the official minima, and officials tried to reassert control by demanding steady work and regular discipline. This has been analyzed at length in the case of dockworkers:

the docks were decasualized during the mid-1950s, while supervision was tightened (Cooper 1987). Denied the flexibility to combine wage labor with other economic activities and paid several times prevailing agricultural wages, the dockworker was expected to live his life in Mombasa, raising his children on his wages and in the urban locus of civilization. In 1959, another of the many investigations into dock labor concluded that considerable progress had been made, and the major area where more needed to be done was housing: "The African worker must have a place where he can keep his wife and children. . . . Attempts to meet these needs are being made by the creation of housing estates, with shops, community halls, playing fields, churches, etc." (Kenya 1959: 19).

When the government accepted definitively the principle of the family wage, it enshrined the principle above even that of the market wage. As the Colonial Secretary (a Tory), put it, "[E]ven where the 'bachelor wage' still represents the supply price of labor, it may be below the level of wages necessary to secure efficient production."[5] Why this was so was explained in cultural terms: "We cannot *hope* to produce an effective African labour force until we have first removed the African from the enervating and retarding influence of his economic and cultural background." The state had to take the lead to provide "such conditions, both social and economic, as will induce the African to sever his ties with tribal life and virtually start afresh in a new environment" (Kenya 1954: 11, 16). The pronoun in this official report was masculine, but its reference was actually women. Unless they joined their men—and lived off the men's wages—they were the epitome of tribal life and retarding influence.

TOWARD FAMILY ALLOWANCES IN FRENCH AFRICA

National stereotypes aside, French conceptions of the relationship of African culture and industrial society were not very different from British officials' views in the post-war era. A French study of 1953 insisted that it was necessary but difficult to remake African attitudes toward work discipline, and to do so implied a cultural revolution:

> It is exceptional that a black accepts the need to carry out his effort beyond the simple task in order to increase his gains. For that to happen, it is necessary that he has been profoundly Europeanized, that he has adopted our motivations and accepted our own necessities. In a word, that he has retained nothing African except the color.[6]

As in British Africa, the idea of industrial man had deep roots in metropolitan ideology, but the timing of its application to Africa was a consequence of collective action. In particular, the Senegalese general strike of 1946 threw awry officials' hopes, expressed only two years before at Brazzaville, that a "politique du paysannat" would lead French Africa out of the era of forced labor and into a period of increased production that did not disrupt African communities. That eleven-day general strike—the climax of a two-month strike movement in French West Africa's leading city—served notice that workers existed and would have to be treated as such (Cooper 1990). Unable to handle the disruption within the framework of the colonial structure of authority, officials called in a labor expert from Paris and set about using metropolitan techniques of labor management to resolve the dispute. In so doing, they recorded the social map of Africa, defining a domain in which the African worker—whoever he was, wherever he came from, and whomever he was connected to—would be treated juridically and, increasingly, politically as a worker. As the strike wound down, the imported expert gloated, "There is a technique to organizing work, as with everything, and it cannot be improvised."[7]

The resolution of this strike—and the basis of the actions of the Inspection du Travail in ensuing years—was the standard French form of the "convention collective," or collective bargaining agreement. The work force was divided into occupations and each occupation into a hierarchy of jobs: the structure attempted to reduce contestation to a question of filling in numbers corresponding to the wages of each category. Of course, things did not evolve so simply, and African trade unionists immediately seized on the rhetoric of French officials and turned it into a claim for entitlements for African workers (Cooper 1996).

The key issue, for both sides, was family allowances. By this time, French citizens received a series of benefits, on a per household or per child basis, designed to ease the financial burden of family formation and thus to promote natality. For French trade unionists, family allowances became an entitlement whose form and amounts were an object of struggle, but for employers, church leaders, and officials of the state, family allowances made sense too, promoting family stability and reproduction. French governments saw family allowances as a means of augmenting the French population. That logic implied that family allocations for Africans would augment the wrong population, and in case this was not self-evident, officials pointed out that Africans produced children at rapid rates and would use any family aid to marry more wives. A few elite African civil servants—"évolués" in the charming vocabulary of French imperialism—received family allowances, but in 1945 the issue seemed to most officials to be far removed from the ordinary worker.

But soon, family allowances were on the agenda of both workers' organizations and the Inspecteurs du Travail. In the 1946 strike, civil servants—who had joined laborers and commercial workers on the front—had demanded family allowances equivalent to those of European civil servants. They had only gone back to work when a compromise was worked out, by which low ranking civil servants received either a quarter or half of the rate given the elite. Equality this was not, but an ordinary watchman working for the government was now getting family allowances. Unions were demanding them for everybody, and the issue would remain at the center of trade union issues until a family allowance law for all wage workers became a fact in 1956.

Labor officials, in the post-1946 situation, saw family allowances as a useful part of their program of social engineering: they would promote family stability within the essential class of wage workers. Their thinking was similar to that of their British colleagues: the industrial age was making its own cultural demands, and an African working class had to be separated out from its backward brethren, acculturated, and socialized to behave in appropriate ways. This was not the work of a single generation, and the reproduction of the family had to take place in the worker's milieu, with its very reproduction linked to the workers' continuity of employment.

They had a specifically demographic concern, a belief—based on survey data of unknown reliability—that wage workers, "who were the most able-bodied, and as a result the most useful element from a demographic point of view," faced such difficult conditions of family life that they tended toward "abstention in the domain of marriage and of procreation."[8] The argument has an unpleasant eugenic tinge to it, as if the New African of the post-war era had to be selected from the virile ranks of wage laborers and not the genetically less desirable rural population. But the main conclusions were sociological, an argument that the family was "the only possible framework for the growth of individuals and that this basic psycho-sociological structure dominates all economic and demographic phenomena."[9]

The argument about the peculiar nature of African modes of reproduction was now rebutted by the contention that workers—unlike other Africans—tended to form families of a "European type" and adopt European culture—a tendency which social policy had to support:

> . . . the African wage-earner, head of a family, above all the detribalized urban worker, runs into particular difficulties from the fact of having to support a family, notably when, having attained a certain level of social evolution and of stabilization as a worker, he tends to base his conditions of life on those of the European worker.[10]

The plan for family allocations introduced in 1956—modest in its levels of support—was based on the assumption that the unit being supported was centered around the male worker. Whereas in France, all citizens were eligible for family allocations, in Africa only the families of workers as defined by the Code du Travail (that is, those remunerated by wages) were eligible. The worker's paycheck would be augmented by a series of payments during pregnancy and childhood—as long as the mother submitted to a series of medical examinations and the child attended school.[11] The corollary of the support given to workers' wives was their submission to surveillance—to the certification by doctors, nurses, and teachers that they were raising their children correctly.

CONCLUSION

As colonial regimes, in their final decades of rule in Africa, tried to construct a vision of a future society toward which they were guiding their subjects, they constructed that vision in gendered terms, re-creating in the colonies a set of gender roles that were sociologically inaccurate and politically contestable in the metropoles themselves. The old anthropology of a quaintly backward Africa was to be replaced by a modern sociology, cordoned off from those parts of Africa too large and too backward to be amenable to rapid transformation. This vision was a fantasy, its conflation of universalism and ethnocentrism a reaction to loss of control over the complex social processes colonial regimes actually faced in Africa, a loss underlined by the strike wave of 1935–1947 and by the dangerous violence of events like the Madagascar rebellion of 1947 and the Mau Mau Emergency of the 1950s. Whether the family wage and the family allocation actually remade the African worker's family is another question (see Lindsay this volume).

African trade unionists in fact turned the rhetoric of social engineering into a rhetoric of entitlement, becoming themselves activists in favor of family wages and family allowances. So powerful were these claims—turning the language of French imperialism against itself in the context of planning general strikes—that the Governor-General of French West Africa warned in 1955 that unless family allocations were speedily enacted there would be "generalized agitation" and "social malaise" that would "undermine our authority."[12] Once again, the actual implementation of an innovative social policy came as much from below as above.

But turning rhetoric around enmeshed African trade unionists in a discursive structure, in which their experience and interests as men were reinforced by their experience as actors in an increasingly international debate about development and social change. As African bureaucrats, politicians, and intellectuals became more and more involved in a circuit that included stops at the United Nations, the International Labour Organization, foreign universities, and donor organizations, the limits of the social language of these global discussions—reinforced by the forms in which foreign aid was delivered—had a powerful impact on specifying the realm of the possible in domestic social policy. How categories like "worker" and "family" were to be defined became major questions in the shaping of post-colonial politics. Colonial regimes did not make African women into workers' wives and nothing more. But the rhetorical construction of African women as workers' wives helped to shape the terms in which women's activities outside of this boundary would be discussed. Defining the workers' wife also defined other roles of women as "informal" or "illegal." Such labels—with their implications for law and social and economic policy—mark the long-term significance of the colonial construction of industrial man, with his wife and his family.

NOTES

1. The paper that became this chapter was originally presented at a conference on masculinity in Africa organized by Luise White in 1990. I have since published (Cooper 1996) a much longer work that incorporates arguments set out here into a wider treatment of labor issues in the era of decolonization. I have decided to reproduce the original essay for this volume, with only minor changes, for two reasons. First, the stark, single-minded version of the argument lends itself to comparison with the other chapters of this book, and readers can turn to my own book for more evidence, for more precision in chronology, and for a more nuanced analysis. Second, the most important new research that delves into subjects germane to this chapter is represented in the book itself, notably Lisa Lindsay's study of family life among railway workers in Nigeria, which takes up the issue that my chapter brackets, namely the actual ways in which the rethinking of the labor question, family relations, and gender reshaped the lives of the people most in question.

2. The earlier roots of the debate over where Africans were to be reproduced—and the ways in which women redefined the space allotted to them—are discussed perceptively by Chauncey (1981).

3. Acting Labour Commissioner to Colonial Secretary, 6 February 1945, EST 13/1, Railway Archives, Nairobi. On the General Manager's copy of the letter, someone scrawled "Nonsense."

4. Kenya, Legislative Council Debates, 35 (21 December 1949), c. 648.

5. Oliver Lyttleton, Circular Letter, 2 June 1954, copy in Railway Archives, Nairobi, EST 26/26/1.

6. Afrique Occidentale Française, Inspection du Travail, Office d'Etudes Psychotechniques, "Quelques aspects de la psychologie africaine," July 1953, filed with annual reports, series 2G, Archives du Sénégal (hereafter AS).

7. Inspecteur Masselot to Minister of Colonies, 23 February 1946, Affaires Politiques, 960, France, Archives Nationales, Section Outre-Mer (hereafter ANSOM).

8. Afrique Equatoriale Française, "Note sur l'instauration d'un régime d'allocations familiales en Afrique Equatoriale Française," 16 February 1951, IGT 17/1, and Minister, Circular to Governors General, 3 September 1953, IGT 15/3, ANSOM, both generalizing on the basis of a survey done in equatorial Africa in 1949.

9. Service des Affaires Sociales, Note, 20 January 1955, IGT 15/1, ANSOM.

10. Note of Inspecteur Général du Travail, Afrique Equatoriale Française, "Etude préliminaire de l'institution de prestations familiales," 28 September 1954, IGT 16/1, ANSOM.

11. There was a provision for payments to the families of women wage earners. But in Gabon, for instance, the funds for men were thirty-two times as high as those for women. Afrique Equatoriale Française, Note au sujet des possibilités d'amélioration pratique du fonctionnement du régime de prestations familiales, n.d. [early 1957], IGT 15/2, ANSOM. For the implementation of family allocations, see the files in cartons 15 and 16 of fond IGT, ANSOM.

12. Governor General to Minister, 22 November 1955, telegram, K 418 (144), AS.

REFERENCES

Amsden, Alice. 1971. *International Firms and Labour in Kenya, 1945–70*. London: Cass.

Chauncey, George, Jr. 1981. "The Locus of Reproduction: Women's Labour in the Zambian Copperbelt, 1927–1953." *Journal of Southern African Studies* 7: 135–64.

Cooper, Frederick. 1987. *On the African Waterfront: Urban Disorder and the Transformation of Work in Colonial Mombasa*. New Haven, CT: Yale University Press.

———. 1990. "The Senegalese General Strike of 1946 and the Labor Question in Post-War French Africa," *Canadian Journal of African Studies* 24: 165–215.

———. 1996. *Decolonization and African Society: The Labor Question in French and British Africa*. Cambridge: Cambridge University Press

Kenya. 1945. *Report of the Committee of Inquiry into Labour Unrest at Mombasa*. Nairobi.

———. 1954. *Report of the Committee on African Wages*. Nairobi.

———. 1959. *Report of a Board of Inquiry Appointed to Inquire into Employment in the Port of Mombasa*. Nairobi.

Northcott, C. H., ed. 1949. *African Labour Efficiency Survey*, Colonial Research Publications No. 3. London: It is Majesty's Stationery Office.

Orde Browne, G. St. J. 1946. *Labour Conditions in East Africa*. Colonial No. 193. London: It is Majesty's Stationery Office.

8

MONEY, MARRIAGE, AND MASCULINITY ON THE COLONIAL NIGERIAN RAILWAY

Lisa A. Lindsay

The Yoruba-speaking women of southwestern Nigeria are known for their history of market trading and financial independence (Sudarkasa 1973; Mann 1985). Yet since the beginnings of hired labor, Nigerians have considered formal-sector wage-earning to be men's work, and women's economic contributions to working people's households have declined over time. How is it that in an area where women's trade and independent earning have been long established, women and men now assume that wage-earning is a male preserve? How, in a place where wage work is a relatively recent and small-scale phenomenon, did men come to be defined—at least publicly—as their families' providers?

Wage labor in Nigeria largely originated in the colonial period. The government began constructing the Nigerian Railway in 1896 and hired thousands of workers to clear land, lay and maintain tracks, and—as the system became operational—man the trains and railroad stations. Government employees, and railway workers in particular, remained the largest category of wage earners throughout the colonial period. But mobilization for World War II brought a dramatic expansion of the Nigerian work force as well as a new direction in colonial labor policies. New policies of labor "stabilization" were intended to define a distinct working class, separated from the mass of casual laborers moving between city and country and from job to job. As Frederick Cooper suggests in this volume, part of the hoped-for transformation in African labor had to do with families. Workers' nuclear families were to reside not in remote villages but near the industrial workplace, where they would both sustain and be provided for by their employed patriarchs. Officials hoped that workers' wives would socially reproduce the male labor force through unpaid domestic labor and raise the next generation of urban workers in a "modern" milieu, acculturated to urban living and steady wage employment.

Yoruba culture would seem to both hinder and facilitate such change. On one hand, in southwestern Nigeria the gendered ideals implicit in colonial policies met an equally powerful but very different body of assumptions about the respective roles of men and women. Yoruba gender norms have historically associated women with trading and men with farming, with members of both sexes controlling their own incomes and expenditures after marriage (Sudarkasa 1973; Fapohunda 1988; Mann 1985). Thus there was relatively little predisposition to create families of the type European officials idealized. But Yorubaland's long tradition of economic diversity and commercial activity has meant that people there place special importance on money (Barber 1994; Falola and Adebayo 2000). A new relationship with money, such as through stable wage labor, would therefore be likely to have an important impact on men's places in their homes and communities, as well as their self-definitions as men.

This chapter explores the relationship between wage labor, money, and gender through a study of railway workers in southwestern Nigeria from the late 1930s to the mid-1960s (see Lindsay 1996). The government railway was the colony's largest single employer, with over 30,000 employees by the early 1950s (Nigeria 1953: 36). By the late 1940s it was in the forefront of moves to stabilize a portion of the work force. In exchange for long-term commitments to consistent labor and urban living, workers gained opportunities for job advancement, regular earnings, and benefits. I argue that these wage-earning men increasingly came to be defined as family providers for three overlapping reasons: male wage labor contributed to new domestic patterns, both because of changing conditions of work and because of pre-existing notions linking money to gender and status; wives of wage earners actively participated in the creation of a male breadwinner ideal as part of their own financial strategies; and workers used the discourse of breadwinners instrumentally, to advance wage and benefits claims in disputes with their colonial employer.

MONEY AND MASCULINITY IN EARLY
TWENTIETH-CENTURY YORUBALAND

In early twentieth-century southwestern Nigeria, there were three broad and potentially overlapping types of masculinity for grown men: adult masculinity, senior—or elder—masculinity, and the "big man." All three reflected biological sex and age, although these were not the only factors at work and theoretically one could become a "big man" at any point in adulthood. More importantly for my discussion, all three normative masculinities were related to having access to and command over material resources, particularly money. Furthermore, none was premised on the ideal that a man should provide exclusive financial support for his wife or wives.

Yoruba peoples have historically lived in large communities surrounded by farms, with compounds forming the residential and political units within towns and villages.[1] These compounds were economic, political, and residential units, as well as important bases of kinship. Through membership in a compound, people gained access to land as well as dependents to provide assistance and support. In the early twentieth century, the organization of households, relations between generations, and the social and economic independence of young men all related to control over labor. Junior men formed a dependent labor force for their elders' farms, and as long as they remained unmarried they could not claim a share of the compounds' land or control their own labor. After getting married, a man could set up his own household, acquire his own dependent domestic labor force, and become the household head in relation to his wife and children. Thus, a man's "first marriage was the foundation of his future existence as a social being" (Barber 1991: 216).

This change in status required money, and transactions in cash, goods, and labor formalized marriage ties between individuals and families. In spite of the efforts of colonial-era officials and anthropologists to make the rules for Yoruba marriage more rigid, "custom" varied over time and by locality (Guyer 1994). Marriages were contracted in several stages, often extending over a period of years, almost always requiring transfers of money and goods. Ideally, regardless of whether the parties practiced Christianity, Islam, or Yoruba religion, without a bride-price (*owó-gbéyàwó*, literally "money to carry the wife"), there was no marriage. For most men, the amount involved proved formidable. In Ondo Province in the late 1930s, total costs usually exceeded £14, representing about sixteen months of wage labor. In Ife and other cocoa-growing areas in the 1950s, total marriage expenses were estimated at £50, or about one year's agricultural wages (Ward 1938: 64; Galletti et al. 1956: 214, 265). Ideally, young men expected money for marriage to come from their fathers. In fact, though, fathers could delay funding their sons' marriages on the grounds that the money was not available, thereby prolonging their access to the young men's labor. Sons then were forced to fend for themselves, and conflict about the availability of marriage money produced tensions between different generations of men (Peel 1983: 118–9; Barber 1991: 217).[2]

The need for marriage money was the primary reason men undertook migrant wage labor in the first half of the twentieth century. With the expansion of such opportunities, young men were increasingly able to "abbreviate the period of their juniority" (Peel 1983: 118–9) by earning cash away from home. Retirees who had gone to work for the railway in this era stressed that what had appealed to them most about their job was the steady pay and the status this money brought to them. "When you have a [wage] job at hand it's then your relatives know your value and respect your opinion," one retired railwayman noted (Aruna 1993). M.O. Adegbite (1993) summarized the benefits of working on the railroad this way: "I married, I got children, I built this place [his house]."

These comments indicate that adult masculinity was only the beginning of men's gendered aspirations. Eventually a married man hoped to father and educate children, exercise progressively greater influence in lineage and community affairs, and build his own house, a capstone in the attainment of senior masculinity. To the extent that wage labor made this possible, it speeded up an individual's attainment of senior masculine status. But even when wage labor provided the cash that gave a man his start as an independent adult, his "real career of self-aggrandisement . . . could only be conducted on home ground, and was based on the expansion of the household his earnings had helped to found" (Barber 1991: 218). Temporary "target workers" eventually returned home to establish themselves in their own farms or businesses, growing and marketing a cash crop like cocoa or establishing any of a number of other types of productive enterprises (Berry 1985).

Some senior men became prosperous and influential enough to be known as "big men." Since at least the early nineteenth century, Yoruba men have competed with each other for followers, wealth, and reputation. Aspiring "big men" struggled to establish themselves at the center of a circle of people, whose labor was invested in the expansion of their farms or trading enterprises. A large household and wealth thus reinforced each other: a big man attracted dependents by his ability to provide for and protect them; in turn, they supported his claims to be "big" by contributing labor or productive resources, serving him personally, or enhancing his reputation for generosity.[3] Although being a big man remained an ideal through the twentieth century (to the present), changing political and economic circumstances affected the ways in which people pursued and displayed such status. In the late nineteenth century, seniority was crucial for social standing. But by the 1930s the spread of education and the growth of the cocoa industry had resulted in the development of a group of literates and wealthy businessmen in many towns, who exercised growing influence on local politics. In spite of the fact that many eventually lived or operated outside of their towns of origin, these "new" elites remained connected to their homes, building houses, investing money, and providing the leadership of new progressive unions being formed (Peel 1983; Eades 1980; Berry 1985). In this arena, seniority could help a man's position but was not as necessary as ambition and ability. But whatever their origin, big men gained their hyper-masculine status through wealth, followers, and connections to political power—attributes which in turn supported each other.[4] As the still extant proverb states, "I have money, I have people, what else is there that I have not got?" (*Mo lówó, mo lénìyàn, kí ló tún kù tí mi ò tíì ní?*) (Barber 1991: 183; 1994: 213).

In spite of the fact that the pinnacle of success was to be a "big man," Yoruba gender relations in the first half of the twentieth century were not predicated on a male breadwinner norm. As household heads, men ideally were to take care of their dependents by contributing some food staples, building and repairing the family house, sending children to school, and paying for medical treatments and medicines. But running a farm or business and investing in seniority were high priorities as well. Men's extra-household expenses often meant that women were the ones to maintain domestic budgets, especially when a man's circle of influence and wealth was limited.

Yoruba speakers generally saw women who did not work outside of the home as lazy, and nearly all women engaged in trade or food processing. A 1952 survey of households in cocoa-producing areas showed that three-fourths of Yoruba wives were working on their own accounts, and only 5 percent were totally dependent on their husbands (Galletti et al. 1956: 77). Trading gave women a way of providing for themselves and their children, while at the same time maintaining a flexible enough schedule to accommodate domestic obligations. Work outside of the home, and especially market trading, was a crucial component of womanhood (Sudarkasa 1973).

Women became exasperated with husbands who were not financially responsible or who channeled too much of their income outside of the household. In divorce cases, women's most common complaint was lack of sufficient financial maintenance.[5] Marital tensions about money partly related to the fact that trading gave women readier access to cash than farming brought to men. This meant that husbands on occasion were compelled to borrow from their wives, who usually kept careful accounts of the transactions. Women seem to have made a distinction between the necessary household budget—to which they readily contributed—and money for a husband's personal expenses—which was offered as a loan, at their discretion. If the couple was getting along well, the debt might never be mentioned again; if there were quarrels, however, the debt might become a source of conflict and the woman could even go to court to claim it (Krapf-Askari 1969: 71).[6]

Men also conceptualized inter-household transfers as loans and went to court to reclaim money when relationships went sour. Furthermore, men paid "begging fees" to make amends after offending wives or in-laws. These transactions appeared frequently in my survey of Ibadan customary court cases from 1930 to 1965. Men paid their wives to win favor after an argument, to atone for physical abuse, or to apologize for having spent too much time away from home. Current or future mothers, fathers, and brothers-in-law received begging money in exchange for favorable intervention, consent to the marriage, or forgiveness for a breech of etiquette.[7] Similar payments could be required by lineage elders and customary courts as a form of dispute resolution (see Mann 1982).

Such payments represented men's attempts to maintain marital harmony. Although their efforts to become "big men" often were directed outside of the household, keeping a wife was crucial, and money was an important way to do so. This is not to imply that payments were cynical attempts to "buy" favor in the absence of underlying affection. Money, as an integral part of individual identity and status, had the power to show sentiment as nothing else could (Barber 1994). Thus money was linked to masculinity in colonial Yorubaland. By marking marriage and helping to reconcile marital differences, payments symbolized and facilitated social agreements between parties; and by paying money a male suitor was able to become a husband and father. Later in life, money allowed adult men to take on the attributes of seniority by providing for children's education, assisting lineage members, investing in the community, and building a house. Even more money could translate into greater social influence, patronage, and the status of "big man." Yet these normative ideals did not include the notion that men should be the sole financial providers within their households, or that their wives should not earn money as well. The "male breadwinner" was a specific creation of colonial-era wage labor.

WAGE-EARNING AND CHANGING MASCULINITIES

The target labor pattern, in which wage-earning gave young men their start back in the hometown, was changing by the 1940s. Increasing numbers of migrants were making progressively longer or even permanent commitments to life in the bigger cities. Expanding economic opportunities and the growth of the public sector created booming populations in Lagos and Ibadan. Within the Nigerian Railway, increasing proportions of workers were classified as part of the "permanent establishment."[8] In exchange for long-term commitments to work wherever the railway sent them, these employees earned regular salary increases, fringe benefits, and pensions. In the process many also adopted new kinds of marital behavior and ideas about what it meant to be a man.[9]

I have suggested so far that money was important within Yoruba marriages, even as men primarily directed it elsewhere for what Barber (1991, 1994) has called "self-aggrandisement." What happened, then, when a man earned a steady paycheck? Did it make him, in his own or his wife's eyes, a different kind of man? What was the relationship between steady wage labor and the emergence of a male breadwinner ideal? I address these questions by drawing on life histories of retired railway workers and their wives based in Ibadan, Lagos, and other towns of southwestern Nigeria (see Lindsay 1996). These retirees are officially classed as "pensioners," meaning that they retired from

Photo 8.1. Apprentice Engine Drivers' Training School, Nigerian Railway, Lagos, 1956. Photo courtesy of A.A. Salako (back row, third from right).

pensionable appointments, including stationmaster, locomotive driver, or various grades of clerks. They were career railway men who, by and large, worked their way from unskilled labor to skilled and supervisory posts. The life histories of these men and their wives suggest that salaried men's relationships with women were refined in large measure because of two aspects of railway life: steady paychecks and transfers around the country. In the context of pre-existing links between money, status, and marital relations, men's paychecks helped them to maintain harmonious relations with their wives and, indeed, made them attractive mates to begin with. Wives actively claimed portions of men's paychecks for the kinds of regular expenses—like food and school fees—that otherwise they might have had to pay. Their husbands' incomes allowed them to reduce their own money-generating activities, a situation reinforced by living in unfamiliar surroundings without the benefit of childcare and marketing networks. These households experienced more marital stability and more resource pooling than others of the same period. At the same time, salaried men developed new self-images as family breadwinners, even when in practice their wives continued to make financial contributions to the household.

The longevity of salaried railway workers' marriages seems to have been linked to their steady paychecks. Overall, nearly three-quarters (71%) of the

Photo 8.2. Engine driver (now railway pensioner) A.A. Salako, Aro station, Abeokuta, 1966. Photo courtesy of A.A. Salako.

167 retired railway men I questioned had never experienced divorce or a marital breakdown resulting in separation. In a period during which administrators and social scientists noted dramatically increasing divorce rates (Denzer 1994: 18), those rates actually declined for salaried railway workers. Railway men seem to have experienced drastically fewer unsuccessful marriages than other men their age.[10] Since lack of financial maintenance was one of the most frequent reasons women sought divorce, railway men's ability to provide their wives and children with at least some consistent support likely was decisive in their marriages. Biweekly paychecks also would have given railway employees ready cash to use as "begging fees" or loans in the event of disputes with their wives. As Rebecca Uchefuna (1994), who married a railway clerk in 1955, put it, "If anybody who works in the railway comes your way you would like to marry him. At that time, railway paid very well . . . , so people loved them [the employees] and liked to mix with them." Steady wage earners could be relied upon more frequently than other men for daily household needs as well as periodic payments like school fees. Whereas otherwise wives might have covered food expenses without being repaid, they expected employed husbands to reimburse them after the paycheck came. This made both parties see husbands more and more as family breadwinners.

In spite of financial help from their husbands, railway wives were not keeping more of their own earnings. Mostly, the "extra" money from their trade went into children's education and the expenses of urban living. This was particularly true in the southwest. "In our area [Yorubaland]," Florence Owolabi (1994) told me, "if one is not working, they would say she is a liability to the husband; she is the one consuming all the husband's income." But railway men's income gave their wives greater flexibility in their own careers than many other women had. On average, railway wives began working three to five years after marriage, as opposed to others who began before or immediately after marrying (Sudarkasa 1973: 117). This period without trading corresponded to children's infancy and can be seen as a relative luxury. Although the household clearly needed a woman's income when children were going to school, it could afford to have the wife not work so many hours, or at all, before that.

Railway households were also forced into this situation by transfers to unfamiliar parts of the country. In the mid-1950s, Bernard Aruna and his first wife lived in the town of Offa, where they had no family connections. With two children born in quick succession (and two more later), money was tight, in spite of the overtime he worked. But his wife did not spend much time trading because she had no one in town to help her with the children. "We eat the whole salary and wait for the next month," Aruna (1993) said of that period in his life.

But why should wives have necessarily moved to new parts of the country with their husbands? In southwestern Nigeria rural and urban married couples frequently lived apart for parts of the year. Women might stay in towns or villages while their husbands worked at outlying farms; husbands might be in one place while their wives traded in another (Sudarkasa 1973: 132; Marris 1962: 158–9). Indeed, nearly half (43%) of the railway men I questioned had lived apart from at least one wife for six months or more during their careers. But largely they preferred to move together (see Lindsay 1996: 219–22). Railway workers had little leave time in which to travel to hometowns, and spouses wanted to be together more frequently than that. Wives feared that their husbands would establish new conjugal units in their new places of work and/or neglect them in the hometown, a scenario prevalent enough among migrants to be a legitimate fear. Moreover, many workers and their families felt that spousal togetherness was part of a "modern" identity. Thus many railway wives relocated with their husbands, forming households largely dependent on men's wages.

Their disparity in incomes made it rather pointless for husbands and wives to maintain separate budgets. Unlike the kinds of conjugal units described in the previous section, many railway couples in the 1950s and 1960s pooled their incomes and jointly met expenses. David and Florence Owolabi (1994), who were married in Lagos in 1966, took care of the home "hand by hand," with her contributions equaling about one-fifth of his. M.O. Adegbite (1993) used the same metaphor in discussing his family's budget: "We use hands to wash hands together." This was in contrast to other urbanites: a 1958–59 survey of central Lagos showed that households rarely pooled money, although spouses helped each other (Marris 1962: Chap. 4); and a much later survey in Lagos showed a small proportion of pooling households, mostly among low-income migrants (Fapohunda 1988). This suggests that in addition to relying largely on a steady wage, living outside of one's home community might have fostered resource pooling.

Part of this cooperation extended to earning as well as spending. Several railway pensioners reported engaging in joint ventures with their wives. Felicia Adeyemi (1994), for instance, had been a seamstress in Ibadan before her marriage in 1953. She relocated to Lagos to join her new husband, a railway storekeeper, and together the two of them opened a shop to sell uniforms. Over the ensuing years, they used their combined income for children's education, housekeeping, and "family affairs." "For instance, if it is the time for school fees and his salary is ready he paid it and I will take care of feeding; but if not, if I have the money I would pay the school fees and vice versa." Similarly, assistant locomotive driver Bernard Aruna (1993) paid for rent, ceremonies, and school fees, but his wife chipped in for food, her own clothes, and children's expenses. When he got extra money from overtime, he invested it in her trade.

In spite of such cooperation and women's contributions, railway men made it clear that they were considered heads of the households. Although a husband would not generally interfere in his wife's trade, Aruna (1993) said, still "the husband runs the home's affairs." In the late 1960s, for example, J.B. Adekanola and his new wife lived in a town where they had no social connections. After a year of marriage, he gave her some money to start a trade. Once children started coming, although she had no one to help her, she had to continue working because his salary was not enough to support their growing family. Mrs. Adekanola's income was crucial, she knew, as was help she secretly solicited from an uncle back home. But she did not tell her husband for fear of offending his masculine pride and his sense of himself as the sole earner. "He would be thinking that the money he gave is enough but it is not so I have to add to it" (Adekanola 1994).

This example reveals something of the fragility of the breadwinner ideal among wage earners. Only the most highly paid were able to support their households without assistance—a situation not unique to Nigeria—and, furthermore, women's work outside the home was widely accepted. Yet as we have seen, money and expenditures were vital to masculine identities. Stressing their breadwinning capabilities was a way for men to exert their importance and power at home and, as the next section details, demand improved wages and benefits from their colonial employer.

MALE BREADWINNERS AND FAMILY ALLOWANCES

This idea of railway workers as family breadwinners was forged in relation to British administrators as well as wives and children. In the 1940s and 1950s, trade unionists and colonial officials debated the desirability of state-sponsored family allowances for African workers.[11] In official petitions, Nigerian labor leaders described workers as family providers, responsible for the support of their wives and children. This discourse reflected labor leaders' strategies for improving wage levels as well as the kinds of domestic arrangements described above. It was particularly instrumental given the colonial government's insistence that African men did not support families and therefore did not qualify for wage increases and family allowances comparable to those earned by Europeans.[12]

During the 1930s and 1940s (and even later), European officials and employers argued that formal sector wages could be kept low because men were assisted financially by their wives. Workers, however, stressed that women's trading income was not enough to keep a family afloat, and that men should be considered primary breadwinners. Moreover, by the 1940s they demanded family allowances as a counterpart to payments made to European workers in Nigeria. These "children's (separate domicile) allowances" were to compensate for the fact that officials' children lived apart from them and reflected the administration's assumption that European men were responsible for the maintenance of their children at home. Trade unionists argued that the same situation applied to Nigerian workers compelled to relocate away from their families, and therefore they should be granted the same allowances.

Nigerian labor activists also made the broader argument that wages were not sufficient for workers to support wives and children and that the government should pay family allowances in the interest of social reproduction. According to union leader I.S.M.O. Shonekan, in a 1944 radio broadcast,

> Some employers forget that his [a worker's] children are not given free education, but he tries his best . . . to educate them. They forget that his children are a valuable contribution to society who in the future, will assist mentally or physically in developing the wealth of the nation and defend the State. He is not paid any family allowance by either the State or the employer for these. He is forced to distribute his scanty wages on these important items which go to make him and his family good citizens.[13]

Eight months later, Shonekan raised the issue at the annual congress of the Federated Trades Unions of Nigeria. Arguing that "many of us have wives and children to support," and that wage levels were insufficient, Shonekan recounted arguments in favor of family allowances made by politicians in Europe and South America. His motion, "That the Government of Nigeria be requested earnestly to formulate schemes for family allowances, and to enact an Ordinance sanctioning their payment by all employers to all married African workmen throughout the country," passed unanimously amid cheers by those present.[14]

The Nigerian trade union movement of the 1940s was dominated by the Railway Workers' Union, the colony's largest and the first to be formally organized. This union was at the forefront of the 1945 general strike in Nigeria, which united workers throughout the country in calling for cost of living increases and other benefits. Family allowances, as a counterpart to European "separation allowances," were part of the workers' demands and were brought to the attention of W. Tudor Davies when his commission investigated labor conditions in the strike's aftermath. Tudor Davies' report called for greater stabilization of the Nigerian labor force, but it did not fully support African family allowances. Still, it did recognize the legitimacy of union claims and endorsed a male breadwinner norm for Nigeria. Tudor Davies wrote, "The sooner the male ceases to rely upon the economic contribution of the female to the family exchequer, the sooner will the wage structure be founded upon a more correct basis" (Tudor Davies 1946: 48).[15]

For the next decade trade unionists pressed for the extension of family allowances to Africans. Government officials refused, at first arguing that Nigerians could be expected to move their families any place within the territory rather than maintain two homes.[16] Then the 1946 Harrigan Commission, which addressed wages in the civil service, dismissed the claim for family allowances on the grounds that this was none of the government's business and it would be too complicated in a West African context, where "the word 'family' may be taken to mean not only a wife and children but every near relative" (Harrigan 1946: 8). Still, through the late 1940s and into the 1950s union demands and directives from Whitehall pushed the colonial government toward greater emphasis on male workers as family providers. In 1953 the Secretary of State for the Colonies conducted an inquiry into the extent to which a family wage system prevailed in Africa. Nigeria's reply indicated that family obligations were taken into consideration in calculating men's wages.[17] At least some recognition of family obligations appeared in the 1955 Gorsuch Commission report on civil servants, as its calculations for necessary wage levels were based on the "assumption that the recipient has more than one mouth to feed" (Gorsuch 1955). Still, Gorsuch did not explicitly recommend family allowances for junior officials, and by 1957 at least some unions continued to include them in their demands.[18]

It was somewhat ironic that British administrators in Nigeria resisted the idea of African male workers as breadwinners. Missionaries had for decades stressed the ideal of monogamous families based on male economic and moral authority. Formal education, including vocational instruction, was targeted primarily at men and boys, as officials discounted the potential contributions of women to household and national economies (see Denzer 1994). And within the Nigerian Railway, personnel policies were often based on the assumption that social reproduction was the responsibility of workers' wives, who were engaged primarily in domestic tasks (Lindsay 1998). But in spite of this background, as well as the development of a male breadwinner norm and generalized "family wages" in Britain (Rose 1992; Pedersen 1993), administrators were not willing to extend such principles automatically to Nigerians. And although most wives of Nigerian workers were employed outside the home, union officials agitated for wages that recognized men as household providers.

The most obvious explanation for these developments is economic. When administrators wanted to keep wages low, they pointed to women's trade as an excuse for not paying men a family wage. This does not mean that colonial officials in Nigeria did not support the idea that male workers should financially support their immediate families. Similarly, in a period of inflation and increasingly assertive trade unions, labor activists called for family allowances or family wages as a strategy for raising general salary levels. There was not necessarily a contradiction between male breadwinners and women's work, and female trade coexisted with the expression of patriarchal ideals. But a notion of masculinity resting on the "male breadwinner" was, like others, a fragile and insecure one, in constant need of reiteration. Colonial administrators sent contradictory messages, valorizing the male provider while suggesting that this model did not fit African men. Low wages frequently made it impossible for a worker to meet all of his household's financial needs. And within Yoruba households, both men and women valued women's income-earning activities.

CONCLUSION

Workers generally came to stable wage labor to become adult men, that is, to earn money to marry, build houses, or build up relations of patronage. Within marriages, their paychecks helped them to maintain their wives' goodwill, much as gifts or "begging fees" did for nonsalaried men. Over time, though, railway workers' spending, and its gendered significance, at least partially diverged from normative patterns. Wives made active claims on their incomes for household maintenance, so that such contributions came to be seen as less and less discretionary, while time spent away from the hometown undermined women's opportunities for independent earning. Gradually such circumstances led men to describe themselves in new ways. While aspiring "big men" based their self-esteem on recruiting followers, salaried railway workers did so on their regular control of money, which they focused on the urban household. Steady paychecks earned them dependent wives—which nonsalaried men might lack—and their self-portrayal as breadwinners gave them enhanced bargaining power with European employers. Stable workers' sense of themselves as men was shaped by practices linking money, marriage, and masculinity, influenced by new structures and life styles associated with colonial-era wage labor.

EPILOGUE

The research that resulted in this chapter was conducted in the context of financial insecurity for railway pensioners. In 1993 when I began this project, many former locomotive drivers, senior station staff, managers, and skilled craftsmen were not receiving the pensions that they had looked forward to during their careers. In interviews, they expressed anger and frustration at an employer they felt had cheated them, along with humiliation because many were being supported by their wives. Women who 30–50 years ago were able to shape their own careers around a husband's steady paycheck were now unable to retire from trading because they largely supported their households. As one retired locomotive driver put it (Salako 1994), "I live at the mercy of my wife [who] runs up and down going to farms to buy some fruits . . . that she sells to get us food." When I returned to Nigeria in 1998 the situation had improved somewhat, yet inflation had rendered pensions largely symbolic. The male breadwinner ethos described in this chapter may be under its greatest threat in these days of massive economic insecurity. I end, then, with this perhaps obvious point: gender transformations are not necessarily linear, and they must be considered within their material contexts. In southwestern Nigeria, the image of the working-class male breadwinner, which came into being through processes described above, may not outlive its sixth decade.

ACKNOWLEDGMENTS

This chapter is based on research conducted during two trips to Nigeria: in 1993–94 through a grant from the Joint Committee on African Studies of the Social Science Research Council and the American Council of Learned Societies with funds provided by the Ford, Mellon, and Rockefeller Foundations; and in 1998 through a Junior Faculty Research Grant from the University of North Carolina at Charlotte. I am grateful to both institutions, as well as to Jide Oyeneye for his valuable research assistance. Different incarnations of this chapter were presented at the Berkshire Conference on the History of Women in Chapel Hill, NC, in 1996, the North American Labor History Conference in Detroit in 1999, and the European Social Science History Association Conference in Amsterdam in 2000. I thank the participants in those panels for their helpful suggestions, along with Stephan Miescher, whose comments prompted the final and most significant revision.

NOTES

1. Much of the discussion in this and the following section appears in Lindsay (1998).

2. Analogous situations existed throughout colonial Africa. See, for example, Beinart (1982: Chap. 3), Harries (1994), White (1990: Chap. 2), and Bravman (1998).

3. Barber (1991: Chap. 6). For the life history of an urban "big man," see Mann (1991).

4. Berry (1985: Chap. 3), Eades (1980), Lloyd (1967), and Barber (1981, 1991).

5. Nigeria (1956: 10) and innumerable divorce cases involving financial "neglect."

6. For example, see Oke Are I Civil Court, Vol. 21, 1693/30, *Ayi vs. Lawani*, September 1930, pp. 231–7; Bere I Civil Court, Vol. 23, 233/42, *Foyeke vs. Obasawi*, February 1942, pp. 125–6.

7. Oke Are, Vol. 47, 529/33, *Lamuni vs. Rihonatu Foyelle*, March 1933, pp. 2–9; and Oke Are I, Vol. 83, 64/51, *Lamidi vs. Raji*, May 1951, pp. 103–4. Other examples include Bere, 912/36, *Selia vs. Lajide*, April 1936, pp. 321–3; Bere I, Vol. 18, 286/41, *Barikisu vs. Yesufu*, March 1941, pp. 200–2; Oke Are, Vol. 47, 529/33; Oke Are I, Vol. 83, 64/51; Bere I, 816/37, *Ayi vs. Salau*, May 1937, pp. 53–5; Bere, I, 517/36, *Adenike vs. Johnson*, August 1936, pp. 311–3; Bere I, Vol. 23, 193/42, *Joseph Abioye vs. Ainke*, February 1942, p. 88; Oke Are 4B Divorce Court, D946/60, *Bolatito Adunni vs. Gabriel Ayoade*, July 1960, pp. 527–30.

8. The "permanent establishment" included 11.5% of railway employees in 1939–40, as opposed to 34.5% in 1946–47 and 50.3% in 1964–65. Nigerian Railway *Annual Reports*; and "Transfer of Daily-Paid Staff to Permanent Establishment," in GMS 316, Vol. 1. Lagos: National Railway Corporation [hereafter NRC] Headquarters.

9. For the links between labor stabilization and domestic behavior elsewhere, see Moodie (1994), Parpart (1986), and many studies of the Copperbelt from the Rhodes-Livingstone Institute in the 1950s and 1960s.

10. In 1963 Lloyd reported a divorce rate of 3% per year (Lloyd 1963: 37). Also see Guyer (1994), where she noted that fewer than half of older men had sustained stable marriages.

11. For more on family allowances and family wages in colonial Africa, see Cooper (1989, 1990) and Lindsay (1999).

12. This section is based on Lindsay (1999).

13. Excerpt from 26 April 1944 speech on Lagos Radio Distribution Service, in *The Nigerian Worker*, published by the Federated Trades Union of Nigeria, Vol. 1, No. 5, April 1944, p. 4, in GMS 310/2, "The Nigerian Worker." Lagos: NRC Headquarters.

14. Excerpt from speech titled "Family Allowances" in *The Nigerian Worker*, Vol. 1, No. 7, December 1944, p. 2, in ibid.

15. For background on the call for family allowances, general strike, and the Tudor Davies Commission, see Ananaba (1970), Cohen (1974), and Lindsay (1999).

16. Minutes and correspondence in CSO 26/46820/S.1 (NAI).

17. H.J. Marshall, Acting Governor General of Nigeria to Secretary of State Oliver Lyttelton, 15 April 1955, PRO, CO 859/810.

18. See "List of Allowances" n.d. [November 1957] in GML 302/2, Vol. 1 (NRC Lagos), which includes children's allowances for senior officials only. "Rapson Recommendations: Rail Workers to Lead Delegation to Government," *Daily Service* (5 August 1957), mentions a protest advocating children's allowances for junior officers. Interestingly, by 1968 the railway workers' union (NUR) opposed the payment of children's allowances altogether, on the grounds that they only applied to senior servants and they were unnecessary in the context of high salaries and other perquisites. "NUR Demands Abolition of Allowances," *Morning Post* (2 April 1968).

REFERENCES

Adegbite, M.O. 1993. Interview with the author. Ibadan, 28 December.

Adekanola, Ruth. 1994. Interview with the author and Funmilayo Carew. Ibadan, 17 February.

Adeyemi, Felicia. 1994. Interview with the author. Ibadan, 11 February.

Ananaba, Wogu. 1970. *The Trade Union Movement in Nigeria.* New York: Africana Publishing Corp.

Aruna, Bernard. 1993. Interview with the author. Ibadan, 28 December.

Barber, Karin. 1981. "How Man Makes God in West Africa: Yoruba Attitudes Towards the Orisa." *Africa* 51, 3: 724–45.

———. 1991. *I Could Speak Until Tomorrow: Oriki, Women and the Past in a Yoruba Town.* Washington, DC: Smithsonian Institution Press.

———. 1994. "Money, Self-Realization, and the Person in Yoruba Texts." In *Money Matters: Instability, Values and Social Payments in the Modern History of West African Communities*, Jane I. Guyer, ed. Portsmouth, NH: Heinemann.

Bascom, William. 1969. *The Yoruba of Southwestern Nigeria.* New York: Holt, Rinehart and Winston.

Beinart, William. 1982. *The Political Economy of Pondoland, 1860–1930.* Cambridge: Cambridge University Press.

Berry, Sara S. 1985. *Fathers Work for their Sons: Accumulation, Mobility, and Class Formation in an Extended Yoruba Community.* Berkeley: University of California Press.

Bravman, Bill. 1998. *Making Ethnic Ways: Communities and their Transformations in Taita, Kenya, 1800–1950.* Portsmouth: Heinemann.

Cohen, Robin. 1974. *Labour and Politics in Nigeria, 1945–71.* London: Heinemann.

Cooper, Frederick. 1989. "From Free Labor to Family Allowances: Labor and African Society in Colonial Discourse." *American Ethnologist* 16: 745–65.

———. 1990. "The Senegalese General Strike of 1946 and the Labor Question in Post-War French Africa." *Canadian Journal of African Studies* 24: 165–215.

———. 1996. *Decolonization and African Society: The Labor Question in French and British Africa.* Cambridge: Cambridge University Press.

Denzer, LaRay. 1994. "Yoruba Women: A Historiographical Study." *International Journal of African Historical Studies* 27: 1–39.

Eades, J.S. 1980. *The Yoruba Today.* Cambridge: Cambridge University Press.

Fadipe, N.A. 1970 [1940]. *The Sociology of the Yoruba*, Francis Olu. Okediji and Oladejo O. Okediji, eds. Ibadan: Ibadan University Press.

Falola, Toyin and Akanmu Adebayo. 2000. *Culture, Politics, and Money among the Yoruba.* New Brunswick and London: Transaction Publishers.

Fapohunda, Eleanor R. 1988. "The Non-Pooling Household: A Challenge to Theory." In *A Home Divided: Women and Income in the Third World*, Daisy Dwyer and Judith Bruce, eds. Stanford, CA: Stanford University Press.

Galletti, R., K.D.S. Baldwin, and I.O. Dina. 1956. *Nigerian Cocoa Farmers: An Economic Survey of Yoruba Cocoa Farming Families.* Oxford: Oxford University Press.

Gorsuch, L.H., chair. 1955. *Report of the Commission on the Public Services of the Governments in the Federation of Nigeria, 1954–55.* Lagos: Government Printer.

Guyer, Jane I. 1994. "Lineal Identities and Lateral Networks: The Logic of Polyandrous Motherhood." In *Nuptiality in Sub-Saharan Africa: Contemporary Anthropological and Demographic Perspectives*, Caroline Bledsoe and Gilles Pison, eds. Oxford: Clarendon Press.

Harries, Patrick. 1994. *Work, Culture, and Identity: Migrant Laborers in Mozambique and South Africa, c. 1860–1910*. Portsmouth, NH: Heinemann.

Harrigan, Walter, chair. 1946. *Report of the Commission on the Civil Services of British West Africa, 1945–46*. Accra: Government Printing Department.

Krapf-Askari, Eva. 1969. *Yoruba Towns and Cities: An Enquiry into the Nature of Urban Social Phenomena*. Oxford: Clarendon Press.

Lindsay, Lisa A. 1996. "Putting the Family on Track: Gender and Domestic Life on the Colonial Nigerian Railway." Ph.D. dissertation, University of Michigan.

———. 1998. " 'No Need . . . to Think of Home'? Masculinity and Domestic Life on the Nigerian Railway, c. 1940–61." *Journal of African History* 39: 439–66.

———. 1999. "Domesticity and Difference: Male Breadwinners, Working Women and Questions of Gender in the 1945 Nigerian General Strike." *American Historical Review* 104: 783–812.

Lloyd, P.C. 1963. "The Status of the Yoruba Wife." *Sudan Society* 2: 35–42.

———. 1967. "The Elite." In *The City of Ibadan*, P.C. Lloyd et al., eds. Cambridge: Cambridge University Press.

Mann, Kristin. 1982. "Women's Rights in Law and Practice: Marriage and Dispute Settlement in Colonial Lagos." In *African Women and the Law: Historical Perspectives*, Margaret Jean Hay and Marcia Wright, eds. Boston: Boston University.

———. 1983. "The Dangers of Dependence: Christian Marriage among Elite Women in Lagos Colony, 1880–1915." *Journal of African History* 24: 37–56.

———. 1985. *Marrying Well: Marriage, Status and Social Change among the Educated Elite in Colonial Lagos*. Cambridge: Cambridge University Press.

———. 1991. "The Rise of Taiwo Olowo: Law, Accumulation, and Mobility in Early Colonial Lagos." In *Law in Colonial Africa*, Kristin Mann and Richard Roberts, eds. Portsmouth, NH: Heinemann.

Marris, Peter. 1962. *Family and Social Change in an African City: A Study of Rehousing in Lagos*. Evanston, IL: Northwestern University Press.

Moodie, T. Dunbar, with Vivienne Ndatshe. 1994. *Going for Gold: Men, Mines and Migration*. Berkeley: University of California Press.

Nigeria. 1953. *Annual Report on the Government Railway for the Financial Year 1952–53*. Lagos: Government Printing Office.

———. 1956. *Annual Report of the Federal Social Welfare Department for the Year 1955–56*. Lagos: Government Printer.

Owolabi, Florence. 1994. Interview by the author and Funmilayo Carew. Ibadan, 7 January.

Parpart, Jane L. 1986. "The Household and the Mine Shaft: Gender and Class Struggles on the Zambian Copperbelt, 1926–64." *Journal of Southern African Studies* 13: 36–56.

Pedersen, Susan. 1993. *Family, Dependence, and the Origins of the Welfare State: Britain and France, 1914–1945*. Cambridge: Cambridge University Press.

Peel, J.D.Y. 1983. *Ijeshas and Nigerians: The Incorporation of a Yoruba Kingdom, 1890s–1970s*. Cambridge: Cambridge University Press.

Rose, Sonya O. 1992. *Limited Livelihoods: Gender and Class in Nineteenth-Century England*. Berkeley: University of California Press.

Salako, A.A. 1994. "Autobiography of Mr. Ayo-Ade Salako, Retired Locomotive Engine Driver Grade I, 1951–1987." Handwritten, 14 pp. Copy in author's possession.

Sudarkasa, Niara. 1973. *Where Women Work: A Study of Yoruba Women in the Marketplace and in the Home*. Anthropological Papers No. 53. Ann Arbor, MI: Museum of Anthropology, University of Michigan.

Tudor Davies, W., chair. 1946. *Enquiry into the Cost of Living and the Control of the Cost of Living in the Colony and Protectorate of Nigeria*. Colonial Office No. 204. London: HMSO.

Uchefuna, Rebecca. 1994. Interview with the author. Ibadan, 21 February.

Ward, Edward. 1938. *The Yoruba Husband-Wife Code*. Catholic University of America Anthropology Series, No. 6. Washington, DC: Catholic University of America.

White, Luise. 1990. *The Comforts of Home: Prostitution in Colonial Nairobi*. Chicago: University of Chicago Press.

9

A "MAN" IN THE VILLAGE IS A "BOY" IN THE WORKPLACE: COLONIAL RACISM, WORKER MILITANCE, AND IGBO NOTIONS OF MASCULINITY IN THE NIGERIAN COAL INDUSTRY, 1930–1945

Carolyn A. Brown

... we are the people who always got accident in the Mine for this reason the amount of 1/3d ... we are receiving ... is not sufficient for us. Many of us have got wives and children, after receiving our monthly wages is not enough to support ourselves and them. (Tub "Boys," Iva Valley, 21 August 1937)[1]

Then all African workers were titled boy, for example, timber man was called timber boy, peak [sic] called peak boy, tub man called tub boy. Everything, boy, boy! Only the Europeans were called overman and foreman. (interview with Eze Ozogwu, Amankwo-Ngwo, 2 April 1975)

Please note that in [the] future the designation "men" must be substituted for "boys" in all communications referring to the Colliery labour either collectively or individually. No person employed by this department must be addressed as "boy." (announcement by Colliery Manager, 23 December 1941)[2]

INTRODUCTION

West African labor history is only beginning to consider how African male workers' desires to fulfill gender norms affected their behavior in the capitalist workplace and influenced their decisions to protest conditions of work, to initiate wage bargaining, and to place demands on the colonial state. Working-class identity was not only shaped by the workplace but also by the social and political roles male workers played in their homes, communities, and the society at large. During World War II workers throughout Nigeria raised demands that articulated British working-class notions of masculinity and reformulated indigenous masculine ideologies (see Lindsay 1999 and this volume). These demands also reflected a racialized class consciousness that drew upon the nationalist discourse of the period (cf. Cohen 1974). Workers explicitly raised issues of dignity, social justice, and racial parity, which were condemnations of the dehumanizing and abusive systems of industrial discipline. Moreover, they complained of the state's unwillingness to support the life style that working men felt they and their families deserved. These demands expressed a confrontation of workers' self-perception as modern, industrial men and the imaginary "African worker" that managers debased and reviled.

In the racialized discourse of colonialism, African subordination was represented as weakness, effeminacy, or "childlike immaturity" (Cornwall and Lindisfarne 1994). In colonialist racial ideology, being a "native" and being a "man" were incompatible. But mining jobs in the Enugu Government Colliery had an ambivalent impact on men's perceptions of themselves. On the one hand industrial authorities deprecated miners as childlike "boys," but the work itself, with its requisite skill and physical strength, produced important elements of masculinity. The workplace was a site of a masculine work culture, in which solidarity with one's work mates challenged colonial industrial despotism. Additionally, this masculinity was further validated in the communities and villages where these men used their incomes to become "modern," progressive, and politically powerful.

The fall of Southeast Asia in 1942 enhanced the colonial importance of coal, making the behavior of the miners a matter of strategic importance. Nigeria became the primary source of vital minerals like tin and tropical exports such as palm products. At the same time, wartime propaganda sharpened the contradictions in the workplace and encouraged African workers to add their concerns to the generalized critique of colonial rule. They brought customary and insulting industrial practices into the public eye by using the nationalist press and calling their supervisors before the courts. They appropriated a discourse of the male breadwinner norm, which they used with considerable opportunism to underscore demands. They argued that as men they could not protect their families from the indignity and humiliation of substandard, overcrowded housing and escalating inflation, nor could they invest in the education of their children. The global dimensions of the war encouraged colonial workers to compare their sacrifices and conditions of service with those of expatriate government staff as well as European and American coal miners.

Miners' demands expressed new ideas about their responsibilities as working men during a period of intense anticipation of the future of the colonial state. Many wanted to prepare their families for future opportunities, believing decolonization to be imminent. Others sacrificed to construct schools in natal villages. The fulfillment of these responsibilities was reflected in workplace struggles and the demands miners placed on both their employers and the colonial state. In this case the roots of worker activism lay in urban and rural communities in which workers interacted with various social groups—farmers, traders, the urban unemployed and semi-employed, and men/women in the "informal" economy. Moreover, their concerns and motivations suggest that neither gender nor race is a static concept; they are dynamic indicators of shifting power relations.

MAKING "RACE" IN A COLONIAL WEST AFRICAN WORKPLACE

Enugu Government Colliery was a state-owned enterprise and a strategic resource during World Wars I and II. The mines were located in southeastern Nigeria, in a region populated by the Igbo people, one of the three largest ethnic groups in contemporary Nigeria. Its coal was the main fuel source for the Nigerian Government Railway and, during the war, the railways of other West African colonies. The coal market included steamships that plied the West African coast and the tin mining companies of northern Nigeria as well. Although the work force was small, ranging from 2,500 to 7,000 in this period, the central position of the industry in West Africa amplified the power of its workers, and disputes attracted the attention of the Colonial Office.

All of the colliery's workers were Igbo, with two-thirds hailing from a group of villages, the Agbaja "clan," within fifteen miles of Enugu. There, severe land shortages prevented reliance on subsistence farming.[3] When the colliery opened in 1914 mine work replaced slavery and a pre-colonial migration of young men to work on farms elsewhere.[4] The Agbaja claimed a special right to colliery jobs because the mines' location on their land deprived them of important farmlands. The Nkanu were a second group of "locals," who lived on the fertile plateau to the east of Enugu. For them mine work competed with commercial farming, made especially lucrative with the development of Enugu. Mining was a job of last resort: "A man might as well be buried alive" (Hair n.d.: x). The few Nkanu employed in the colliery would only work in the less dangerous surface jobs while the Agbaja worked underground. In this way work became an important factor shaping a colonially imposed "clan" identity.[5]

There were two mines during this period, Iva Valley and Obwetti. Both used the *pillar and stall* system of extraction in which the entire mine is divided into sections to be extracted by hewers. This system of extraction encouraged a series of values that became important for the development of miners' self-identity. In the Enugu mines the division of tasks followed the system used in the northern coal fields of England. In Northumberland and Durham, the home of the colliery's first manager, all tasks preliminary to the actual coal getting were performed by specialized workers.[6] This is called the "Derbyshire system," and hewers (miners) only hew the coal and put it in the tubs. Other workers set timber, lay the rails and remove stone to make roadways of sufficient height, and build packing walls. To William Leck, the first and—until 1943—only manager, this fractionalized division of labor seemed appropriate for "the African worker," whom he deprecated as being incapable of handling more than a single task. However, despite what the white bosses thought about the workers' lack of skill, the Derbyshire system encouraged the men at various points in production to recognize the intuitive knowledge required of their jobs. This gave them power and personal pride, which was expressed in their demands during the war.

The mines exemplified the racialized colonial workplace and drew upon the association of "race" with coal mining in England. Anne McClintock (1995: 115) has noted that race was one of the ideological weapons employed by mining capital in the 1840s in an attempt to bring British coal miners under factory-like discipline. Mining officials initiated a public discourse that characterized the fierce independence and protest culture of the coal miners as evidence that they were a "race" apart, "outcasts, historically abandoned, isolated and primitive." Derogatory drawings of miners appeared in newspapers in which they mimicked apes and, by association, the savage Africans. Their militance, today celebrated by labor historians, was considered a badge of their backwardness.[7] For men like William Leck, the colliery's manager, this association must have been especially salient in Enugu, where the miners were truly a distinguishably different race. The fact that the British had well-formed ideas about this race—the black race—and where it was situated in the evolutionary hierarchy facilitated all types of racialized assumptions about the physiological impact of these working conditions on African labor. This was reflected in the general conditions under which Enugu's miners were forced to work.

Racism was an organizing principle of power in the colonial labor process (Burawoy 1985: Chap. 5). European staff saw their supervisory tasks as necessary to ensure that Igbo "boys" performed their jobs. This paternalism was enshrined in the job titles of laborers and their "native" supervisors. *Pick "boys"* (hewers) undercut coal and loaded the tubs, which *tub "boys"* conveyed to the main underground roads. *Rail "boys"* and *timber "boys"* reinforced the roof with timber. The typical work group was one rail man, eight tub men, eight hewers, and two timber men.[8] All were supervised by *"boss boys,"* a discursive paradox if ever there was one. A second representation of race was the "hammock tradition," by which all expatriate underground foremen and overmen were transported daily to work from their residence high on a hill to the mines in a hammock. It was quite clear to the workers that these men could have walked to the mines, and they resented this flagrant demonstration of their own subordination. The tradition clearly emphasized the difference, power, and privileges of the "European man" over the "native" laborer. To be available as transportation, the men who carried the white "boss" lived in special quarters in an area called "Hammock Camp." The "hammock tradition" continued until World War II and was such an accepted aspect of the colliery that "hammock boys" were noted perfunctorily in the classification of jobs in a 1947 study.[9]

In Enugu, race also factored into management's assumptions about the kinds of conditions under which Africans could and should be forced to work. The men worked barefoot, wearing only loincloths. They had no protective clothing and sustained numerous injuries. Without the danger of gaseous explosions, management was less than diligent about ventilation in its general engineering scheme. Racist stereotypes about African tolerance of heat and humidity reinforced this neglect. Oxygen deficiency,[10] humidity levels of 80–100% saturation, and temperatures of 85–90°F visibly impeded work in the mines, but it was never acknowledged that these conditions could interfere with Africans' work performance. Contrary to management's opinion, not even African workers could be expected to work productively under such conditions on a consistent basis. Therefore workers created an underground tradition in which two miners worked one site, in a system that resembled the *marras* of the Durham coal fields.[11] Since conditions prevented either from working a full shift, one worked while the other rested, fanning himself in the main airways to recover from the heat. Although management reviled workers for their absentee rates, which approached 20%, they simply hired redundant workers, sometimes over 100% more than the daily requirement, rather than improve conditions.

STRENGTH, DANGER, AND THE CULT OF MASCULINITY IN THE WORKPLACE

Labor historians often associate mining with a type of rough-hewn masculinity.[12] The possession of mining skills, the danger of the workplace, and "the aggressive celebration of physical strength" were key contributing factors to the masculine work culture of European coal mining. Hewers, proudly called "pit men," had a self-identity of skilled workers and were independent, self-improving men with a work culture oppositional toward supervision (Klubock 1998: 146; Colls 1987: 12).[13] These values defined a social hierarchy within mining communities in Britain that coincided with the ranking in production and similarly emerged as important bases of a proud identity among hewers in Enugu.

In Nigeria the hewers' independent self-identity was encouraged by a number of workplace traditions. First, the hewer was the only worker whose wages were based on piece rates. As Alan Campbell and Fred Reid noted about Scottish miners (1978: 58), piece rates reinforced the hewers' sense of skill "since their earning depended . . . on their ability to use a wide range of hand tools, and to interpret the geological and other conditions under which they worked." Second, because of the high worker-to-supervisor ratio, miners had an extraordinary degree of workplace autonomy. While typical of non-mechanized coal mining in the United States and Europe, miners' workplace control in Enugu was heightened by their persistent involvement in farming. Third, when extraordinary mortality rates during the 1918 influenza pandemic created a labor shortage, hewers became labor contractors heading their own work groups in a local work system similar to the "butty" system in England.[14] The miner brought in "helper" hewers and tub men to work in his production team. His was the only name on the colliery payroll and the output of his work team was attributed to him.

THE "MAN" IN THE VILLAGE

The mines, like many colonial enterprises, were reluctant to encourage the development of a fully proletarianized work force. To political officials the "proletarian" African, whom they saw as "detribalized," was dangerously autonomous. Therefore, the mines encouraged men to remain rooted in their communities and, in effect, considered the entire male population as a pool of labor to be hired and retrenched as the need arose. These roots tied workers into rural systems of masculine validation with significance for the labor movement in the industry.

By the 1940s most adult and junior men commuted daily or weekly from Agbaja and Nkanu, where a stint at the colliery had become a crucial part of the life cycle of men. As young unmarried men, they came to the mines to earn income to pay bride price. Later, as married men they worked to earn the fees to join prestigious rural societies. Membership in a title society was a compelling goal for many Igbo men because it allowed them to exert political influence within the village (Afigbo 1974: 442). While there were numerous such societies, the most prestigious in most Agbadja village-groups was the *Ozo* title (Talbot 1969: 775).

Rural masculinity was not just physical but also moral, with many contradictory norms (Moodie 1994: 38): aggression, perseverance, stoicism, restraint but determination, achievement through hard-fought effort, bravery and courage, and generosity. A man had a social obligation to "uplift" his family, village, and village group. This ranged from helping the less fortunate with resources from one's household to sponsoring some development project in one's village. Either action brought notoriety as a "big man" and benefactor and established important ties of obligation of benefit in village politics. Thus, while individual success and achievement were compelling male norms, a responsible man must always contribute to the common good.[15]

Miners used their incomes to buy prestige goods such as bicycles and certain types of western clothing and to dispense patronage and largesse to their neighbors and family. They financed social rituals that were important for village cohesion and personal status. To these miners, being a "responsible" worker did not necessarily mean an industrially "disciplined" man. Rather, they used mine work to finance such improvements as construction of schools and churches, educating one's or the village's children, and assisting others in gaining jobs in the colliery. Often they used their income in eclectic ways, both "traditional" and "modern." One miner, Samuel Onoh, noted:

> The development of [the] coal industry did a lot to my village. But for coal industry civilization would have not reached us as early as it had reached us. The coal industry initiated me into Ozo title. Now I am Ozo Samuel N. Onoh. I was able to train up my children, build good houses. We contributed money and build schools and churches.[16]

One miner who worked in the early years cited these obligations as an incentive for entering the mines:

> I joined the mine when I felt like. In those days what normally happened was that whenever the villages wanted to celebrate certain feasts, people will rush to the mine to get money; that is, to work for sometime and get money for their feast. When you must then you retire home to celebrate the feast with the money you got from mining work. When the money finished you go back again to another money. (Alo interview)

The mines did not require that workers sign contracts so they could make individual determinations of the time and duration of their work. To the dismay of management, miners sold their labor-power in small and irregular units. Treasuring their involvement in the village, where they were "big men," they absented themselves from the mines to participate in the planting and harvesting seasons in their villages and to fulfill social obligations (i.e., funerals, marriages, festivals, etc.) to their families and communities.

British managers and political officials interpreted workers' rurally based independence as confirmation of their racialist assumptions about the irrationality, insolence, and irresponsibility of African workers. And although miners in Britain often used farm work to lighten the burden of their arduous jobs, no one saw the similarity in the behavior of Nigerian miners. But miners' activism was motivated by goals not so different from those of European and American miners: to contribute to the support and uplift of their families and communities with dignity, respect, and honor. Like the "independent miners" of England and Scotland, Enugu's workers were proud, self-improving men who were a social force for change and progress in their communities. They were powerful, "modern" men despite the mocking of district officers, who called them "coal gentlemen with their flashy clothes, bicycles and air of jaunty self confidence."[17]

NEGOTIATING THE CITY: WORKERS' STRUGGLES ON THE EVE OF WORLD WAR II

During World War I colliery and railway clerical workers and artisans established all-male urban improvement unions. Originally called *Nzuko* or "meetings," these organizations combined consultative village political traditions with self-help programs to socialize new immigrants, funnel money into rural improvement projects, and to assist the state in preserving urban order.[18] At the colliery, men transformed the *Nzukos* into workers' organizations that met to discuss "food shortages, token cheating, bribery and corruption in the obtaining and retaining of jobs and in the allocation of work on hard or soft coal faces."[19] These "meetings," *Nzuko ifunanya*,[20] were structured by job category, with each class of men holding their own meeting under a president and secretary. Although management came to meet with them regularly to discuss the men's' complaints, they were often quite violent toward management spies or "snitches" and defended the secrecy of their meetings by physically blocking Europeans from entering the mines. "Boss boys" and other staff were distrusted and prevented from attending. *Nzuko* used oathing to ensure solidarity and to deter informers (Anyasado interview). They were just the type of workers' organization that the Colonial Office feared most— autonomous and potentially volatile, operating in semi-secrecy.

In 1937–38 the workers launched a number of successful strikes in which the underground *Nzuko ifunanya* played a leadership role. The leaders were men with "good mouth,"[21] steadfast in resisting unjust authority, and diligent in attacking problems. Management saw them as demagogues, men of "energy, personality and slight extra knowledge of affairs," who manipulated the "ordinary unsophisticated local men" (Croasdale 1938: 29–30). But to the men they were an important component of their individual strategies to resist authoritarian abuses in the workplace. The economic recovery after the depression and the gathering tensions in pre-war Europe gave them the opportunity to secure Colonial Office attention.

In March 1937, the colliery's hewers struck to recoup wage losses during the depression and to underscore their demand for such welfare provisions as workmen's compensation and better housing.[22] They timed the strikes to coincide with the railway's heavy coal demand to evacuate the annual ground nut (peanut) crop. The hewers were the elite of the work force. All jobs in the mines, from office clerk to lowly "tub boy," relied on the hewers' effort, intuitive skill, and bravery. As a group, their demands incorporated the desires of working men to fulfill obligations to their families and to play leadership roles in the adjacent villages. Implicitly they reminded the state that it had social responsibilities for the living standards of its employees.

Among other complaints, the hewers attacked the immorality of their overcrowded accommodations, which exposed their families to unhealthy substandard conditions and were beneath their status as working men. At that time the colliery camps were free and offered "foreign" workers an important alternative to high-cost rental housing in Enugu. But the camps were built in the style of range-type housing first used for indentured workers and now declared unacceptable for family life by the International Labour Organization and the British government. They were a row of $12' \times 12' \times 10'$ rooms separated by partial petitions and topped with corrugated roofs. They were insufferably hot during the day and had an average of 5.5 inhabitants.[23] The overcrowding violated Igbo marital norms, and the men considered the quarters to be demeaning and immoral. Perched at the top of the production hierarchy, the hewers felt morally compromised by the conditions in which they were forced to place their families. They were especially outraged by the necessity of boarding a single "pick boy" with their family or of sharing a room with another family. They also recognized that such overcrowding was a health hazard and complained that "our current mode of living is rather an inconvenience and far out of sanitation so well."[24] Conditions were especially unpleasant for polygynous families because this rural symbol of masculine status clashed with the spatial constraints of urban living. Some rooms had an employee, three to four wives, seven to ten children and one or two servants![25]

The strikers argued that the industry made it difficult for them to support their families. They cited the hazards of their job as well as their positions as breadwinners:

. . . your humble petitioners beg to inform you that we are the people who always got accident in the Mines for this reason the amount of 1/3d (one shilling and three pence) we are receiving per diem is not sufficient for us. Many of us have got wives and children, after receiving our monthly wages is not enough to support ourselves and them.[26]

THE SHIFTING RACIAL PROTOCOL
OF WORLD WAR II

The 1938 protests embarrassed the Colonial Office by demanding colonial conformity to metropolitan industrial standards on the treatment of workers on the job and in their homes. Workers called for improved conditions for their families, compensation for injuries and death, and financial rewards for long-term service. Moreover, the men demanded that the government monitor the conditions under which they worked. The strikes pressured the Colonial Office to urge a negligent management and local officials to improve the conditions of work and upgrade housing in the labor camps. But the strikes were only successful in attracting state attention to a disastrous condition. It was the necessity to increase colonial production during the war that resulted in concrete improvements in the lives of the men, their families, and their conditions of work.[27]

In Enugu this more intensive attention to the details of African life initiated a period of state intervention into the domestic and work life of the colliery workers. As Europe moved toward certain war, metropolitan officials were less patient with bungling colonial bureaucrats and managers, like William Leck. The 1938 strikes occurred just as Governor Bourdillion was deflecting pressure from Ormsby-Gore, the Colonial Secretary, to become more systematic in dealing with colonial workers: to establish a labor department, to appoint labor inspectors, and to become more involved in securing better social conditions for African labor. When the miners went out on strike, Ormsby-Gore responded in bewildered exasperation to the backwardness of the Nigerian government:

> The conditions at Iva Colliery revealed in connection with this strike occasion me considerable concern. The existence of a colliery owned and managed by Government in a territory where there are no effective Trade Unions or other associations for safeguarding the interests of the workmen calls for a more vigilant government supervision than would appear to have hitherto been exercised in this case and if the facts revealed in your dispatch under acknowledgment were widely known, I should find great difficulty in defending the Nigerian Government from the criticisms which would inevitably be provoked.[28]

The war marked a skepticism and lack of confidence in local managers' competence to use the most "scientific" methods of labor control and consultation. In 1940 the visit of Major Granville Orde-Browne, the Colonial Office's first official labor adviser, corroborated the Colonial Office's worst suspicions. He argued that management neglect, poor labor practices, deplorable underground conditions, the lack of a labor consultative system, and few amenities (e.g., housing, medical care, etc.) led to the 1938 disruptions.[29] Furthermore, officials became increasingly concerned with the connections between control of the labor process (i.e., industrial discipline and productivity) on the one hand and urban order on the other (see Cooper 1987). To the Colonial Office, management (i.e., the state) had too little control over the colliery's underground workers, and this had produced problems for the city. Since the men worked so erratically the colliery had to house hundreds of workers in the camps to meet daily requirements. Some were absent because they were physically unable to put in a full week working under such severe conditions. Others, as noted above, simply remained engaged in the rhythms of the village economy. Moreover, management still had problems in controlling the workplace. Even when on the job the men seldom worked with the intensity that management felt was possible, resting frequently to preserve their strength and often simply leaving the pit when they felt that had worked enough.

By 1939 the Colonial Office had pushed colonial governments to establish unions as "the surest means of securing industrial stability and the removal of extremist tendencies."[30] As Ormsby-Gore had noted earlier, not to do so would "encourage the formation of illegal organizations which may easily develop into 'secret societies' and extend their operations into the political field."[31] But colonial unions were not permitted to operate with the full rights of metropolitan unions. They faced compulsory registration under terms to be decided at the discretion of the government and were subjected to special restrictions: a six-month waiting period, frequent imprisonment of militant leaders, and a close monitoring of finances.[32] Nonetheless throughout the war workers struggled to make them represent their interests.

Two unions were established at the colliery: the Colliery Surface Improvement Union and the Underground Colliery Workers Union. Although plagued by leadership struggles and corruption, they were relatively successful in articulating the grievances of workers through the war. One of their first targets was the emasculating use of corporal punishment. Until the war, assaults against workers were protected by the state's refusal to allow Africans the right to contest this treatment in the courts. Now beatings, insulting forms of address, and management's dismissive attitude toward worker complaints were no longer tolerated. But it was not until 1947 that the manager issued a directive instructing the men that the word "boy" was no longer to be used in addressing the men or as a part of job titles.

GENDER AND THE CITY: ENUGU, THE MINERS, AND WORLD WAR II

Wartime Enugu had many of the problems of colonial cities throughout Africa: severe overcrowding, escalating inflation, and deplorable public sanitary conditions. By 1945 the city's population had grown to 40,000 from 13,000 before the war. With colonial production focused on the defense of the metropole, imperial governments were loath to devote resources to raising inhabitants above the squalor and chaos that characterized urban life. The colliery tried to do its part by focusing recruitment on adjacent villages, assuming that the men would commute daily to work. But in 1945, when its work rolls grew to 6,800 from 2,500 in the 1930s, many men still moved to the city. The work force fell into three residential categories. One-third, predominantly "foreign" Igbos, had always been permanent residents in the "native" areas of Enugu township and the labor camps. A quarter of the remaining two-thirds, largely "locals," lodged in the labor camps but left their wives and children in the adjacent villages, to which they returned every weekend. The remainder lived in the villages and walked up to 15 miles daily to work.[33] In 1938, some 1,600 of the over 2,400 men living in the Iva Camps, Coal Camp, and Alfred's Camp (an unofficial camp) were from Udi, presumably comprising the weekend commuter category (Croasdale 1938: Appendix A).

The urban adaptation of the "large compound" was another area of state concern. In the early part of the century most men aspired to head large households with many wives, children, and slaves. As a productive unit these households allowed patriarchs to produce surpluses by employing the labor of subordinates. Although the economic rationale for this household form had declined by the 1940s it nonetheless retained some appeal for many men during the period of this study. Working men tried to express their status by establishing polygynous households despite the scarcity of adequate rooms and deplorable housing conditions. Moreover, the income earned by many government employees led their relatives to expect them to re-create these rural models. The burden of supporting an escalating flow of rural relatives to the city weighed heavily on colliery men and figured in their calculations of what constituted a "just" wage.

"Foreign" and "local" urban residents established different types of households in Enugu but retained similar expectations of gender roles in domestic space. Foreign men's wives cooked, cleaned, and laundered their clothes. Local men created a new type of household in which adolescent boys assumed "female" domestic roles. Established rural gender norms forbade men from performing certain domestic tasks (i.e., cooking, cleaning, washing clothes), and they contracted with relatives to bring their sons to the city as servants. It was not uncommon for several men to share one "boy servant." While there was a practical rationale for having domestic servants—the burden of cooking after work—and having someone to watch their property while at work, it also reflected male ideologies about status, age, and prestige (see Lindsay 1998). Mature men did not cook, and they did not trust others, nonrelatives, to cook for them. But other responsibilities of the servants symbolized the man's position in the hierarchy of production: "small boys" carried the "pick boy's" tools to work daily (Croasdale 1938: 23).

THE STATE VENTURES INTO THE AFRICAN BEDROOM: HOUSING SCHEMES AND FAMILY CONTROL

The all-male domestic units began to decline when the state, seeking to mold a "responsible" working class on the foundation of a nuclear family, began to put resources into the construction of housing. For the first time officials studied African domestic arrangements and proposed policies to encourage a familiar stability based on the male breadwinner norm. Workers astutely appropriated this discourse and used it to support their arguments for improved wages and conditions.

In 1941 workers' persistent demands raised in the context of war resonated with the state's realization that undifferentiated poor conditions facilitated dangerous political alliances. An alliance of the stable and, for the war effort, crucial urban working class with the city's lumpen proletariat was a dangerous alchemy for urban disorder, political unrest, and imperial vulnerability. Colonial labor officials believed that by encouraging Africans to form stable, nuclear families they could produce the type of efficient, disciplined worker that the industry needed (see White this volume). Moreover, by creating a model mining estate, in which they would regulate the occupancy rate of rooms, policymakers tried to encourage subtle changes in African home life. Once in the estates, African families were to be subjected to a number of other regulations to change their nutritional habits, expose them to modern medical care, and provide recreational activities that would structure their leisure and working time.

In November 1942 the treasury approved a £104,000 loan for the construction of 461 semi-detached houses, providing 922 rooms.[34] From its inception, the project was envisioned as a model of state ownership and a demonstration to Africans of the correct, "modern" way to construct houses. Construction began in February 1943. A colliery "Housing Committee" had finalized the plans in a series of meetings from October 1940. Membership in the committee touched all major government agencies involved in land use and social welfare, as well as labor officials and colliery welfare staff, but at no point did it include either the workers or their representatives in the unions.[35]

The estates were an excellent example of an "imagined" English mining village, an illustration of the fantasies colonialists entertained in the world of African workers: two-room cottages on 40′ × 60′ plots, with verandahs, electric lights, and small gardens. The camps had wide roads, open spaces, bath-rooms, social halls, and chlorinated water. Officials ignored the miners' own modern homes built with zinc roofs in the village. It was assumed that once the communities saw how beautiful and modern these buildings were, they would modify their own construction in the villages.[36] Officials assumed that the estates would not become the rowdy type of English village that encour-aged solidarity and militant worker unrest. They modeled the camps instead on the "garden city" type of town planning: ordered houses, bright and airy with sufficient vegetation. In fact, the Udi Siding Camp was called Garden City.[37]

Female welfare officers supervised women and children, operating chil-dren's clinics and entering homes to teach nutrition and health. Initially the wives of the staff welfare officer and deputy manager held these posts and visited adjacent villages.[38] The unions resented these intrusions and asked that the women welfare officer stop "supervising and molesting their wives when they went to work." The men underscored this request by reminding the officials of "the substantial quota the colliery workers were contributing towards the war effort."[39]

The central conflict concerned the core issue of the project: the size and composition of the African household. Occupancy rates were set at three and a half people per room in the largest camp, Garden City. At a meeting with the senior resident and acting manager, Augustine Ude of the Colliery Workers Union complained that under the occupancy limits of three and a half people per room in Garden City, residents would have to leave part of their family "behind or throw them away."[40] The men resisted the most invasive aspects of the project. Those with polygynous families insisted on adequate housing for their families and servants as well. They organized a boycott of the estates and fined people who agreed to occupy them. When only 100 people con-sented to live in the houses, the Colonial Secretary complained: "No one had apparently attempted to find out the sort of accommodation which, while sat-isfactory from the health point of view, would be acceptable to the Africans."[41] It was one thing to design the physical space that workers and their families occupied. It was quite another to make them occupy it accord-ing to the abstract standards developed by remote colonial labor experts.

CONCLUSION: STRUGGLING FOR DIGNITY AND FAMILY IN A COLONIAL INDUSTRY

Enugu Colliery workers joined the small but strategically placed Nigerian working class in protesting the severe economic conditions during and after the war. Between 1939 and 1942, the cost of living increased by 75% in Nige-ria, forcing the miners to endure deplorable housing conditions and prevent-ing their support for village development projects. They became more sensitive than before to the disparity between their living standards and those of expatriate bosses who often had the same skills but were protected by the color bar. And they resented the humiliating treatment they suffered at the hands of white bosses.

Against all odds, these workers struggled to implement their own models of development in the village. The village group of Ngwo, for example, built and maintained their own maternity home, employed a midwife, and contracted with the colliery to have a doctor and nurse visit periodically (Anyasado interview). Later, after the war, the district officer reported "a quite phenomenal outburst during 1946 and 1947 of building of large stone-built primary schools paid for to a large extent from the wages of colliers and wage earners living in Enugu."[42] In many respects the strikes and agitations of the war expressed the views of working-class African men about the meaning of "development." These ideas were grounded in a worldview that valued individual pride, social standing, and community improvement. Their initiatives in utilizing income, forming associations, and tapping into a generalized nationalist discourse of the period give us some insight into the new ways in which men were restructuring their roles. They reveal their perspectives on how best to position their children for the future and their view of the state and its responsibilities toward its employees. An examination of these new and old ideologies provides us with a crucial understanding of the nature of working-class masculinity during a period of rapid political change.

NOTES

1. Nigerian Archives Enugu (hereafter NAE), NIGCOAL 2/1/94, "Petition from Southern Native Location, Enugu Township, to the Colliery Manager, Colliery Department Enugu, through the Under Manager, Iva Valley Coal Mine, Enugu, 21 August 1937."

2. Nigerian Coal Corporation Files (NCC), New No. P.1, "Letter from Colliery Department to All Officials and Staff—European and African, 23 December 1941."

3. These villages are Ngwo, Abor, Nsude, Ebe, Ukana, Obioma. See Hair (n.d.). A considerable proportion of all adult males in these villages worked at some point in the colliery.

4. Jones (1949). The people of Agbadja were known for selling their children to get food to support other members of the family. For a discussion of the importance of slavery in this region even into the twentieth century, see Brown (1996). In an interview one mine worker responded to a question about the impact of coal mining on the villages: "People did not have to sell others into slavery" (Noisike interview).

5. This is a theme that will be further explored in Brown (forthcoming); Akpala (1965).

6. For a good discussion of the system of work in the Northumberland fields see Daunton (1981: 582).

7. McClintock (1995: 116) notes that authorities considered one indicator of the backwardness of coal miners, an indicator that cast aspersions on the "manliness" of the profession, to be the inclusion of women, who were being "unsexed" by work in the mines.

8. Powell Duffryn Technical Services, "First Report to the Under-Secretary of State for the Colonies, on the Government Colliery, Enugu, the Characteristics of the Coal Pro-

duced and the Investigation into the Other Coal and Lignite Resources," mimeograph, London, 1948, p. D-19.

9. In 1947 the Colonial Office commissioned the Powell Duffryn Technical Services, a major mining engineering firm, to do a study of the Enugu Colliery to see how it could be developed more efficiently. Their report, which is a richly textured technical document on the industry, lists these "hammock men."

10. Powell Duffryn, Section D, Part IV, "Ventilation."

11. *Marras* are two hewers who work the same coal face, either during the same shift or on alternate shifts. They are paid by piece rates for the total output of the coal face that they share. The close working relationship encourages personal friendships that extend beyond the workplace. See Douglas (1977: 227–8).

12. The literature on mining and masculinity is quite extensive. For just a sample see Klubock (1998), Nash (1979), Dennis et al. (1956), Burawoy (1972), Moodie (1994), and Harries (1994).

13. Colls (1987: 12) explains the distinction between "pit man" and "collier": "The word 'pit man' carried with it meanings of social bearing; other men were 'colliers' compared to 'pit men,' and others again were labourers compared to colliers."

14. The "butty" is a master hewer who contracts with the colliery owner to mine a particular area at a certain price. He then brings in his own work crew and they extract the coal under his supervision. The pay is by the ton and given to the master hewer, who in turn pays the work team. See Douglas (1977).

15. Nwala (1985: 194), Uchendu (1965: Chap. 1), Cole and Aniakor (1984: 24).

16. Onoh interview. Onoh began work in 1915 as a "tub boy" and worked up through the ranks until he became an underground foreman after World War II.

17. NAE/NIGCOAL 2/1/94, Colliery Manager to Director of Transport, 20 June 1938.

18. *Nzuko* is a generic term meaning any type of "meeting." The urban "tribal" unions were also characterized as *Nzuko*.

19. Croasdale (1938: 28–9). This report was destroyed during the Nigerian civil war, and I thank Dr. Hair of Liverpool University for sending me a xerox of his copy.

20. This roughly translates to "self help meetings" or "mutual aid" groups. Their history has not been documented. The only study that explicitly mentions them is that of Croasdale (1938).

21. This refers to men with considerable oratory skills. See Amadiume (1987).

22. Documentation of the strike is found in Public Record Office, London (hereafter PRO), CO 583/216, 1937, "Nigerian Railway. Strike at Udi Colliery."

23. PRO/CO 583/263/30544, Colonial Office Press Section, 11 May 1943, "Model Villages for African Miners."

24. NAE/NIGCOAL 2/1/94, Letter from Colliery Department, Iva Valley, to the General Manager (hereafter GM), Railway, Lagos, 12 July 1937 and Colliery Manager (hereafter CM).

25. This information followed a survey of the camps during the period of labor force stabilization in 1939. PRO/CO 583/237, Bourdillon to MacDonald, 30 August 1939.

26. Ibid., "Petition from the Southern Native Location, Enugu Township to the Colliery Manager, Colliery Department, Enugu through the Under Manager, Iva Valley Coal Mine, Enugu," 21 August 1937.

27. For the most extensive treatment of the African strikes of the late 1930s see Cooper (1996). For a discussion of the post-war conjuncture see Oberst (1988) and Weiler (1984: 370). For a similar case study of the connection between economic recovery, urban unrest, and labor protest see Cooper (1987).

28. In the original draft he had written "some" concern, but he crossed this out and wrote "considerable." PRO/CO 583/216, Ormsby-Gore to Bourdillion, 13 May 1937.

29. While Orde-Browne (1941) was to represent a "progressive" direction in labor policy, he did not support trade unions, considering the miners "too primitive and uneducated" to *be trusted* (emphasis mine) to form trade unions. For an attack from the left (British C. P.), see Woodis (1954). Although the Committee was only established in 1942, informal meetings had been held in the Colonial Office since 1931 to discuss labor policy. The documentation is available in the PRO, file series CO 323/1117 and CO 888/1. Files CO 888/2-11 contain the documents of the Committee.

30. Royal Commission on disturbances in Trinidad, as cited in Weiler (1984: 374).

31. PRO/CO 1766/37, Ormsby-Gore, "Circular," 24 August 1937, as cited in Weiler (1984: 372).

32. PRO/CO 554/132/33729, Secretary of State Oliver Stanley, to H.V. Tewson, Assistant Secretary, BTUC, 8 July 1943.

33. Hair (n.d.: 71). Concern with the cost in physical stamina of such a trek never materialized in a subsidized transport system to the mines.

34. PRO/CO 583/263/30544, "Report of a Committee Appointed to Review the Question of Housing Accommodations for the Employees of the Government Colliery, Enugu," 27 September 1941.

35. Members included the Resident, Onitsha; Manager Leck; and F.J.W. Skeates, the colliery's staff welfare officer. PRO/CO 583/263/30544, "Report of the Committee."

36. PRO/CO 583/263/30544, Gerald Wormal, "New Homes in Old Africa," n.d.

37. According to an informant, it was better placed than the others. People were encouraged to beautify their compounds, and competitions were held for the best-looking garden. The district officer and colliery manager awarded prizes. Anyasado interview.

38. Hansards, *37th Parliament. Debates 1942–43*, 11–17 November, 1943, p. 344.

39. They also asked for a woman who was not married to be the lady welfare officer. The current officer was the wife of the staff welfare officer, Skeates. NAE/UDDIST 3/1/104, "Enugu Colliery Workers and the New Housing Scheme."

40. UDDIST 3/1/104, "Enugu Colliery Workers and the New Housing Scheme." Ude interview.

41. PRO/CO 583/261/30425, "Notes on Points Arising in Discussions with the Secretary of State on Wednesday 27 October and Thursday 28th October 1943."

42. NAE/UDDIST 9/1/1, "Annual Report 1947—Udi Division."

REFERENCES

Afigbo, A.E. 1974. "Southeastern Nigeria in the 19th Century." In *History of West Africa*, 2nd ed., Vol. 2, J.F.A. Ajayi and M. Crowder, eds. New York: Columbia University Press.

———. 1981. *Ropes of Sand: Studies in Igbo History and Culture*. Ibadan: Oxford University Press.

Akpala, Agwu. 1965. "The Background to the Enugu Colliery Shooting Incident in 1949." *Journal of the Historical Society of Nigeria* 3, 2: 335–64.

———. 1972. "African Labour Productivity—A Reappraisal." *Africa Quarterly* 12, 3: 233–55.

Amadiume, Ifi. 1987. *Male Daughters, Female Husbands: Gender and Sex in an African Society*. London: Zed.

Brown, C. A. 1996. "Testing the Boundaries of Marginality: 20th Century Slavery and Emancipation Struggles in Nkanu, Northern Igboland 1920–1928." *Journal of African History* 37: 51–80.

———. Forthcoming. *"We Were All Slaves:" African Miners, Culture and Resistance: The Enugu Government Colliery, Nigeria 1914–1950*. Portsmouth, NH: Heinemann.

Burawoy, Michael. 1972. *Another Look at the African Mine Worker*. Lusaka: University of Zambia.

———. 1985. *The Politics of Production*. London: Verso.

Campbell, Alan and Fred Reid. 1978. "The Independent Colliery in Scotland." In *The Independent Collier: The Coal Miner as Archetypal Proletarian Reconsidered*, Royden Harrison, ed. New York: St. Martin's Press.

Cohen, Robin. 1974. *Labour and Politics in Nigeria, 1945–71*. London: Heinemann.

Cole, Herbert M. and Chike C. Aniakor. 1984. *Igbo Arts: Community and Cosmos*. Los Angeles: UCLA Museum of Cultural History.

Colls, R. 1987. *The Pitmen of the Northern Coalfield: Work, Culture and Protest, 1790–1950*. Manchester: Manchester University Press.

Cooper, Frederick. 1987. *On the African Waterfront: Urban Disorder and the Transformation of Work in Colonial Mombasa*. New Haven, CT: Yale University Press.

———. 1996. *Decolonization and African Society: The Labor Question in French and British Africa*. Cambridge: Cambridge University Press.

Cornwall, Andrea and Nancy Lindisfarne. 1994. *Dislocating Masculinity: Comparative Ethnographies*. London: Routledge.

Croasdale, C.H. 1938. "Report on Labour at the Enugu Government Colliery," mimeograph Enugu.

Daunton, M.J. 1981. "Down the Pit: Work in the Great Northern and South Wales Coal Fields, 1870–1914." *Economic History Review* (2nd Series) 34, 4: 578–97.

Dennis, N., F. Henriques, and C. Slaughter. 1956. *Coal Is Our Life*. London: Eyre and Spottiswoode.

Douglas, D. 1977. "The Durham Pitman." In *Miners, Quarrymen and Saltworkers*, R. Samuel, ed. London: Routledge and K. Paul.

Hair, P.E.H. n.d. "Enugu: A West African Industrial Town," mimeograph. Enugu: Nigerian National Archives.

Harries, Patrick. 1994. *Work, Culture, and Identity: Migrant Laborers in Mozambique and South Africa, 1860–1910*. Portsmouth, NH: Heinemann.

Jones, G. I. 1949. "Igbo Land Tenure." *Africa* 19: 309–23.

Klubock, Thomas Miller. 1998. *Contested Communities: Class, Gender, and Politics in Chile's El Teniente Copper Mine, 1904–1951*. Durham, NC: Duke University Press.

Lindsay, Lisa A. 1998. "'No Need . . . to Think of Home'? Masculinity and Domestic Life on the Nigerian Railway, c. 1940–61." *Journal of African History* 39, 3: 439–66.

———. 1999. "Domesticity and Difference: Male Breadwinners, Working Women and Colonial Citizenship in the 1945 Nigerian General Strike." *American Historical Review* 104, 3: 783–812.

McClintock, Anne. 1995. *Imperial Leather: Race, Gender and Sexuality in the Colonial Contest*. London: Routledge.

Moodie, T. Dunbar, with Vivienne Ndatshe. 1994. *Going for Gold: Men, Mines and Migration*. Berkeley and Los Angeles: University of California.

Nash, June. 1979. *We Eat the Mines and the Mines Eat Us: Dependency and Exploitation in the Bolivian Tin Mines*. New York: Columbia University Press.

Nwala, Uzodinma T. 1985. *Igbo Philosophy*. Lagos: Lantern Books.

Oberst, Timothy. 1988. "Transport Workers, Strikes and the 'Imperial Response': Africa and the Post-World War II Conjuncture." *African Studies Review* 31, 1: 117–34.

Orde-Brown, Granville St. G. 1941. *Labour Conditions in West Africa*, Cmd. 6277. London: HMSO.

Talbot, T. Amury. 1969. *The Peoples of Southern Nigeria*, Vol. 3. London: Oxford University Press.

Uchendu, Victor. 1965. *The Igbo of Southeast Nigeria*. New York: Holt, Rinehart and Winston.

Weiler, Peter. 1984. "Forming Responsible Trade Unions: The Colonial Office, Colonial Labor and the Trades Union Congress." *Radical History Review* 28–29: 367–92.

Woodis, Jack. 1954. *The Mask is Off! An Examination of the Activities of Trade Union Advisers in the British Colonies*. London: Thames Publications.

Interviews

Alo, James. Okwojo Ngwo, Nigeria. 6 July 1975.

Anyasado, B.U. Mbieri, Owerri, Nigeria. 23 July 1975.

Noisike, Thomas. Owa Imezi, Udi. July 1975.

Onoh, Samuel N. Ngwo-Etiti, Nigeria. 9 August 1975.

Ozogwu, Eze. Amankwo-Ngwo. 2 June 1975.

Ude, Augustin. Umuaga, Udi. August 5, 1975.

PART III

GENDERED NATIONALISMS

10

MATRIMONY AND REBELLION: MASCULINITY IN MAU MAU[1]

Luise White

One way to think about the 1940s in Africa is that those years included an attempt to refashion African men. There had been many efforts to transform African masculinity into something more disciplined, and more domestic, starting earlier, but this had mainly been the domain of missionaries (Strayer 1978; Shaw 1995; Hunt 1999). Starting in the 1940s, though, there were worldwide colonial concerns about masculinity. They were not stated exactly in those terms, of course, but as Fred Cooper points out in this volume (see also White 1990), there was a desire to create urban homes for urban Africans, men—and the women who would passively help them transform into something better—who had stable, skilled lives and a stake in urban respectability, wage labor, and the orderly running of urban and, indeed, national life.

Recent scholarship (White 1990; Cooper 1996; Thomas 1996; Robertson 1997; Barnes 1999; Lindsay, Hodgson, and Mann in this volume) has shown that this was not an imported piece of top-down colonial social engineering. African men were not in some passive, untransformed state until the 1940s. African men had their own visions of what a man should be, and they had debated them actively, and passionately, for generations: John Lonsdale has done a better job than anyone else of showing how, in central Kenya, that debate reached a new, politicized intensity in the late 1940s and early 1950s (Lonsdale 1992). My argument in this chapter is that one context in which men debated the conduct of masculinity was in the Mau Mau rebellion of the

1950s. There, I argue, the debates were not simply about reclaiming land and the best ways it could be redistributed, but about marriage, fatherhood, domestic labor, and all the things it meant to be a man.

The sources I use for this are a specifically Kenyan autobiographical form, Mau Mau memoirs. These are typical of war memoirs from Zimbabwe or Namibia, and they are mainly written by men (see Likimani 1985 for a dubious and fictionalized exception). A few Mau Mau activist authors were "discovered" by a foreign scholar who edited their stories, and these became very complicated texts. The best example is Donald Barnett's 1966 endeavor to make Karari Njama's story a coherent picture of "the Movement," while Njama uses the text to legitimate and democratize Dedan Kimathi's hierarchical Kenya Parliament.

With the laudable exception of Marshall Clough (1998), these books have not figured in academic studies of Mau Mau (Rosberg and Nottingham 1966; Throup 1987; Maughan-Brown 1986; Lonsdale 1992; Kanogo 1987a; Furedi 1989; Maloba 1993), in part because of intellectuals' distrust of popular literature and in part because these autobiographies are often so intensely personal that they contain more information about a man's private life than they do about Mau Mau. This is the very reason, of course, that I find these books such excellent sources with which to examine African men's ideas about African masculinity. In these books, men wrote about defining gender, about courtship, about whose task it was to cook, and fetch water. They wrote about being husbands, lovers, and fathers, gender roles that were an integral part of their political struggles.

As Cooper, Lindsay, and Brown show in this volume, these men were not alone in thinking about male genders in Africa. This was a continent-wide postwar obsession, but in Kenya it took the form of anxieties about the kinds of political culture migrant labor engendered. The short version of the idea was that men living together, in dormitories or hostels, bred crime and dissent; married men were fulfilled and complacent. According to such policies an African man with no one to talk to, no helpmate, no companion, was a man in danger, not from his sexual desires—which could be met by prostitutes—but from his emotional needs. Such a man would be drawn to political action because there was no home life to contain him. The estranged African man, drifting into militancy because there was no one to talk to, was a potent colonial fantasy. Journalists and scholars attributed just such qualities to Jomo Kenyatta in the early 1950s: Peter Abrahams, to show how his despair led him to lead Mau Mau, and David Throup, to show how marginal he was to postwar politics in Kenya. "He had no friends. There was no one in the tribe who could give him the intellectual companionship that had become so important to him in his years in Europe" (Abrahams 1960; see also Throup 1985, 1987). The colonial fantasy of what the lonely man might do was equaled by the political fantasy of what a wife could do for an African man. An educated wife, wrote the governor in 1939, would give her husband someone to talk to, and he would not go out and talk dissent with his fellows (White 1990: 142). Within a few years, officials claimed that the happiest and healthiest migrants had their wives with them in town (White 1990: 223–4). The psychologist who explained Mau Mau—even as it was going on—linked it to migrancy, and wives left behind and children disturbed when their mothers and fathers had different values (Carothers 1953: 9–10, 23–4). Married men were happier; their wives contained them.

I argue that Mau Mau challenged these notions to their very core. During Mau Mau the educated men and skilled workers who fought in the forest wanted companionate marriages: one wife with whom to share all they experienced. The illiterate, unskilled Mau Mau army, the Kenya Riigi, banned rank and relationships. The state's belief that a respectable working class was one that would be restrained by marriage and cohabitation was taken over and inverted by a generation of men the state called terrorists. The response of colonialists—in the 1950s a timely combination of officials, missionaries, and the Special Branch—was to dismantle the gender in revolt. Eighty thousand African men were jailed during Mau Mau, and one of several marks of their rehabilitation was their willingness to do women's work in the detention camps.

REBELS' LOVE

In postwar Central Kenya the official debate about gender, sexuality, and the precise nature of companionate marriage—whether or not it calmed men out of protest—was joined by African men, with conviction and substantially more dissent than had been seen in the colonial administration. There is not enough evidence to say with any certainty if these were colonial ideas taken over by Africans or if these were African ideas taken over by colonialists, but it also hardly matters: these ideas were in the air, sites of struggle and resistance in which many people, black and white, acted.

According to the autobiographies of participants, Mau Mau practice and organization in Nairobi involved married and bachelors' quarters, stabilization of the labor force, and the illusion of family life in ways undreamed of by postwar officialdom. For example, single men did not drive each other into activism by grumbling, but by trying to protect themselves and each other. The most apolitical roommates took Mau Mau oaths, willingly, so that no one could be accused of harboring a loyalist (Kabiro 1973: 54–5). But it was in the dense forest that separated the Kikuyu reserve from the settled areas of the Rift Valley that Mau Mau experimented with and reconstructed gender relations and the myths and rituals around them. Usually men went into the forest alone, but sometimes couples went together, and occasionally unmarried women went alone. It was said that 15,000 Kikuyu went into the forest, which they used as a staging ground for raids that were often ill-advised and, after mid-1953, were little more than attempts to secure food and ammunition.

There is no narrative history of Mau Mau from 1952 to 1956, let alone one of the operations in the forest. A political chronology might read: December 1952, leaders in the forest; June 1953, breakup of the joint leadership of Dedan Kimathi and Stanley Mathenge; February 1954, Kenya Parliament and probably Kenya Riigi formed; February–March 1955, surrender negotiations; October 1956, Kimathi captured; December 1956, British Army withdrawn. I want to suggest another, gendered chronology: December 1952, leaders in the forest; July 1953, first conference called to insist on monogamous marriage; August 1953, women given warrior status; March 1954, Mathenge's Kenya Riigi banned sexual relations in the forest; March 1955, Dedan Kimathi made prime minister of the East African Empire in a Kenya Parliament ceremony in which his lover, Wanjiru, was made his queen, "Knight Commander of Gikuyu and Mumbi" (Barnett and Njama 1966: 449–58; Wachanga 1975: 24–9, 35–8, 96–103). Mau Mau issued many more statements about the nature and proper organization of marriage than it did about land or freedom.

Monogamy and companionate marriage were not the arrangements men and women took with them into the forest. According to Jomo Kenyatta, polygyny proved a man's worth, "his capacity to look after the interests of the tribe" (Kenyatta 1937: 169), but in the forest leaders and generals did not take more than one wife at a time. There were not enough women, after all. Starting in July 1953, however, the forest fighters split along the same lines that divided men in the wider society, or at least in Nairobi's labor markets: literacy, skill level, respect for rank and hierarchy, and differential access to cohabitation. Among the forces loyal to Kimathi, there was a new emphasis on monogamous marriage in which all women were to be married and live with their husbands, separate from unmarried men. Some said women chose their mates (Barnett and Njama 1966: 221–2, 227).

Literacy divided the forest fighters far more than marriage did. By late 1953 most of the considerable intelligence security forces had obtained came from the very bitter enmity between the literate and illiterate factions (Clayton 1976: 34–5). When that enmity became institutionalized, the Kenya Riigi claimed that they represented the majority of Kenyans and that the literates' leadership in the Kenya Parliament was illegitimate and autocratic, that they were too Europeanized. The Kenya Parliament responded by accusing the illiterates of the same thing the state accused Mau Mau of—reliance on witchdoctors, magic, and regional loyalties (wa Kinyatti 1987; Barnett and Njama 1966: 335, 397–401; Wachanga 1975: 41–3). Very little attention has been paid to Mau Mau's initial ability and subsequent failure to contain both its literate and oral factions (but see Lonsdale 1992; Clough 1998), but ideas about writing and ideas about love and marriage seem to have been intertwined among the Kenya Parliament's leadership. Thirty years after his execution it was said that Dedan Kimathi proposed to his wife—not Wanjiru—by writing her three letters. She could never understand why her neighbor could not "communicate his tender feelings by word of mouth rather than write love letters. But that was his way" (Mutahi 1986: 15).

Among Kenya Parliament forces, marriage and hierarchy were intimately entwined. Kimathi's appointed commander on Mt. Kenya, General China, had been a dormitory dweller all his working life, from the railway to the King's African Rifles. He had a wife with whom be had rarely lived until she joined him in restriction in Marsabit, but by his own account he demanded a fearsome monogamy among his soldiers starting early in 1954: all ranks had to make public even contemplated adultery. More importantly, he conflated rank and gender and made courtship subject to rank: no officer could "play about with girls in front of his soldiers," nor could he "hunt for a girl but must meet her through our women commanders" (Itote 1967: 288–300).

After mid-1953, the Kenya Parliament insisted on hierarchy and monogamous marriage, while the Mathenge forces practiced no marriage at all. The Kenya Riigi spurned ranks altogether; they used the term "big leader." When Karari Njama, one of three men and two women in the forest with a secondary school education, visited Mathenge as Kimathi's secretary, he chided him for not having his own kitchen; Mathenge replied that he liked to eat in the company of his soldiers (Barnett and Njama 1966: 290). A close reading of Mau Mau memoirs indicates that Kenya Riigi men did have sexual relations with Kenya Riigi women, without the twenty-four lashes their rules demanded (Gikoyo 1979: 169; Barnett and Njama 1966: 292, 428), but those relations were never institutionalized in any way. Kenya Riigi men and women often fought side by side, but they lived separately and never described themselves as couples. One Kenya Riigi man referred to the woman he later married as his "co-fighter" (Gikoyo 1979: 244). In postwar colonial social engineering, families were a reward allocated by the state to a select few. Mau Mau, whatever else it did, took the allocation of family life out of colonial hands and put it under African control. The Kenya Riigi did not give themselves relationships; they consciously chose to do without the very thing the state had withheld from them during their working lives.

Kenya Parliament marriages were monogamous, egalitarian, and contentious. Mau Mau had joint men and women's councils "where women's voices were heard," and the women who fought in the forest claimed "there was no man or woman leader," as gender was immaterial (Kanogo 1987a: 147). Indeed, "killing people like [Chief] Waruhiu was the work of women and girls" (Presley 1986b: 255). In the early days of the struggle men and women often performed each other's customary tasks: in the camps near Nairobi men brought water in automobiles; elsewhere, women who sometimes cooked went armed with men on raids. Men nurtured women, "giving us strength to fight" (Presley 1986b: 252–5; 1988, 502–7). But starting in mid-1954 the Kenya Parliament issued proclamations to correct deviations in the sexual division of labor, demanding that women cook and gather firewood for men, regardless of their rank. "It is wrong to send men to fetch water and gather firewood when there are women to do it" (wa Kinyatti 1987: 34). At about the same time, however, the Kenya Riigi insisted that men do women's work and administered an oath asking forest fighters to abandon any leader who "did not participate in fetching food and firewood, building his own hut or carrying his own luggage" (Barnett and Njama 1966: 479–81). Many of the struggles within Mau Mau were about housework.

It was not just marriage that was contested in Mau Mau; gender relations were part of the struggle to be sure, but so was the definition of gender. General China wrote that after the bloody and unpopular Lari Massacre the joint committee of Mt. Kenya and Nyandarua troops debated whether loyalist women and children should be killed. The debate centered on defining women, and establishing how they were different from men. Were they primarily mothers or companions? Some argued that since women socialized their children, a loyalist widow could turn her children against her husband's killers, but others said that women, who "work and think like a man," should be captured and reeducated. In late 1953 women argued for a gender-specific notion of motherhood and equal rights with men: China's secretary, a woman with a year or two of secondary schooling, claimed that while "we no longer live in the days when a woman could not eat meat before men," no woman, however militant, could let another woman's child "die of hunger when our own children are eating—in this way we are not at all like men. Even white women" fed hungry children. Others agreed and told the story of the great famine in which only women survived, hid in the forest, and rebuilt the Kikuyu tribe by capturing men and forcing them to stay until they all became pregnant (Itote 1967: 61–70). The new comradeship in arms of Kikuyu men and women in the forest did not remove women from all domestic relationships, but it did infuse those relationships with new meanings and new powers.

There does not seem to have been much debate about the role of men in parenting after 1953, although an army of the Kenya Parliament suggested that they establish a fund to support orphans in 1954 (wa Kinyatti 1987: 38; Presley 1986b: 253). Women provided childcare for the very few children in the forest, but, for the most part, mothers lived there as wives. Where husbands and wives went on armed patrols together, their children lived with maternal or paternal grandparents in the reserve. Wives could be warriors, but mothers could not: if a woman became pregnant in the forest, she "lost the rifle" and "her male partner was subjected to punitive chores" (Presley 1986b: 253).

Companionate marriage had a vital meaning to men in the forest: a Mau Mau hymn called upon men to divorce their wives if their wives left the forest (wa Kinyatti 1980: 94). Like many observers of African society in the early 1950s, Mau Mau held that couples should not disagree. But women in the forest seem to have valued their status as companions with identities separate from those of their spouses. When Kimathi's lover Wanjiru was captured in 1956, she raged against being called "Kimathi's woman" rather than by her own name (Henderson 1958: 149–50). Indeed, the male, internal criticism leveled at Wambui, the executioner for Nakuru's Mau Mau Court, had nothing to do with her politics or her maternal skills, but that she refused to remarry: "she could not be ruled, she knew everything . . . she could easily kill a useless husband" (Kanogo 1987b: 94).

One way to look at all of these ideas about gender is that these were the social rearrangements of women and men in intense crisis; another way to look at these ideas is that Mau Mau was the movement of women and men whose definitions of gender were in intense crisis. In such an atmosphere—one that we know about from sources written and sung by men—women were discussed almost abstractly, but for men in Mau Mau the debate about their own gender was practical, complicated, and often painful. Men discussed how gender roles should be defined and how familial responsibilities were apportioned. Kiboi Murithi, who fought with General Tanganyika's forces vaguely affiliated with the Kenya Parliament, chided a fellow soldier for thinking of his family—"How can you be married if you never see your wife and totos?"—even as he admitted that he worried about his mother. His comrade rebuked him: "Shame! Mothers have daughters to look after them. The old wazee are always there to see if they're all right" (Murithi and Ndoria 1971: 61).

The most detailed authority on forest life, Karari Njama, was himself somewhat stodgy on sexual matters and never got over his initial dislike of women in the forest. Yet he and others chronicle, in Njama's case in spite of himself, how men grappled with their own weakening self-image as providers for and protectors of women until it was discarded, by Kenya Riigi and Kenya Parliament alike, by late 1954. Shortly before the ceremony installing Kimathi and Wanjiru, Njama lamented that "we were starving of food and cold and had failed to support ourselves. How then could one support a family?" He had already written his wife, sending some money and warning her "not to expect any sort of help from me for the next ten year's time . . . to take care of herself and our beloved daughter. I trained myself to think of the fight, and the African government." But the sense of women's potential for autonomy was so strong in the forest that Wanjiru was installed in a ceremony that named her previous Mau Mau lovers and praised how she had managed to flee from bomber fire many times over (Barnett and Njama 1966: 4–50, 434–7).

WHITE SKIN, BLACK MASK

African male genders, and the proper conduct thereof, were not the only contest during Mau Mau. To defeat the revolt, white men donned old clothes and black face, yellowed their eyes with a diluted potassium solution, and accompanied Kikuyu countergangs into the forest in broad daylight. It was said that the soldiers in the Kenya Regiment did this best, since they could speak Swahili and perhaps some Kikuyu. The intimacy of counter-insurgency did more than trouble ideas about race and class; it disrupted notions of gender. So fluid were notions of the counter-insurgents' gender that a widespread settler rumor had it that one British pseudo—as the whites in the counter-gangs called themselves—adopted a Kikuyu baby orphaned in forest action and brought it up as his own child (Best 1979: 192; see also Baldwin 1957: 164–8; Henderson 1958: 149–51; Kitson 1960: 171). White men's appropriating the maternal work of African women did not end there. In 1959, shortly after the last detention camp was closed, two white policemen, Robert Griffiths of the General Service Unit and Patrick Shaw of the Special Branch (in which he was to remain well into the 1980s), founded Starehe Boys Centre to raise and educate Nairobi's vagrant boys (Iliffe 1987: 187).

Intimacy permeated every level of counter-insurgency. In Mau Mau, with its mass oaths, every Kikuyu was suspect. Starting in mid-1952, the only Kikuyu speakers considered trustworthy enough for official translations were white. One was the son of a settler, the other the son of a missionary; both claimed to be Kikuyu and both became experts on Mau Mau. Indeed, much of the construction of Mau Mau comes from these two men. One was Ian Henderson, the son of a Scottish immigrant who grew up on his father's farm in Nyeri. He was undistinguished at school and was saved from a career as a Nairobi traffic cop when the Special Branch discovered he spoke Kikuyu fluently. He translated the Kenya African Union rally at Nyeri in 1952, much of which was used at Kenyatta's trial at Kapenguria. He interrogated General China after his capture and translated at some of the negotiation meetings. He led the "hunt for Kimathi" in the Aberdares, often in blackface. He had enough information about forest life to present Kimathi and Wanjiru as Hitler and Eva Braun—perverted, dependent, and pathologically jealous (Henderson 1958: 151). He had so successfully created Kimathi as a villain that two months after Kimathi's capture British troops were withdrawn from the forest.

Louis Leakey was the son of a CMS missionary who claimed, "In language and in mental outlook I was more Kikuyu than English, and it never occurred to me to act other than as a Kikuyu" (Leakey 1952: 32). He was a world-renowned archeologist in the early 1950s, and, within two months of the assassination of Chief Waruhiu, he began to explain Mau Mau to the wider world and the British army. He translated Kikuyu for the Kapenguria trial, at which knowledge of Kikuyu was such a key issue that a Luo politician was acquitted, not because he was innocent, but because he did not speak Kikuyu and therefore could not have organized Mau Mau (Kaggia 1975: 138). Leakey was one of the architects of how Kikuyu could be rehabilitated in detention. He designed the pipeline through which 80,000 Kikuyu passed from detention to stages of rehabilitation between 1953 and 1959. Leakey was never deported from Kenya, but his Kikuyu-ness was not lost on Mau Mau: in 1954 his elderly cousin was buried alive by forces loyal to Mathenge, a story of human sacrifice that settlers and rebels told with detailed self-righteousness (Wachanga 1975: 43; Blundell 1964: 11; Majdalany 1963: 244).

The issue is not how African Henderson or Leakey actually were, of course, but that they were the men whose Kikuyu-ness colonial officials could trust. Men in the forest could not be trusted, however much officials had tried to transform them in the past, and the men who surrendered and joined counter-gangs were considered cowardly, soft, and fickle—in a word, unmanly: "They had surrendered because they could not take it" (Henderson 1958: 37; see also Baldwin 1957: 174–5; Stoneham 1955: 129). Colonial officials provided the fantasies that made the revolt, which was unlikely to attract much metropolitan support in any case, appear more brutal, more bloodthirsty, more frightening than it actually was. The propaganda campaign was at least as intense as the military one and stood in imaginative contrast to the settlers' eyewitness accounts, which portrayed Kikuyu as vain, sadistic children (Maughan-Brown 1986: 77–92). Officials' boyish fantasies of African sexuality added menstrual blood—called "monthlies" in official dogma (Kanogo 1987a: 86)—and severed members to the Mau Mau oaths, which, a medical doctor told a Parliamentary Delegation in 1954, drove Kikuyu mad: "they just kill on being instructed to kill—their own mother, their own baby" (Majdalany 1963: 166–7; see also Corfield 1960: 163–70; Blundell 1964: 171).

But attempts to portray Mau Mau as sadistic savages (with or without the menstrual blood) failed precisely because of the way rehabilitation was envisioned. Examined from the optic of postwar colonial policies, Mau Mau and its repression were a specific dialectical debate about the very issues that were galvanizing the rest of the continent—the nature of manhood, the role of wives, the meaning of marriage. Elsewhere, this debate took the form of the extent to which an African labor force could or should be stabilized (Cooper 1987). The repression of Mau Mau was so extraordinary because it was a complicated, deliberate attempt to dismantle a vision of gender so lovingly engineered by colonial officials.

COOKING, CLEANING, AND MASCULINITY

Families had backfired. Not only did wives not tranquilize their husbands; they seemed to have made them more rebellious. Women raised children "to follow the Mau Mau creed," so their rehabilitation was critical "if the next generation is to be saved," but the considerable efforts of the colonial state went to rehabilitate men. Officials went to Malaya to study rehabilitation there and came back with a model other officials later called a vision of public school, detention camps emphasizing "hard work, washing, discipline, and games" (Rosberg and Nottingham 1966: 338; Presley 1988; Stoneham 1955: 68, 133). These ideas had a certain charm as a way to deal with people who were said to be willing to kill their own children on command, but as important as the ideology was the scale on which it was carried out. In all there were fifty-six camps for screening, detention, and works; they were firmly under the control of the Ministry for Community Development.

Rehabilitation was to do through detention camps what colonial capitalism had prevented male migrant labor from doing for itself: removing men from their families, socializing them in new norms, and returning them to family life as a reward for their hard work and new discipline. It was a way of constructing a single male gender without class divisions. Starting in the 1920s in Kenya, the paltry attempts to house and make permanent skilled workers began the construction of two male genders—one more skilled, richer, healthier, and presumably happier—the other, tolerably weak in body and spirit, with a sordid social life. In the forest, skilled literate men had stable, companionate marriages and illiterates had no wives and communal kitchens. In other words, literate men and illiterate men (those who while in the work force lived in dormitories) had separate and distinct social lives with separate and distinct ideologies of marriage, domestic life, and the responsibilities therein. The cure for Mau Mau was to dissolve the two genders. Dormitory life was the punishment, marriage was the reward earned by hard work, but this time the reward was for all men.

As a system for manufacturing a certain kind of African man, the camps worked well. All detainees were to receive a "moral and political re-education" to counteract the Mau Mau oath. In theory the unjustly accused and the rehabilitated were sent home. For those who remained in the camps, detention attempted to reconstruct Kikuyu manhood as a progression: a pipeline grading a hard core of black (men who refused to cooperate or confess at all) to intermediate grey to white was developed. Most detainees commented on the symbolism of the color codes (Kariuki 1963: 89; Muchai 1973: 55). Detainees were often first taken to screening camps, where their degree of involvement was ascertained by less than voluntary methods (Blundell 1964: 198–9; Mathu 1974: 62–4). Without formal charges, men had to confess, at least to taking one of the first Mau Mau oaths, so that their cure could begin. If men confessed—and the greatest care and determination was taken to see that they did—they were moved to special detention camps where their re-education began in earnest: they learned crafts and heard lectures by loyalists and former Mau Mau. Detainees' ideals about gender and family were different from those that had obtained in the forest. One Mathenge supporter told the woman who had fought alongside him in the forest what to say in her confession (Gikoyo 1979: 101–2).

Cooperative detainees could go on to work camps, where discipline and re-education continued—often in the form of beatings—but where they could receive visits from their families (Rosberg and Nottingham 1966: 334–42; Clayton 1976: 16–7, 49–52). And by then, a great many men had been changed. They resented or were saddened by their wives' independence while they had been away, and the visits of loved ones often broke many detainees faster than years of beatings had done. Seeing their wives and siblings often "demoralized many detainees: it left them feeling that they had been cheated; that they had wasted the best years of their lives." Most painful of all were the children their wives had had while they were in the forest or in detention. In confessing adultery, wives often made themselves secondary to other familial ties: "In many such cases wives let their mothers-in-law see their sons first so they could break the horrible news" (Wamweya 1975: 196–7).

Other men changed in unexpected ways. Educated detainees taught illiterates to read in the camps; Manyani "was one big literacy class," as were Tiola and Lodwar. J.M. Kariuki ran a huge primary school at Saiyusi in Lake Victoria. Those who could read and write Kikuyu and Swahili were taught to read English (Kariuki 1963: 141; Wamweya 1975: 185; Muchai 1973: 60; Wachanga 1975: 143; wa Wanjau 1988: 161–7). New bonds were created according to who taught whom English: General China claimed that Kenyatta taught him the language (Itote 1967: 212–7). The greatest division within Mau Mau was leveled in detention. Kahinga Wachanga cooperated in 1959 and was made a supervisor of a works project at Hola Open Camp. Sounding very much like a community development officer himself, Wachanga boasted about his supervisory position, his salary, and the crops grown in the irrigation scheme and noted that the new processes of accumulation favored the married, not necessarily the skilled and literate. Four acres of land were given to detainees who brought their families to the Open Camp, and two acres were given to detainees who did not (Wachanga 1975: 152; Mwanamwende n.d.: 18–9). Unskilled and semi-skilled detainees earned two-thirds to one-third less than supervisors and built the family housing for the camp (Muchai 1973: 70–1). The new men were given every opportunity to flourish.

Detention was a violent, expensive version of everyday life. Kariuki, who took 2,800 shillings into detention with him, described the severity of the beatings, how goods were bought and sold, how information was presented and evaluated. What made detention different from everyday life was that men did women's work—the very labor that some men had struggled valiantly against in the forest. The state did not provide laundresses, or cooks, or cleaners; detainees did those tasks. Money was not the object; detainees were paid more (sometimes in tokens and sometimes in cash) than women employees would have earned (Clayton 1976: 15–6; White 1990: 152–4, 186–8). All Mau Mau memoirs remark on the ironies of men's detention camp labors. At Lokitaung, Jomo Kenyatta, who had been detained because he was believed to have organized Mau Mau, was declared "unfit for hard labor" and given the task of cooking for the other detainees (Kaggia 1975: 139). At Athi River, cleaning and cooking duties were rotated through the four hard-core compounds (Mathu 1974: 67). Cooking and gathering fire-wood were required of the hard core on Manda Island (wa Wanjau 1988: 45). At the work camps in Kiambu men carried water cans, which, according to a man who had not been in the forest, "men, in all the history of our tribe, had never learned" (Mwanamwende n.d.: 28). In Manyani in 1954, cooking was a punishment for the hard core; these men had never cooked before and took hours to prepare dinner (Kariuki 1963: 95; Wamweya 1975: 84; wa Wanjau 1988: 8).

By 1956, when there were about 20,000 men still in detention and a coher-ent policy to accelerate confessions with "compelling force" (Rosberg and Nottingham 1966: 342–3), women's work was sought after by even the most uncooperative detainees. The hard core at Manda had to be weaned from kitchen work with reduced pay (wa Wanjau 1988: 167). At Manyani in that same year detainees were elected to the cooking staff, as candidates from their district: "kitchen work was the one duty in Manyani every detainee had his eye on." Men accused of any loyalist activity could not get elected. It had become so important that it was "the one place where one could win popular-ity or dislike for himself." Joram Wamweya, during his second, more cooper-ative stay at Manyani starting in 1956, took pride in his skills as a soup server and knew that others appreciated his impartiality. He wrote about the care he took to fill each soup measure full, about his scalded fingers, about how he "graduated in soup serving" (Wamweya 1975: 181–3).

This was not simply a man in a specific context performing women's work with dignity and self-confidence; it was the transformation of women's work from punishment into a way men could serve other men, through hard work and discipline. Dormitory life blurred any gender-specific concept of domesticity—a concept that had been intensely debated and contested in the forest. In detention, men performed women's work with pride and discipline to calm and to please and to silence other men, the very thing women had failed to do a few years before. Here was detention at work. Mau Mau memoirs con-tain numerous examples of detainees making homes for themselves—sharing cooking tasks, sewing, and cleaning cells, kitchens, and offices of the staff who ordered their beatings (Kariuki 1963: 96–7; Muchai 1973: 64; Mathu 1974: 77–8; wa Wanjau 1988: 76, 154–60). By 1956 or 1957, by which time many of the hard core had been in detention for years, they worked hard at making themselves and their fellows comfortable, without overt cooperation, confession, or ever thinking of themselves as anything but hard core (Kariuki 1963: 164–5; Mucahi 1973: 71; wa Wanjau 1988: 198–203).

CONCLUSIONS

This essay is perhaps less about Mau Mau as a unique movement than it is about a gendered reading of the literature Mau Mau has generated as a debate about masculinity, and how conflicts around that masculinity formed colonial and anti-colonial policies in the late 1940s and early 1950s. I do not doubt that Mau Mau was about land and freedom, of course, but it was also about marriage, masculinity, and how household chores might be allocated in the new relationships open rebellion engendered. The politics of Mau Mau were not only the politics of peasant revolt, but of everyday life, of childcare and male responsibility and who would cook and clean. And it was these politics that the repression of Mau Mau addressed with great force, in which men could rehabilitate themselves by living without women and by doing domestic chores until they too could re-enter society, calmed and cleansed of the ideas about marriage and domesticity they had taught themselves while in revolt.

NOTE

1. This is a reworking and updating of some of the material in "Separating the Men from the Boys: Constructions of Sexuality, Gender and Terrorism in Central Kenya, 1939–1959," *International Journal of African Historical Studies* 23, 1 (1990): 1–25.

REFERENCES

Published

Abrahams, Peter. 1960. "The Blacks." In *An African Treasury*. Langston Hughes, ed. New York: Crown Publishers. 40–59.

Baldwin, William. 1957. *Mau Mau Manhunt: The Adventures of the Only American to Fight Terrorists in Kenya*. New York: Doubleday.

Barnes, Teresa A. 1999. *"We Women Worked So Hard:" Gender, Urbanization, and Social Reproduction in Colonial Harare, Zimbabwe*. Portsmouth: Heinemann.

Barnett, Donald and Karari Njama. 1966. *Mau Mau from Within*. New York: Monthly Review Press.

Best, Nicholas. 1979. *Happy Valley*. London: Andre Deutsch.

Blundell, Michael. 1964. *So Rough a Wind*. London: Macmillan.

Carothers, J.C. 1953. *The Psychology of Mau Mau*. Nairobi: Government Printer.

Clayton, Anthony. 1976. *Counter-insurgency in Kenya*. Nairobi: Transafrica.

Clough, Marshall S. 1998. *Mau Mau Memoirs: History, Memory and Politics*. Boulder, CO: Lynne Reinner.

Cooper, Frederick. 1987. *On the African Waterfront: Urban Disorder and the Transformation of Work in Colonial Mombasa*. New Haven, CT: Yale University Press.

———. 1996. *Decolonization and African Society. The Labor Question in French and British Africa*. Cambridge: Cambridge University Press.

Corfield, F. 1960. *Survey of the Origins of Mau Mau*. Nairobi: Government Printer.

Furedi, Frank. 1989. *The Mau Mau War in Perspective*. London: James Currey.

Gikoyo, Gucu G. 1979. *We Fought for Freedom*. Nairobi: Kenya Literature Bureau.

Henderson, Ian. 1958. *Man Hunt in Kenya*. New York: Doubleday

Hughes, Langston, ed. 1960. *An African Treasury*. New York: Hougton-Mifflin.

Hunt, Nancy Rose. 1999. *A Colonial Lexicon: Of Birth Ritual, Medicalization, and Mobility in Belgian Congo*. Durham, NC: Duke University Press.

Iliffe, John. 1987. *The African Poor*. Cambridge: Cambridge University Press.

Itote, Warihiru. 1967. *"Mau Mau" General*. Nairobi: Heinemann.

Kabiro, Ngugi. 1973. *Man in the Middle*. Life Histories from the Revolution, Vol. 2. Richmond, BC: Liberation Support Movement.

Kaggia, Bildad. 1975. *The Roots of Freedom*. Nairobi: Kenya Literature Bureau.

Kanogo, Tabitha. 1987a. *Squatters and the Roots of Mau Mau*. London: James Currey.

———. 1987b. "Kikuyu Women and the Politics of Protest: Mau Mau." In *Images of Women in Peace and War*, Sharon MacDonald, Pat Holden, and Shirley Ardner, eds. 87–102. Madison: University of Wisconsin Press.

Kariuki, Josiah. 1963. *"Mau Mau" Detainee*. Harmondsworth: Penguin Books.

Kenyatta, Jomo. 1937. *Facing Mount Kenya*. London: Secker and Warburg.

Kitson, Frank. 1960. *Gangs and Counter-gangs*. London: Barrie and Rockliffe.

Leakey, L.S.B. 1952. *Mau Mau and the Kikuyu*. London: Methuen.

Likimani, Muthoni. 1985. *Passbook Number F.47927: Women and Mau Mau in Kenya*. London: Macmillan.

Lonsdale, John. 1992. "The Moral Economy of Mau Mau: Wealth, Poverty and Civic Virtue in Kikuyu Political Thought." In *Unhappy Valley: Conflict in Kenya and Africa*, Book 2: *Violence and Ethnicity*, Bruce Berman and John Lonsdale, eds., pp. 315–504. Oxford: James Currey.

MacDonald, Sharon, Pat Holden, and Shirley Ardner. 1987. *Images of Women in Peace and War*. Madison, WI: University of Wisconsin Press.

Majdalany, Fred. 1963. *State of Emergency*. Boston: Little, Brown.

Maloba, Wunyabaru O. 1993. *Mau Mau and Kenya: An Analysis of a Peasant Revolt*. Bloomington, IN: Indiana University Press.

Mathu, Mohammed. 1974. *The Urban Guerilla*, Life Histories from the Revolution, Vol. 3. Richmond, BC: Liberation Support Movement.

Maughan-Brown, David. 1986. *Land, Freedom and Fiction*. London: Zed Books.

Muchai, Karigo. 1973. *The Hardcore*, Life Histories from the Revolution, Vol. 1. Richmond, BC: Liberation Support Movement.

Murithi, Kiboi and Peter Ndoria. 1971. *War in the Forest*. Nairobi: East African Literature Bureau.

Mutahi, Wahome. 1986. "The Letters Dedan Kimathi Wrote." *Daily Nation*, July 25, p. 15.

Mwanamwende, K. n.d. [1985] *My Life in Detention Camps*. Privately printed, n.p. [probably Nairobi].

Okihiro, Gary Y., ed. 1986. *In Resistance: Studies in African, Caribbean, and Afro-American History*, Amherst, MA: University of Massachusetts Press.

Presley, Cora Ann. 1986a. "Kikuyu Women and the Mau Mau Rebellion." In *In Resistance: Studies in African, Caribbean, and Afro-American History*, Gary Y. Okihiro, ed. pp. 115–37. Amherst, MA: University of Massachusetts Press.

———. 1988. "The Mau Mau Rebellion, Kikuyu Women and Social Change." *Canadian Journal of African Studies* 22, 3: 502–27.

Robertson, Claire C. 1997. *Trouble Showed the Way: Women, Men and Trade in the Nairobi Area, 1890–1990*. Bloomington, IN: Indiana University Press.

Rosberg, Carl G. and John Nottingham. 1966. *The Myth of "Mau Mau."* New York: Praeger.

Shaw, Carolyn Martin. 1995. *Colonial Inscriptions: Race, Sex, and Class in Kenya*. Minneapolis, MN: University of Minnesota Press.

Stoneham, John. 1955. *Out of Barbarism*. London: Chatto and Windus.

Strayer, Robert. 1978. *The Making of Mission Communities in East Africa*. London: Heinemann.

Thomas, Lynn M. 1996. "*Ngaitana* (I Will Circumsize Myself): The Gender and Generational Politics of the 1956 Ban on Cliterodectomy in Meru, Kenya." *Gender and History* 8: 338–65.

Throup, David. 1985. "The Origins of Mau Mau." *African Affairs* 84: 399–434.

———. 1987. *Social and Economic Origins of Mau Mau*. London: James Currey.

Wachanga, H.K. 1975. *The Swords of Kirinyaga: The Fight for Land and Freedom*. Nairobi: Kenya Literature Bureau.

wa Kinyatti, Maina. 1980. *Thunder from the Mountains. Mau Mau Patriotic Songs*. London: Zed Press.

———. 1987. *Kenya's Freedom Struggle: The Dedan Kimathi Papers*. London: Zed Press.

Wamweya, Joram. 1975. *Freedom Fighter*. Nairobi: Kenya Literature Bureau.

wa Wanjau, Gakara. 1988. *Mau Mau Author in Detention*. Nairobi: Heinemann.

White, Luise. 1990. *The Comforts of Home: Prostitution in Colonial Nairobi*. Chicago: University of Chicago Press.

Unpublished

Presley, Cora Ann. 1986b. "The Transformation of Kikuyu Women and Their Nationalism." Ph.D. thesis, Stanford University.

11

GENDERED NATIONALISM: FORMS OF MASCULINITY IN MODERN ASANTE OF GHANA

Pashington Obeng

Otuo pae a, esi obarima bo. (When a musket or a gun explodes, it lands on the chest of a man.)

Akan Twi proverb for bravery

This chapter is an exploration of the cultural and historical constructions of masculinities in twentieth-century Asante, with particular reference to two moments of nationalist crisis. It focuses on the Yaa Asantewaa war of 1900 against the British and the 1954 National Liberation Movement (NLM), led by the Asante "youngmen" (*nkwankwaa*). The first revolt was directed against British colonial rule, and the second was a struggle within Ghanaian nationalism about the form of independence for the future Ghana. Both nationalist movements provided opportunities for new leaders, including women or juniors, to challenge senior men for political leadership. But while Yaa Asantewaa, a woman, effectively assumed the helm of a military confrontation with British colonizers, the youngmen of the NLM were unsuccessful in their bid for electoral support against Nkrumah's Convention People's Party (CPP).

A comparison of the two movements sheds light on the opposing, interlacing, alternating, and subversive constructions of the relations between femininity and masculinity, seniority and juniority among the Asante of Ghana. It shows both the flexibility of a gender system in which kinship ties, religious oaths, the ideology of the Golden Stool, historical contexts, and agency were implicated in Asante notions of masculinity, and the limitations placed on such flexibility. In pre-colonial Asante, the notion of senior masculinity was closely linked to men's authority over their wives, women, and junior males, as well as their bravery demonstrated in warfare. Such dominance was also expressed in senior males' accumulation of wealth (McCaskie 1981, 1995). Yet wealth alone did not guarantee the qualities of seniority: *Wode kokuroko na edi amim a, anka esoneo to fie.* ("If sheer huge size or brute force determined leadership, the elephant would be ruling at home.") Since political and military leadership was intertwined with ideologies of senior masculinity, it was unusual for a non-senior male to exercise political leadership.

Both Yaa Asantewaa and the junior men, the *nkwankwaa*, tried to take on the attributes of dominant senior masculinity—including bravery, royalty, and religious authority—to rally a unified military or electoral effort. Thus senior masculinity was not always defined exclusively by biological sex (see Amadiume 1987) or age. But although forms of masculinity may transcend a biological divide among the Asante, this is only possible in certain contexts. Yaa Asantewaa was able to embody senior masculinity in a political crisis because she was a senior person herself and because she was of a royal lineage and connected with significant religious power. The 1954 youngmen struggled to gain the authority of senior masculinity. Even though they were biologically men, they were social juniors, and their attempts to gain royal and religious legitimacy were insufficient to give them the status of senior masculinity and thus widespread political support. They did not possess the socially and historically constructed masculine attributes that would have given them the power and political influence they sought to achieve. Hence, senior masculinity relates to both biological sex and age; transcending biology to become a "senior man" may have been possible, but it was clearly difficult.

ASANTE ORATURE AND GENDER IDEOLOGIES

It is important to situate Yaa Asantewaa's and the youngmen's struggles within Asante gender ideals, which often were articulated through orature. Since the inception of the Asante nation in the seventeenth century, its orature—including war victory songs, pithy sayings, and proverbs—seemed to valorize masculine notions and behavior patterns. Most of Asante praise poetry (e.g., Arhin 1986) foregrounds men's bravery in warfare and accumulation of wealth. Beneath such stereotypes, however, Asante orature may also include attention to women's achievements and the possibility for women to act "as men."

Asante social comments and institutions tend to devalue women's roles and activities and put women with the youth in an anomalous category. At times, unspoken but dramatized forms and cultural mechanisms—such as the rites based on Asante notions of pollution regarding menstruation, childbearing, and puberty rites for girls and not for boys (see Sarpong 1977)—and socio-political systems that have ambivalent attitudes toward women and youth have portrayed an apparent asymmetrical relation between maleness and femaleness. Both Ivor Wilks (1993) and T.C. McCaskie (1995) assert that in pre-colonial Asante, male elders controlled the land, agricultural products, the production of youngmen, and the reproduction of women. Specifically, the "good citizen" (*okaniba*) according to McCaskie (1981: 486) was defined with reference to the accumulation and consumption of wealth. The underlying logic thus led to a highly ranked society in which the domestic economy included women as part of the accumulated wealth. It is not surprising that in the nineteenth century, a disgraced member of the political elite would be forced to lose his "office, gold, land, subjects, all but a few of his slaves, and all but one wife" (McCaskie 1981: 487). A man who had one wife was considered to have achieved the minimum index of citizenship. Furthermore, the jural institution of *ayefere sika*, compensatory fines for adultery, implicitly treated the woman involved as the property of her husband. The fine paid by the male offender was to compensate the husband whose property was stolen by the adulterer. Since adultery located women as goods and infidelity attracted monetary compensation to the offended husband, McCaskie (1981) contends that power relations between men and women were tilted against women. For the colonial period, Jean Allman and Victoria Tashjian emphasize the continuity of male dominance while, for example, the power of the father and husband was remade, mirroring "the authority of the nineteenth-century Asante pawn-holder" (2000: 222).

The history of pre-colonial Asante triumphalism highlights heroes engaged in a series of wars, conquering lands, taking captives, beheading some, and keeping their skulls as war trophies (Tordoff 1965; Wilks 1975; Arhin 1986; McCaskie 1995). Since war was a male preoccupation, historical accounts about Asante conquest tended to reinforce the construction of valor along the male gender. Kwame Arhin (1980) points out that all potential successors to the Asantehene's (Asante king's) stool (royal office) bore the title *barima*, which stands for a male warrior. The first Asante king, Osei Tutu, for instance, carried such titles as *Bediako* (one who came to fight) and *Katakyie* (the brave one). On public occasions, performed by drum language and ceremonial horn messages, the fearlessness and military power of the kings were evoked. In Asante praise poetry, military prowess defined a masculine ideal for Asante heroes: for example, *Obarima nsuro wuo* ("A brave man does not fear death") and *Obarimatwereboo na ne ho bon atuduru* ("The warrior or the brave man smells of gunpowder").

Such Asante oral narratives give the impression that forms of masculinity have always been essentialized and structured along a biological divide.

However, since not all men went to war, ideas about masculinity need to be further examined to unearth aspects of courage that may transcend differences between men and women. The titles *Bediako* and *Katakyie* do not necessarily refer solely to either male or female fighters. Thus, attributes of masculinity need to be historicized and contextualized.

Some sayings indicate that women could engage in warlike activities as well as men, even if such activities might be deemed inappropriate. Take, for instance, Asante explicit declaratives such as *Obaa sene bomma, ye kyem, to tuo a, etwere obarima dan mu* ("If a woman carves a drum, a shield or buys a gun all are stored in a man's house") or *Obaa ton nnuadewa, na onton atuduro* ("It is appropriate for a woman to sell garden eggs but not to indulge in the sale of gunpowder"). Although at one level, the former proverb may suggest a strict division of labor along gender lines, one historical event discussed in this chapter shows that women like Yaa Asantewaa were in a position not just to make such weapons but also to wield them. Furthermore, even though in pre-colonial Asante direct involvement in warfare was seen as the preserve of men, women participated through *mmobome*, a ritual performed by Asante women who did not go to war in ancient times (cf. Akyeampong and Obeng 1995: 492). During *mmobome*, women paraded in partial nudity while chanting to perform spiritual warfare. They pounded empty mortars with pestles to symbolically torture the enemies, or, at times, they beat discarded cooking utensils. These female public acts were an expression of solidarity with male warriors, deploying distinctive women's spiritual warfare against Asante enemies. There are also proverbs that emphasize the importance of women and others, which subvert certain displays of maleness or masculinity. *Obaa nya sika a, odane barima* translates as "When a woman becomes wealthy, she turns into a man" and indicates a certain flexibility about the attributes of masculinity. *Obaa na owoo barima* ("It is the woman who gave birth to the man") indicates that success or strength may emanate from a place that appears not to hold any promise.

Although these proverbs stem from Akan traditional lore, their meaning is, as Kwesi Yankah argues (1989a, b), determined by specific historical contexts. Gendered values and ideas appearing to be systematic may contain contradictions that allowed for women and men to provide alternative constructions and notions of gender roles in Asante society, as did Akyaawa Yikwan, who was involved in the Asante war against the British in 1824. Akan proverbial lore related to masculinity and femininity thus must be understood in a larger historical and sociocultural context. Orature as is— including proverbs, praise poetry, legends, and songs—is a flexible text for understanding changing notions about gender. When Yaa Asantewaa was praised as a "woman who could withstand cannons" (*Obaa basia a ogoro aprema ano*), the appellation was also an allusion to the Asante king's praise poem. Moreover, when the youngmen in the 1950s evoked Yaa Asantewaa's name, they were deploying Asante rhetoric about former heroic deeds and simultaneously affirming their pride, connected to this historical tale, and expressing their preparedness to resist exploitation like Yaa Asantewaa. When we contrast the above with *Obaa ton nnuadewa, na onton atuduro* ("It is appropriate for a woman to sell garden eggs but not to indulge in the sale of gunpowder"), we may glean additional gendered expectations. In Asante, like other Akan societies, one virtue of an ideal woman was to refrain from speaking publicly so as not to draw attention to herself. In "mixed-gender situations" (Yankah, 1998: 17), only men were supposed to speak. However, there is evidence about female chiefs in Akan societies who were known within court settings as orators with "expressive competence" (Yankah 1998: 18). Proverbs as encapsulated reflections do not always refer to the male–female dichotomy. Rather, the proverb comments on fluid gender roles with allusions to expectations of women in Akan traditional lore. The proverb, *Akokonini gyae akuntunakuntun, na yen nyinaa ye kesua mma* ("O, cock, stop this ostentation and bravado for we all came out of the eggshell") elaborates on this idea, reminding humans of their mortality. Hence, there is no need for anyone to be arrogant. The lessons of polyvalent proverbs—and their potential as historical sources—lie in their specific constructions of local norms and values for women, men, and places within a given society.

Proverbs and proverbial arts are attention grabbing, as they may also subvert and challenge certain cultural assumptions—for example, *Opanin wo ho ansa na wo wo hene* ("Age does not make one a chief or king"). If one does not belong to a royal family, one may be the oldest in the community, but one cannot be enstooled. Or *Esono kokuroo adowa ne panin* ("Size alone does not determine seniority") shows that if political leadership depended merely on size, the elephant would always rule over the deer. Thus among Akan societies, an eligible heir to the throne may be passed over for a younger contender because of the latter's wisdom, virtues, and personality. The proverb implies that Akan people are not taken simply by size or appearance; they know maturity and experience are more important than age and immensity not backed by substance. Moreover, proverbs may be used to embellish conversation, but they "do not guide the speakers' judgement; neither do they take over his reasoning" (Yankah 1989b: 338). Thus the force of Akan proverbs does not lie solely in their appropriate use. The audience and the users apply their own assessment by looking at all facts of a given situation to give meaning to the proverb and decipher its gendered implications.

FEMALE SENIOR MEN

The fluidity and context-driven nature of gender in Asante may be seen through reference to legendary female heroes, like Yaa Asantewaa and her precursor, Akyaawa Yikwan, who took on the military leadership roles of male elders. Wilks (1993: Chap. 10) points out that postmenopausal women formed a separate gender in nineteenth-century Asante, and indeed Akyaawa Yikwan and Yaa Asantewaa were senior women. They also marshaled royal and religious connections into a formidable challenge to Asante leaders in the context of threats from British invaders.

The Asante recall that masculine ideals were applied in the nineteenth century to the woman Akyaawa Yikwan. Akyaawa Yikwan has been described as "she who blazed a trail" (Wilks 1993: 329). C.C. Reindorf wrote that among the royal family "was one Akyiawa, a woman of masculine spirit" (1895: 198). Akyaawa, a princess, was part of the Asantehene Osei Yaw's war campaign against the British in 1824. According to Reindorf, Akyaawa's participation in this war campaign showed her as a courageous person; she was a woman of valor. She also wielded some authority derived from serving as a priestess of Taa Dwemo, an Asantehene war deity (Wilks 1993). Thus, her affiliation with this royal deity, her masculine spirit, and her postmenopausal status accorded her the capacity to taunt King Osei Yaw for pulling back his forces instead of fighting the British. Her religious status coupled with her advanced age provided legitimacy and authority for her to castigate a king who was cowardly. By implication, the Asantehene and his forces had been emasculated, whereas the princess showed masculine spirit. Ayaawa was a woman who demonstrated *abannimsem* or *akokoduru* (great courage). This was again manifested in Akyaawa's key role in negotiating peace settlements between the Asante and the British. Wilks highlights Akyaawa's great accomplishments: "It was an extraordinary invasion of a sphere that was, in Asante, all but totally male dominated. Yet the fundamental role of the Asante women was to see to the reproduction, not only in a biological but also in a social and economic sense, of her lineage" (1993: 353). Akyaawa asserted the prerogatives of male leadership, although perhaps within the discursive sphere of maternalism. Furthermore, her membership within the royal family and her position as priestess of Taa Dwemo, a royal deity, buttressed her ability to construct an "extraordinary" female masculine form. Akyaawa was one of those few women who took on men's positions in pre-colonial Asante—thus providing examples of female senior masculinity.

Just as Akyaawa in the 1820s challenged the masculinity of men in times of crisis, Yaa Asantewaa, in 1900, stirred up in men their need to pick up arms to end British domination. With the exile of the Asantehene Prempe I, his courtiers, and other prominent chiefs in 1896, the British began to entrench themselves in Asante. The Asante people grew resentful of how the British were undermining their system of government, traditions, religions, and economic activities—especially the sale and purchase of slaves (Tordoff 1965: 105; Lewin 1978: 217ff.). Despite the fact that the Asante had come close to rebelling against the British between 1898 and 1900, it was Governor Arnold Hodgson's taunt that Prempe I would never return and that the Golden Stool would be given to him (the governor) to sit on that caused decisive action. Since Hodgson and other Britons knew about the symbolic significance of the Sika Dwa Kofi (Golden Stool) to the Asante, he wanted to consummate the colonization of the Asante by owning it. Asante without a king appeared and felt like a nation in limbo, and so the governor did not expect any opposition. The governor would discover his error at great cost. At a secret meeting on the night after Hodgson's inflammatory speech, the sixty-year-old queen mother of Edweso, Yaa Asantewaa, called on the gathered male elders and the Asante nation to wage war against the British. Her words, as cited by Agnes Aidoo (1981: 75), spelled out her notions of the divide between femininity and masculinity and what was required during that national crisis: "How can a proud and brave people like the Asante sit back and look while the white-men took away their king and chiefs, and humiliated them with a demand for the Golden Stool. . . . I shall not pay one *predwan* [£8.2s] to the governor. If you, the chiefs of Asante, are going to behave like cowards and not fight, you should exchange your loincloths for my undergarments [*Montu mo danta mma me na monnya me tam*]."

This female leader of Edweso gave muscle to the "leaderless" and dispirited Asante nation. Through the challenge to the chiefs, Yaa Asantewaa—whose grandson, the Edwesohene Akwasi Afrane Kuma, had been exiled with king Prempe I—was also summoning the men and the rest of the nation to male potency to be manifested in a struggle for freedom. She is said to have whisked a rifle from a chief and fired it at the ground (Aidoo 1981: 74f.). There and then the chiefs accepted the challenge and swore an oath to fight the British. Yaa Asantewaa, wearing a leather belt and sword, provided much-needed leadership during the war. Her military challenge forced the government and Christian missionaries in Kumasi to lock themselves up in a fort as the Asante cut off their food, water, and ammunition supply. When the governor sent telegraph messages for reinforcements, the two hundred men on the way to rescue were ambushed and beaten back by Yaa Asantewaa's army. It was not until Colonel Burroughs from Sierra Leone and his battalion of the West African Regiment and other troops loyal to the British stormed Kumasi that Yaa Asantewaa was defeated. By then the war had been waged for eight months. In the end, the remaining people in the fort were released and the Asante surrendered. The leaders of the resistance, including Yaa Asantewaa, were exiled from the Gold Coast (Donkoh 2001; Lewin 1978; cf. Edgerton 1995). Yaa Asantewaa's influence was also demonstrated when Governor Hodgson wanted to negotiate with leaders of Asante. It is said that Yaa Asantewaa sent word to the governor that she would not attend the meeting and that she had her loaded gun and was giving orders to her captains in Kumasi and its surrounding towns.[1]

Yaa Asantewaa's activities and leadership need to be understood in the context of her lineage politics (Akyeampong and Obeng 1995). Yaa Asantewaa's female ancestor, Afranie I, fought and won Lake Bosomtwe for the Asantehene in the late seventeenth century (Akyeampong's field notes 1994). She brought the ethos of senior female royalty to shape and articulate Asante nationalist resistance against the British. But as the Edweso native Sarkodie-Mensah informed Emmanuel Akyeampong in 1994, male residents of Edweso after the 1900 war argued that Yaa Asantewaa was a man disguised as a woman. Such a male perspective underscores how masculinity was redefined by a woman despite the feeble attempt by the men to freeze and harden the divide between male and female in Asante. Yaa Asantewaa became the locus of male–female reconfiguration as she marshaled royal lineage, spiritual and political powers, and courage to challenge her own people to resist the British in 1900. Moreover, by meeting the challenge of her generation, Yaa Asantewaa was reformulating her identity in "relation to the cultural representations of what is male and what is female" (Moore 1996: 179).

Agnes Aidoo (1977) has argued that Akan political status was intertwined with military position, and thus rulers of territories were simultaneously military leaders for their areas. There were few times when women occupied male stools in nineteenth-century Akan societies (Arhin 1983). Among them were Dokua of Akyem Abuakwa and the Dwabenhemaa (queen mother) Ama Seiwaa who in 1843 took over as chief of Dwaben and led her people back to Asante from exile in Akyem Abuakwa (Donkoh 2001). Although, by implication, these female rulers assumed military responsibilities, this was not unproblematic. Yet, during the 1900 uprising, Yaa Asantewaa's activities went beyond those of a female ruler who dared her men to fight: she became the first female commander-in-chief, *sahene*, in Asante, and "took on the might of the technologically superior British" (Donkoh 2001: 7). Thomas Lewin (1974: 44) quotes the recollection of Kwadwo Donko, sub-chief of Asokewa: "Yaa Asantewaa was the military leader of the Asante army. She [even] appointed individuals to be leaders." As part of her role as *sahene*, Yaa Asantewaa traveled from one battlefield to another, encouraging the Asante fighters, and "supplied gunpowder" to her field commanders (Lewin 1974: 264). In an earlier conflict, the Asante civil war of 1886–1888, Afrane I, the Edwesohene, had been the king's keeper of guns, *Atufoohene* (Lewin 1974; Aidoo 1977). By 1900, it was the female occupant of the Edweso Stool, Yaa Asantewaa, who was *Atufoohene*—responsible for supplying gunpowder. No doubt this role of her being in charge of the armory contributed to the redefinition of her gendered female position as one who not only kept gunpowder but also supplied it to men—in contrast to the proverb, "Women sell garden eggs but not gunpowder." This historical context provided the proverb with new meaning. By wearing Asante battle dress and bearing a gun, Yaa Asantewaa not only subverted conventional gender folklore, but created an opening to connect ideas about masculinity with a woman.

In pre-colonial Asante military practice, commanders-in-chief sought spiritual protection and support to ensure victory. In 1900, Yaa Asantewaa consulted Asante deities, decided on strategies, and organized women to back up the efforts of the troops. In this last stand against British imperialism, Yaa Asantewaa "demonstrated unusual but outstanding leadership qualifications and qualities"; she defied Asante values that "women were to be submissive and meek (at least in public)" (Donkoh 2001: 7). Rather, as a woman, she took on the role of military leader, which was explicitly public and considered masculine. A praise poem captures Yaa Asantewaa's indomitable spirit:

> Kookoo hin ko
> Yaa Asantewaa
> The mere woman
> Who faces the cannon
> Kookoo hin ko
> Yaa Asantewaa

This poem, which is part of the oral tradition around Edweso, parallels sentiments in a praise reserved for the Asante king: *Kaekae Gyame a ode ntutua ko apremo ano* ("Kaekae Gyame who fights the cannon with the musket") (Brempong 2000). Yaa Asantewaa's valor was being compared to that of the Asante king. She became *Bekoe* (the one who fights), whose bravery was displayed not at home but in war. Thus, her biological femaleness was subsumed by her public and masculine role as war leader.

The Yaa Asantewaa war of 1900 revealed important issues about gendered nationalism and military leadership. The Akan Twi proverb cited at the beginning of the chapter is applicable here: *Otuo pae a, esi obarima bo* ("When a musket or a gun explodes, it lands on the chest of a man"). In this case, a female was valiant, the one who rose to the occasion. Despite the fact that femininity appeared to be defined and structured through marriage, motherhood, and adultery damages, and that masculinity was channeled via public office, military prowess, as well as material and social wealth, Yaa Asantewaa challenged these norms. Also, Yaa Asantewaa's example shows that individuals and groups—through cultural re-enactment, utterances, and symbolic gestures—play out notions of gender and dramatize conflicting, complementary and alternating, as well as innovative conceptions of femininity and masculinity. It was precisely during a moment of national crisis when the apparent sociopolitical malaise created a space for the power and status of senior masculinity—expressed in public military leadership—to be occupied by a woman. This chapter argues that in twentieth-century Asante established understandings of senior masculinity were challenged and reformulated. Still, they continued relating to ideas about religion, royalty, age, individual, and personality, while embedded in a context of specific historical forces at work. As Yaa Asantewaa restructured notions of masculinity in 1900, she became a heroine and symbol of national resistance to oppression;

she became a model to other movements like the NLM in challenging Nkrumah and the CPP.

YOUNG SENIOR MEN?

The social gradation in Asante tended to privilege senior men over juniors (McCaskie 1981). Since male elders wielded power as "good citizens," they determined when juniors could enter their own adulthood. Juniors, without any assets, depended on their male elders for land and other resources. In effect, while marriage was used to subjugate women, kinship ties and age were used by male elders to subordinate "youngmen," who have formed a recognized social category (*nkwankwaa*) since at least the mid-nineteenth century. But not all youngmen were literally young; rather their "youth" referred to their "subordination to elder and chiefly authority" (Allman 1993: 29). Wilks suggested that the nineteenth-century *nkwankwaa* "belonged to old and well-established families but whose personal expectations of suc-ceeding to office or even of acquiring wealth were low" (1975: 535). In the 1880s, they included radicals who refused to pay taxes and fines and engi-neered the overthrow and suicide of several Asante chiefs (Aidoo 1977: 26), including Asantehene Mensa Bonsu in 1883 (Lewin 1978; Tordoff 1965). Structurally subordinate to their elders, youngmen found it necessary to forge alliances with other Asante groups "to further their own aims, be it an end to conscription, the abolition of communal labor, a lessening in taxes, or the opening up of free trade with the coast" (Allman 1993: 30). Youngmen needed to form coalitions with rich people (*Asikafo*), the poor (*Ahiafo*), and the chiefs and other members of the ruling elite to support, legitimize, and foster their goals (cf. Wilks 1975). Other youngmen were moderates who wanted to see the coexistence of British rule and the Asante regime.[2]

After 1900, the youngmen became an important pressure group who ini-tially gained a new sense of independence under colonial rule. Anshan Li (1995) shows that the *nkwankwaa* at times helped to enforce ethical injunc-tions on their political leaders. Some youngmen, because of their Western education, experienced social mobility, occupying new positions as teachers, clerks, and accountants in European companies and the colonial bureaucracy (see Austin 1964; Allman 1993; Miescher this volume). Yet with the intro-duction of indirect rule in Asante, the political aspirations of the *nkwankwaa* were capped. In 1936, the Asante Confederacy Council officially abolished the *nkwankwaa*, including the *nkwankwaahene* (the leader of the *nkwankwaa*), although groups of youngmen continued to exist unofficially (Tordoff 1965). Since the colonial authorities considered chiefs to be the legitimate channels of communication between the Asante and themselves, that situation excluded the youngmen from greater participation in political leadership. Had the youngmen gained greater participation in colonial politics, that would have given them access to the economic opportunities foreign capital created in the country (Rathbone 1973).

However, the economic boom of the 1940s in cocoa, timber, and minerals fostered the emergence of a wide range of aspirant entrepreneurs in Asante, many of whom belonged to the *nkwankwaa*. In the following decade, the same youngmen were instrumental in the split of Nkrumah's Convention People's Party (CPP) in Asante, forming the National Liberation Movement (NLM). They had become painfully aware that the ruling CPP and foreign firms controlled the economic activities in the Gold Coast. According to Richard Rathbone, between 1940 and 1955, the NLM became the only viable channel through which "a new generation of aspirants could enter the gainful sectors of the economy" (1973: 398). Though their determination to acquire wealth was not the only motivation behind the activity of the NLM of the 1950s, economics played an important role in their struggle.

Jean Allman (1993: 8) has analyzed the activism of Asante youngmen in the NLM between 1954 and 1957 in two contexts: as a challenge to the politics of nation-building spearheaded by Prime Minister Kwame Nkrumah's CPP and as part of a local struggle with Asante "established powers." The youngmen were social and political juniors, and to meet the latter challenge, they pursued the same strategies as earlier generations of youngmen had— seeking allies. Akyeampong points out that the expulsion of 81 Asante members from Nkrumah's CPP was a major catalyst in the formation of the NLM under the Asante youngmen (1996: 132). The expelled youngmen tapped the support of Asante chiefs and local farmers who had been alienated by Nkrumah's Cocoa Duty and Development Funds (Amendment) Bill. The price fixing by Nkrumah's government prevented farmers from determining the prices of their cocoa (cf. Austin 1964: 253ff.). The NLM leadership also sought to include other ethnic groups and organizations, which helped the party to achieve national recognition.

Unlike the "class analysis" that foregrounds the social and political status of the *nkwankwaa* (Rathbone 1973; Allman 1993), this discussion focuses on the intersection of age, gender, and seniority with social and economic forces concerning constructions of masculinity. Since at least the nineteenth century, politics, age, and wealth worked hand in hand within Asante society. Unlike Yaa Asantewaa—whose royal lineage, elder status, and personal courage had enabled her to assert leadership in the form of (female) senior masculinity— the youngmen of the 1950s depended on access to wealth, seniority, and political contacts to restructure ideals of senior masculinity within the public realm.

In times of crises, Asante men have been accused of being cowardly and effeminate, as expressed by Yaa Asantewaa and, before her, by Akyaawa Yikwan, who both challenged men who did not live up to gendered social expectations. The youngmen of the 1954–57 National Liberation Movement were the modern example of those who attempted to rework notions of senior masculinity, articulated in their political struggle against Nkrumah's CPP. In addition to forging alliances, the NLM youngmen worked to appropriate the symbols of senior masculinity, such as bravery, royalty, and religious authority, which would give their movement legitimacy in the eyes of Asante voters.

Members of the NLM followed the example of Yaa Asantewaa, at times explicitly, in their attempts to exert political leadership and thereby act as senior men. Just as the Edwesohemaa Yaa Asantewaa had challenged and invited Asante chiefs to take up arms to fight the British, so leaders of the NLM encouraged its members to free themselves and resist a perceived oppression by the Convention People's Party. They, like Yaa Asantewaa, drew on spiritual forces and cultural norms such as the Great Oath of Asante. To wage war in 1900, the chiefs and Yaa Asantewaa had sworn the oath of Asante to locate and renew themselves in their heroic history, to regroup themselves and forge a future for Asante. In September 1954, the NLM and others numbering about 40,000 "gathered at the source of the sacred Subin river in Kumasi" (Allman 1993: 16). Some were clad in mourning cloth, shouting their battle cry to begin their struggle against Nkrumah; at the same time they were articulating their determination to free themselves and resist a perceived oppression and inviting the spirits of their ancestors to join in the struggle. When the youngmen inaugurated the National Liberation Movement, they tapped into Asante religion and nationalism by pouring libations, sacrificing sheep, and swearing an oath to free themselves from the apparent political and economic control of Kwame Nkrumah and the CPP. As Yaa Asantewaa had done, they seized the day to show their bravery. Confronting the perceived domination and exploitation by the Nkrumah government, the youngmen had accepted the challenge as those on whose male chest the gun or musket had burst. Spiritual forces on both occasions were deployed to redefine valor and reorder their reality. There were also lineage ties between Asantewaa and the NLM. Yaa Asantewaa, as mentioned, was the descendant of the female war leader Afranie I. Another descendant of Afranie I, Edwesohene (chief of Edweso) Nana Kwasi Afranie, was alleged to have killed Kofi Banda—a member of the Convention People's Party—in the NLM struggles (Allman 1993: 104). Banda was said to possess spiritual powers that enabled him to disappear from his enemies, and therefore many Asante people feared him.

As the youngmen realized that they could not successfully assert Asante nationalism without the support of the custodian of the Golden Stool, the Asantehene, they recruited the support of Baffour Akoto, a spokesperson for the king. Akoto's role as liaison between the Asantehene and the NLM provided royal recognition of the group. Furthermore, by 1956, the executive committee of the NLM consisted of the "new intelligentsia," such as K.A. Busia, I.B. Asafu-Adjaye, Joe Appiah, Victor Owusu, and R.R. Amponsah, who had broken ranks with Nkrumah's CPP. Apart from the fact that these men

had been a part of the long-term Gold Coast political struggle for independence and hence were politically astute, they were intellectuals with international experience and contacts. Equally important was the fact that they were
"all sons of the Golden Stool" (Allman 1993: 139), close to the palace and the
elite of Kumasi, thus providing the *nkwankwaa* with the necessary royal connections. Whereas the youngmen of the 1950s required royalty to express their
senior masculinity, Yaa Asantewaa had been senior because of her royal birth.

The stabbing death of E.Y. Baffoe, the propaganda secretary of the NLM,
fostered the establishment of a "paramilitary wing, the Action Groupers"
(Akyeampong 1996: 135) as their response to the CPP "Action Troopers."
These opposing groups fought each other with weapons in the streets of
Kumasi and its neighboring towns. The use of arms became a necessary tool
for defining both the identity and objectives of the youngmen, as military
bravery had for Asante leaders in times past. Allman provides a copy of the
leaflet that was circulated by Osei Assibey-Mensah, a member of the youngmen, in 1954 after the death of Baffoe. The leaflet's call to arms explicitly
invokes a comparison between the youngmen and Yaa Asantewaa:

> Awake
> All ye sons and daughters of
> the Great Ashanti Nation built
> with Blood by King Ossei
> Tutu and Okomfo Anokye
> The Spirit of our Great Queen Yaa Asantewa
> Calls you to ACTION
> The Quills of the Ashanti Porcupine are erect whilst we are
> being slained in cold blood. . . .
> We are doomed if we do not awake to
> fight bribery and corruption, disrespect, hooliganism . . .
> and threat of Dictatorship and Communism . . . We are
> resolute and unless we perish there will never be a second
> exile of our Golden Stool. . . .
> Emmanuel Yaw Baffoe is dead but
> his soul goes marching on . . . (Allman 1993: 59f.)

Assibey-Mensah appealed to and invoked the Asante heroic military past—a
past that included the valiant deeds of Yaa Asantewaa. The youngmen in 1954
were summoning Asante heroes and marshaling the unifying symbol of the
Golden Stool to inspire the Asante nation to fight and placed themselves
within this glorified Asante past. While Yaa Asantewaa had made more
implicit reference to Asante heroic history, the NLM youngmen were very
explicit. Both calls to action, however, were aimed at inspiring courage, an
important aspect of Asante senior masculinity, to resist and rid the Asante
nation of domination.

Despite the fact that much protest resulted from E.Y. Baffoe's murder, the strength of the youngmen waned. The Akan proverb *Enye huuhuu na ode di mmarimasem* ("It takes more than empty threats to be a man") came true in the youngmen's struggle against Nkrumah's CPP. When the NLM lost the 1956 election, its leaders conceded to the CPP. This defeat paved the way for the proclamation and implementation of the CPP vision of an independent Ghana on March 6, 1957. The original NLM members who did not have access to political office and did not hail from royal families felt abandoned by their executive board. Regarding themselves as representing the common-ers of Asante, they could not resolve the internal conflicts of the NLM. Nor were they able to galvanize the party to fight the CPP to reach the goal of political autonomy for Asante. As Allman argues, those who never had "the power, economically or politically, to go it alone. . . . [T]he youngmen were not to transcend their historical impotence as a class" (1993: 136). Or to put it in an Akan proverb, *Kontromfi kyea se akyeafo kyea, nanso ne to ye koo* ("The chimpanzee may walk with the gait as other bipeds do, but it cannot hide its identity, because of its naked brown bottom or rear"). Because the youngmen lacked economic, political, and royal might, as well as the senior-ity to defeat Nkrumah's party, they were vanquished by the Convention Peo-ple's Party.

The youngmen took the mantle of leadership to give voice to the perceived disenfranchised of the society, thus living out their notion of masculinity through the proverb *otuo pae a, esi obarima bo*. They did not shy away from what they saw as a crisis situation and Nkrumah's domination. They ended up being the men who were defeated by forces greater than they could handle. *Anomaa kokokyirika tu abirempong tu a woto no abirempong tuo* ("When the tiny bird flies like a mighty bird, the cannon is used in shooting it down"). The youngmen overstepped their political bounds by seeking the status of senior masculinity; they were crushed. They deployed the known cultural symbols of religious oath and organized themselves around issues they thought represented the interests of the Asante majority. But given the histor-ical circumstances, their "impotence" as regards their specific notion of mas-culinity marked their historic efforts, and they failed to accomplish their objectives. In spite of the fact that the 1954–57 youngmen saw themselves as standing in a long line of agitators who had engineered the overthrow of an Asantehene, Mensa Bonsu in 1883, such identification was not enough to bring them victory. The youngmen could not stand on their own to pursue their goals. *Obaa sene bomaa, ye kyem, to tuo a, etwere obarima dan mu.* They, by implication, bought a shield, carved drums, and owned a gun, but they stored all these items with people who were their superiors, their seniors. It is significant that Asante, as well as other Akan speakers, use the term *nkwankwaa* to refer to both youths and commoners. This designation clearly "denoted their real lack of power" in the lineage and state structures in which chiefs, lineage heads, and great men exercised authority (Aidoo 1977: 26). Therefore, what had begun as something rather anomalous in Asante political and military leadership (a woman as *sanahene*) was later turned into both a symbol of resistance to oppression and a model that the NLM and others used in challenging established gendered leadership.

CONCLUSION

The above discussion has touched on the shifting and overlapping constructions of gendered agency in Asante. Aspects of Akan orature and history were examined to explore understandings of senior masculinity as articulated in a public and political realm. The analysis draws on Asante norms and alternating, subversive and opposing constructions of gender as manifested by Yaa Asantewaa and the youngmen in the NLM. Although during both historical events those who championed Asante resistance were defeated by their opponents, Yaa Asantewaa's show of valor, *abannisem*, was much more formidable than that of the youngmen of the 1950s. She, by virtue of her senior age, royal lineage, and religion, succeeded in forming a resistance movement against the British. Yaa Asantewaa, like the earlier Akyaawa Yikwan, is remembered as possessing a masculine spirit, because she located her actions in religion, economics, lineage, and warfare, to claim for herself, as a woman, the status of senior masculinity, including its political and military connotations.

A little over fifty years later, the youngmen of the NLM drew upon Asante cultural symbols, religion, and affiliation with royalty to assert their notions of senior masculinity and to attempt to gain political power. Their position was that of "emasculated" men. They embraced, though unsuccessfully, a form of masculinity different from that of men with higher status and advanced age, but sought to attain similar political influence and privilege. Thus, there is evidence for the existence of competing forms of masculiniy in twentieth-century Asante, as Stephan Miescher (1997 and this volume) argues for southern Ghana in older colonial and missionary settings like Akuapem and Kwawu towns. In Asante of the 1950s, these different notions of masculinity were determined by older ideas about royal lineage, age, status, religion, and access to wealth, as well as by newer attributes concerning educational credentials, party politics, and salaried positions in a wage-labor economy. However, both historical incidents—Yaa Ansantewaa's war in 1900 and the youngmen in the NLM—underscore the fact that religion, seniority, lineage, local and translocal politics, and agency were implicated in Asante understandings of masculinity that operated in a public and political realm. Furthermore, constructions and deployments of masculinities remained fluid: *Otuo pae a, esi obarima Yaa Asantewaa bo na ensi Asante nkwankwaa bo* ("When the gun explodes, it lands on male Yaa Asantewaa's chest but not on the chest of the youngmen").

Senior masculinity is not always limited by biology, yet senior masculinity is not easily attained by women and juniors either. The links between seniority, sex, and gender are not fixed, but they may be reconfigured only in specific circumstances. The two cases discussed in this chapter show that the production and reproduction of gender in Asante were less a matter of an individual's biology than his or her embeddedness in a pool of sociocultural attributes, such as lineage, status, religion, and age, which became particularly salient in moments of crisis and changing nationalist activism.

NOTES

1. Obrecht to Basel, July 30, 1990 (No. 1990.II.169, Paul Jenkins, Abstracts of the Ghana correspondence of the Basel Mission, Basel Mission Archives).

2. *Gold Coast Times*, II, 84, 2/24/1883: 2: III, 114, 9/28/1883: 2.

REFERENCES

Aidoo, Agnes A. 1977. "Order and Conflict in the Asante Empire: A Study in Interest Group Relations." *African Studies Review* 20, 1: 1–36.

———. 1981. "Asante Queen Mothers in the Government and Politics in the Nineteenth Century." In *The Black Woman Cross-Culturally*, Filomina Chioma Steady, ed., pp. 65–77. Rochester, VT: Schenkman.

Akyeampong, Emmanuel Kwaku. 1996. *Drink, Power, and Cultural Change: A Social History of Alcohol in Ghana, c. 1800 to Recent Times*. Portsmouth, NH: Heinemann.

Akyeampong, Emmanuel and Pashington Obeng. 1995. "Spirituality, Gender and Power in Asante History." *International Journal of African Historical Studies* 28, 3: 481–508.

Allman, Jean Marie. 1993. *The Quills of the Porcupine: Asante Nationalism in an Emergent Ghana*. Madison, WI: University of Wisconsin Press.

Allman, Jean and Victoria Tashjian. 2000. *"I Will Not Eat Stone": A Women's History of Colonial Asante*. Portsmouth, NH: Heinemann.

Amadiume, Ifi. 1987. *Male Daughters, Female Husbands: Gender and Sex in an African Society*. London: Zed Press.

Arhin, Kwame. 1980. "Asante Military Institutions." *Journal of African Studies* 7, 1: 22–30.

———. 1983. "The Political and Military Roles of Akan Women." In *Female and Male in West Africa*, C. Oppong, ed., pp. 91–96. London: Allen & Unwin.

———. 1986. "The Asante Praise Poems: The Ideology of Patrimonialism." *Paideuma* 32: 163–97.

Austin, Dennis. 1964. *Politics in Ghana 1946–1960*. London: Oxford University Press.

Brempong, Nana [formerly Kwame Arhin]. 2000. "The Role of Nana Yaa Asantewaa in the 1900 Asante War of Resistance." *Ghana Studies* 3: 97–110.

Donkoh, Wilhelmina J. 2001. "Yaa Asantewaa: A Role Model for Womanhood in the New Millennium." *Jenda: A Journal of Culture and African Women Studies* 1, 1: 1–11.

Edgerton, Robert B. 1995. *The Fall of the Asante Empire: The Hundred-Year War for Africa's Gold Coast*. New York: Free Press.

Lewin, Thomas J. 1974. "The Structure of Political Conflict in Asante, 1875–1900." Ph.D. dissertation, Northwestern University.

————. 1978. *Asante Before the British: The Prempean Years, 1875–1900*. Lawrence, KS: Regents Press of Kansas.

Li, Anshan. 1995. *"Asafo* and Destoolment in Colonial Southern Ghana, 1900–1953." *International Journal of African Studies* 28, 2: 327–57.

McCaskie, T.C. 1981. "State and Society, Marriage and Adultery: Some Considerations Towards a Social History of Precolonial Asante." *Journal of African History* 22, 4: 477–94.

————. 1995. *State and Society in Pre-Colonial Asante*. Cambridge: Cambridge University Press.

Miescher, Stephan F. 1997. "Becoming a Man in Kwawu: Gender, Law, Personhood, and the Construction of Masculinities in Colonial Ghana, 1875–1957." Ph.D. dissertation, Northwestern University.

Moore, Henrietta L. 1996. *Space, Text, and Gender: An Anthropological Study of the Marakwet of Kenya*. New York: Guilford Press.

Rathbone, Richard. 1973. "Businessmen in Politics Party Struggle in Ghana 1949–57." *Journal of Developmental Studies* 9, 3: 390–401.

Reindorf, C.C. 1895. *History of the Gold Coast and Asante*. Basel: Missionsbuchhandlung.

Sarpong, Peter. 1977. *Girls' Nubility Rites in Ashanti*. Tema: Ghana Publishing Co.

Tordoff, William. 1965. *Ashanti Under the Prempehs: 1888–1935*. London: Oxford University Press.

Wilks, Ivor. 1975. *Asante in the Nineteenth Century*. Cambridge: Cambridge University Press.

————. 1993. *Forests of Gold: Essays on the Akan and the Kingdom of Asante*. Athens: University of Ohio Press.

Yankah, Kwesi. 1989a. *The Proverb in the Context of Akan Rhetoric: A Theory of Proverb Praxis*. New York: Peter Lang.

————. 1989b. "Proverbs: An Aesthetics of Traditional Communication." *Research in African Literatures* 20, 3: 325–46.

————. 1998. *Free Speech in Traditional Society: The Cultural Foundations of Communication in Contemporary Ghana*. Accra: Ghana University Press.

PART IV

MASCULINITY AND MODERNITY

12

Being Maasai Men: Modernity and the Production of Maasai Masculinities[1]

Dorothy L. Hodgson

Mentioning the "Maasai" usually evokes images of warriors, of men herding cattle, of proud patriarchs:

> The most picturesque people in East Africa are those of a tribe which has changed little of its ways since the advent of the White Man—the Masai. The tourist, when he spots a Masai herding his beloved cattle, or leaning gracefully on the haft of his long bladed spear, cannot but feel the spirit of Africa of yesterday. (Kilusu 1956–7: 135)

As this quotation indicates, such romanticized images of Maasai,[2] particularly male Maasai, as immutable icons of traditional Africa have been shared by many Westerners, from the first explorers and missionaries in the nineteenth century to the tourists taking their pictures today. While some people express a conservative longing to preserve the "cultural integrity" of "the once free and beautiful" Maasai, for others such images of Maasai provoke a progressive, modernizing urge.

Such ambivalent attitudes toward Maasai have shaped their long history of engagement with the complex, overlapping cultural processes and material structures of modernity. Structured and propelled by Enlightenment notions of individuality, progress, order, rationality, and civilization, these processes include colonialism, economic and social development, missionization, and nation-building.[3] Although the form, content, and context of the social, political, and economic interventions fostered by these processes vary, the underlying objective has generally remained the same: that is, to protect Maasai culture through preserving and occasionally improving Maasai pastoralism, guided by an image of pastoralism as a purely masculine endeavor. As a result, these processes and their associated interventions have further reinforced and rigidified the distinctions between Maasai as "traditional" and others (whether British colonial administrators or Tanzanian elites) as "modern." The complex intertwining of modernist interventions and reified cultural differences have had substantial material consequences; as an ethnic group, Maasai have been marginalized from both political power and economic resources in first the colonial and now the postcolonial nation-state.

However, at the same time that Maasai as a collectivity have been disenfranchised, these same interventions have reinforced and expanded the political and economic power of Maasai men over women as "individuals," "owners," "citizens," "taxpayers," "workers," and "household heads." In part because of the ambivalent attitudes of colonizers, missionaries, and others toward Maasai culture, the consolidation of male political and economic power occurred simultaneously with the reinforcement of the link between Maasai ethnicity and cattle herding, nomadism, and warriorhood. The result of marking all of these pursuits as male has been to privilege and fix certain masculinities. As a result, not only have Maasai women lost economic rights of control over pastoralist resources and access to new economic and political opportunities, but they have been disenfranchised from a sense of Maasai identity as well. Being "Maasai," as I will demonstrate, came to be understood by Maasai men themselves as being a pastoralist and a warrior: a dominant masculinity forged in opposition to "modernity" and sustained by certain economic and social interventions. Conversely, Maasai men who in some way embraced aspects of modernity, and therefore did not conform to this dominant configuration of masculinity, were stigmatized and ostracized. But these days, as increased land alienation, declining livestock populations, forced settlement, and continuing marginalization from economic and political resources within the state make such so-called traditional pursuits untenable, the dominant Maasai masculinity is being reforged to uneasily embrace both the traditional and the modern.[4]

The consolidation and expansion of their political-economic power has therefore been an uneven and deeply ambivalent process for most Maasai men. They have had to reconcile the contradictions of being constituted as traditional in a world shaped ever more forcefully by modernity. What is it like, one wonders, to live in a world where a certain configuration of attributes—being a nomad, a pastoralist, a warrior—persists for more than a hundred years in defining who you are to other people? How do the men whose masculinity is shaped by such configurations experience and reconcile the contradictions that are produced? Finally, what happens when none of these pursuits is possible anymore, when the structures that sustained you as traditional in a modern world collapse?

To address these questions, this article explores the historical articulation of modernity with the shifting production of Maasai masculinities. The analysis is framed in terms of the shifting meanings and referents of two Maasai masculinities; the dominant Maasai masculinity and *ormeek* masculinity. Maasai have multiple masculinities; the dominant one refers to the masculinity premised on the pursuit of pastoralism and cultural authenticity nurtured, reinforced, and often celebrated by colonial and postcolonial policies. *Ormeek*, in contrast, is a Maa word that emerged in the early colonial period as a derogatory label for "modern" Maasai men and thus refers to a historically subordinate masculinity. To facilitate analysis of the complex articulations of culture with political economy reflected in the use of these terms, I employ an ethnohistorical approach based on archival materials, participant observation, crossgenerational interviews with Maasai men, and life histories.

This ethnohistorical analysis of masculinity and modernity among Maasai contributes to the growing body of feminist scholarship which has recognized that to analyze the production, reproduction, and transformation of gender inequalities we must go beyond just recording the experiences and ideas of women (e.g., Hodgson and McCurdy 2001; Hodgson 2000b, 2001b). Since gender, like patriarchal power, is not a monolithic, ahistorical entity, but is produced and reproduced through the contested actions and ideas of men and women, we must analyze masculinities as well as femininities, men as well as women, male dominance as well as female subordination. In this case, since the contradictions of being figured as traditional in a modern world are particularly acute for Maasai men, analysis of Maasai masculinity is crucial to fully grasp the local experience of modernity. Moreover, by setting the ethnographic analysis within a historical frame, this chapter foregrounds relations of gender, power, and difference to demonstrate that masculinities (like femininities) are multiple, historical, relational, and contradictory. In combining ethnographic and historical analysis to examine shifting Maasai masculinities, I draw on my broader work on Maasai gender relations and femininities (Hodgson 1996, 1997, 1999a, 1999d, 1999e, 2001a, n.d.).

MAASAI MASCULINITIES: GENDER, GENERATION, ETHNICITY, AND HISTORY

Maasai life (and therefore masculinities) had shifted in interaction with historical processes and events prior to the British colonial period. Key moments included the migration of Maa-speaking peoples southward along the Rift Valley to their current locations on the highland plains of contemporary

Kenya and Tanzania, the emergence of pastoralism as a specialized production system, encounters in the early nineteenth century with Swahili slave and ivory traders as well as European travelers and missionaries, the disasters of the 1890s and the ensuing wars and dispersal, and the imperial German occupation (Bernsten 1979; Sommer and Vossen 1993; Sutton 1990, 1993; Waller 1978; Galaty 1993). By the early nineteenth century, Maa speakers coexisted with different economic specialties: as pastoralists, agropastoralists, farmers, and hunter-gatherers. Throughout this time, however, increasing numbers of people became pastoral Maa speakers by conquest, as well as by assimilation through marriage, child adoption, and adopting Maasai dress, cultural practices, and social allegiances. Although the ethnonym "Maasai" was first used in travelers' accounts of the mid-nineteenth century to designate territorial differences among Maa speakers (with Maasai living in certain areas and Iloikop/Kwavi in others), by the late 1870s, the meaning of "Maasai" had shifted to indicate economic differences, with Maasai as pastoralists and Iloikop/Kwavi as agriculturalists or agropastoralists (Bernsten 1980; cf. Krapf 1968 [1860]; Thomson 1968 [1885]; Galaty 1982a).

From their earliest encounters, Western travelers in East Africa portrayed Maasai in words and pictures as the antithesis to modern Europeans. Drawing on the exaggerated tales of Swahili traders, the early vanguards of imperialism wrote vivid descriptions of fierce Maasai who roamed the plains with their cattle, stealing livestock, attacking agricultural settlements, and leading a life free of the domesticating concerns of modern man (see, for example, Thomson 1968 [1885]; Krapf 1968 [1860]). For Europeans who encountered this "nomad warrior race," Maasai *ilmurran* (warriors) represented the epitome of a wild and free lifestyle (see, e.g., Johnston 1886: 408–9).

But the warrior archetype emphasized in European accounts represented an exaggerated reification of only one mode of Maasai masculinity. As everywhere, Maasai masculinity embraced a range of masculinities cross-cut by generation. They were shaped in relation to each other as well as to Maasai femininities, and they were formed and transformed through interactions with broader historical processes and events.

According to sources from the 1890s to the 1930s, relations of gender and age organized the pastoral production system, political power, religious expression and ritual authority, systems of address and respect, and domestic duties.[5] In general, men and women had distinct roles and responsibilities in each of these domains, premised on mutual autonomy and respect, but shared common goals in furthering the interests of their homestead. The reputation of each homestead depended on the success of each category of person in fulfilling these responsibilities. Women played central roles in the pastoral economy as milk managers, caring for young and sick animals, and as traders. They controlled the production and distribution of milk within the homestead and held rights in other livestock products such as hides. They bartered both milk and hides with neighboring cultivators, passing caravans, and at permanent trade settlements for foodstuffs and other household goods. Women were also responsible for the daily mediations with God (*Eng'ai*) through prayer and song on behalf of the people and livestock in the homestead. As they aged, and especially once their sons became *ilmurran*, their respect and authority inside and outside the homestead (*enkang'*) increased. Women felt deep pride in their identity as pastoralists, and as Maasai.

The roles and responsibilities of men varied according to their age grade, a set of life stages that men moved through as part of their age set. As young, uncircumcised boys (*ilayiok*; sing. *olayioni*), they herded first calves and small stock, then, as they grew older, cattle. Once circumcised, they became *ilmurran* (sing. *olmurrani*; literally "the circumcised ones"), a word most often glossed as warriors. *Ilmurran* were responsible for protecting settlements and livestock against raids and predators and serving as messengers for elder men. Eventually the *ilmurran* became *ilpayioni*, or junior elders (and later, with the circumcision of new age sets, elders, senior elders, and venerable elders), through distinct ceremonies. Now they could marry, start a family, and begin managing the affairs of the livestock and people in their homestead. Their political power increased as they grew older, and ideally wealthier in stock, with numerous wives and children, peaking when they were elders/ senior elders. As they continued to age and became venerable elders, however, the management of the affairs of the homestead shifted to younger men.

Each age grade, or generational masculinity, was distinguished by distinct property relations, political rights, domestic responsibilities, respect behavior, and forms of address. The defining contrast was between the collective interests of *ilmurran* and the individualistic imperatives of male elders. Each age grade was also culturally elaborated in dress, ornamentation, hairstyle, and accessories. Metaphorically, the structural tension and contrasts between *ilmurran* and elders could be expressed as a series of dichotomies: communal/individual, wild/domesticated, freedom/authority, sex for pleasure/sex for procreation (cf. Spencer 1988; Llewelyn-Davies 1978, 1981). Of course, as everywhere, such ideals belied a range of practices contingent on individual traits, economic circumstances, and other opportunities and misfortunes. Moreover, all *ilmurran* inevitably became elders and the structural tension was expressed and resolved ritually. But the ironies remained: once they were elders, men spent much time and energy protecting their livestock (and wives) from the predations of *ilmurran*, while simultaneously recalling and recounting their own similar exploits as *ilmurran*.

When the British took control of Tanganyika from the Germans in 1916, they found Maa-speaking peoples scattered throughout northern and central Tanganyika, often interspersed with other communities. Some Maa speakers herded, others cultivated, many did both. All were recuperating from a series of cattle epidemics and smallpox in the last two decades of the nineteenth century, which, together with the ensuing famine and wars between Maasai sections, decimated their livestock herds and killed large numbers of Maa speakers (Waller 1988; Hodgson 2001a).

Haunted by images of Maasai as dangerous warriors and uncontrollable nomads, colonial administrators perceived the dispersed intermingling of Maasai with other tribes as a menace to settlers and African cultivators and a threat to administrative control and order. The scattered presence and diverse production strategies of Maasai disturbed administrative notions of not just political order but cultural order as well; they sought neat alignments of culture, political system, and mode of production in the form of tribes. After lengthy consultation, administrators decided to consolidate and isolate Maasai in a newly created Maasai reserve (Hodgson 2001a). By the late 1920s, the categories of "Maasai" and "Maasailand" were taken as givens by colonial administrators, despite continued contestation in practice as some Maasai farmed, others intermarried with non-Maasai, and many ignored reserve boundaries. When the British spoke or wrote of "the Maasai" they meant Maasai men. And such men were, in British eyes, divided into two categories: elder men who were naturally wise and authoritative, and junior men or warriors, who were considered wild and potentially dangerous. Women of all ages were generally missing from the category "Maasai" and thus from the related categories created and consolidated by British practices, including "taxpayer," "household head," and native "authorities" (Hodgson 1999a, 2001a). Maasai men took advantage of the British neglect of the rights and roles of women to strengthen their political authority and economic control.

These images of Maasai men as pastoralists and warriors shaped not only colonial administrative practices, but development interventions as well, generating contradictory policies: either conservative interventions to protect and preserve Maasai in this image, or progressive interventions to modernize Maasai attitudes and practices. As I detail elsewhere (Hodgson 1999a, 2000a, 2001a), until the 1950s, most administrators were hesitant to support any intervention that might change Maasai culture. Even as pastoralism became less and less viable with increased land alienation of dry-season grazing grounds and permanent water sources (for settler farms, forest reserves, game parks, and government development schemes), colonial interventions like water development, veterinary control, and—eventually—education were designed to restrict Maasai to pastoralism and to the reserve. And all of these interventions (whether control over water sources, veterinary advice, or education) were directed at Maasai men, since Maasai women, by British definition, were not pastoralists.

On the rare occasions when more progressive interests tried to set the development agenda, with proposals to encourage Maasai farming, remove the strict controls to Maasai movement outside of the reserve, or broaden educational opportunities, they confronted self-righteous attacks about destroying Maasai culture (Hodgson 2001a). The ambivalent attitudes of colonial administrators toward Maasai development and culture had contradictory consequences for Maasai themselves. On the one hand, colonial ambivalence provided the space for Maasai to avoid certain modern interventions such as wage labor and indoctrination into Western values through widespread education. But their enforced isolation during this period set them at a distinct political and economic disadvantage in relation to other Tanzanians, provoked deep resentments over their privileged status, and reinforced perceptions of their cultural conservatism and traditionalism. It also posed a dilemma for many Maasai, who wanted some of the changes and opportunities proffered by the state, such as the water projects, access to veterinary medicines, and, for a few, education, but rejected others (such as veterinary quarantines). They especially resented colonial efforts to circumscribe their movements and those of their livestock and limit their interactions with other peoples, including traders and neighboring cultivators.

The 1950s marked a sharp shift in the pace and intensity of development interventions throughout British colonies and protectorates. As part of post-war recovery, the metropole demanded increased productivity from its colonies and protectorates to support their administrative costs and subsidize metropolitan rebuilding. Pastoralists in general and Maasai in particular became icons of the traditionalism and communalism that colonial officials were now so eager to combat in the name of progress. Administrators ignored their own complicity in circumscribing Maasai opportunities for development and social change and launched vigorous campaigns, such as the Masai Development Project (Hodgson, 2000a), to modernize their traditional ways. They exhorted Maasai leaders to rapidly change their attitudes and practices or else be left behind.[6] Administrative frustration with the perceived lack of progress by Maasai generated new perspectives on Maasai men: *ilmurran* were lazy and should be working to earn money and help their communities, and elder men were too conservative and uneducated to promote the necessary changes. Administrators therefore restructured the native administration to incorporate younger, educated Maasai men (some from Kenya) on whom they felt they could depend to guide and implement their mandates for change.

These administrative policies and practices had several lasting consequences for Maasai gender relations. The formation of the native administration, first with elder men and later with younger, educated men, consolidated male control over the emergent political domain, relegating women both conceptually and spatially to the increasingly devalued domestic domain. Other initiatives such as veterinary interventions, taxation, and campaigns to encourage Maasai men to sell cattle for cash privileged and reinforced the rights of men as individual owners of cattle and heads of households, thereby disenfranchising women from their formerly shared rights over cattle. Livestock development projects such as the MDP, which targeted and trained men as the animal husbandry experts, further devalued women's contributions to and identity with pastoralism. As a result, Maasai ethnic identity became profoundly gendered as Maasai men claimed to be the pre-eminent pastoralists.[7]

With independence, development was appropriated and recast as the legitimating project of the postcolonial nation-state in Tanzania; the African elites who took power embraced the modern narrative with its agenda of progress. Intent on integrating the people of Tanzania into a socialist nation by forging links of language, infrastructure, and a sense of national identity, they translated the former racialized distinctiveness of Maasai into a heightened sense of ethnic difference marked by pronounced cultural and visual signifiers (cf. Kituyi 1990). For them, Maasai represented all they had tried to leave behind and persisted as icons of the primitive, the savage, and the past.

Mocked by the elites as primitive, accused of cultural conservatism, and excluded from most state-sponsored development initiatives, Maasai became increasingly impoverished as their land, livestock, and possibilities for viable livelihoods continued to disappear. Most state resources have been directed to other areas and to people perceived as more progressive, easier to reach and work with, or eager for development. And when development initiatives such as the huge, multimillion-dollar USAID Maasai Range Project have been implemented, their objectives have paralleled the ambivalent goals of many colonial projects: to leave Maasai culture intact while trying to develop their livestock industry for the benefit of the state (Hodgson 1999b). Other state-sponsored interventions have been more repressive: the brutal policies such as forced resettlement and sedentarization under the villagization program in the late 1970s (Ndagala 1982) and continuing attempts to force Maasai men to wear trousers and shirts in towns. Not only has Maasai clothing become a politicized issue, but the Maa language has as well: the Tanzanian government has long mandated that all political gatherings, meetings with government representatives, and so forth must be conducted in the national language of Swahili, not local languages (*lugha za kienyeji*).

But nowadays, as tourism has become an increasingly important source of revenue for the development of the Tanzanian nation-state, state officials have put Maasai back into view: to attract tourists, state officials promote Maasai as icons of traditional and primitive Africa through travel brochures and guides, postcards, postage stamps, and other visual and written media. The attentive gaze of tourists has its repercussions for Maasai development, however; the few state-sponsored development initiatives have almost dried up for fear of marring the authentic persona and landscape that captivate tourists and capture their foreign exchange. Simultaneously, however, international nongovernmental organizations have directed increasing attention and resources at sustaining pastoralists and pastoralism as viable livelihoods (Hodgson 1999b). Maasai themselves have begun to use these images of cultural authenticity to their own advantage, linking current efforts to protect their lands and livelihoods and access development resources to global campaigns for the rights of indigenous peoples (Hodgson 1999c, 2001a, n.d.).

NEGOTIATING THE CONTRADICTIONS OF MODERNITY AND MARGINALITY

Historical analysis and interviews with 25 men from the five living age grades of a community of Kisongo Maasai reveal that the relationship between Maasai masculinities and modernity is most clearly seen in terms of the configuration of the masculine category of *ormeek*.[8] (The Maa language is gendered, so "or" is a masculine prefix. *Emeeki*, with the feminine prefix "e," is the rarely used female equivalent.) In contrast to the dominant masculinities described earlier, the origins of *ormeek* as a descriptor of an initially subordinate, even stigmatized masculinity can be traced historically to the early colonial period. Initially it seems that *ormeek* referred to all non-Maasai Africans, whom Maasai also came to refer to as Swahili. During the colonial period, the meaning of *ormeek* expanded from just a derogatory name for Swahilis or non-Maasai to include those Africans who were educated, spoke Swahili, worked in the government, or were baptized. They were often symbolized, for Maasai, by their clothing of trousers, shirts, and occasionally jackets. In time, however, the term was invoked to mark, mock, and ostracize any Maasai man who imitated Swahilis, who adopted the practices or fashions of modernity, who sought to be anything other than a real Maasai man.[9]

Ormeek seems to have first been applied by Maasai to other Maasai men in the 1930s, when it was used to deride elder men who worked for the colonial government as headmen (*jumbes*).[10] In time, the meaning of *ormeek* was broadened to include not only men associated with the colonial government, but those men and boys who attended school. When the government finally opened a Native Authority school for Maasai boys in 1937, a common reason elders gave for refusing to let their children enroll was the fear that they would become *ormeek:* "Those elders who refused to send their children to school . . . said 'Oh! if my child goes he will become ormeek!'" Some feared "losing their children," or, more precisely, "the Swahilis" taking their children. When forced by the government to send at least one child to school, elders reportedly gave the son they liked the least (cf. Saitoti 1986: 53).

Ormeek was also used to describe Maasai men who were baptized. Maasai elders I interviewed perceived baptism to be even more incompatible with Maasai culture and masculinity than education; one said, "If they only learn things like how to write and read, a regular education, but are not baptized, *basi*, when they come home, they will be normal people like other Maasai. But once he is baptized, he will have a different faith. He will separate from us completely." Conversion to Christianity by Maasai men marked a fundamental change in their male identity for several reasons. Maasai men, espe-cially *ilmurran* and junior elders, were not perceived as particularly religious. Male converts had to promise not to marry any more wives, and they had to recognize and submit to another authority as superior to their own ritual and political leaders (Hodgson 1999e).

Ormeek was therefore an implicit critique of all that modernity represented to Maasai: education, institutionalized religion, even the political structure and language of the nation-state. The senior and venerable elders I inter-viewed, who grew up with this strictly enforced dichotomy of the dominant Maasai masculinity and the disparaged *ormeek* masculinity, described the dif-ference between Maasai and *ormeek* in mutually exclusive terms. As opposed to the ideal of Maasai men as pastoralists, for example, *ormeek* were ignorant of herding and cattle. *Meyielo ataramat inkishu*, literally, "They did not know how to care for/about cattle"). The use of *ataramat*, from the verb *eramatare*, is significant here, as *eramatare* denotes more than just herding (*enkirritare*) and encompasses all aspects of cattle care. To care for cattle one must have the pertinent animal husbandry knowledge, but to care about cattle implies an emotional bond and commitment. Given the centrality of caring for and about livestock to Maasai pastoral identity, economic production, social organiza-tion, and prestige structure, this statement marks *ormeek* as profoundly not-Maasai.

Others described them in spatial terms as rootless, ungrounded, wandering: "Those people have no place where they live. They come and go with work. They come like people from far away, but don't distinguish themselves. And their seed is not known." Although this senior elder's description could be read as depicting *ormeek* as roving nomads, the reference to their unknown seed suggests that it is more of a commentary on *ormeek*'s perceived lack of community and attachments. Seed is a symbol of the patriline, occurring con-stantly in discussions of marriage arrangements when parents or elders debate the quality of a future bridegroom's seed, or the seed that spawned a future bride. These descriptions imply profound differences that cannot be easily overcome: one either knows about cattle and herding, or one does not. Nor can one be grounded and rootless at the same time. And one's seed is either recognized and respected, or unfamiliar and suspect.

During this period, the *ormeek*/Maasai opposition refracted the modern/traditional dichotomy in terms of Maasai subjectivities in a manner that rei-fied two extremes within a range of possibilities, masking the complexities and contradictions of cultural change. In many ways, *ormeek* became as much a stereotype as the dominant Maasai masculinities had become by this time, in part because the characteristics of *ormeek* transcended age grades—any Maasai man, *ilmurran*, or elder could become an *ormeek*. But neither the dominant masculinity nor *ormeek* was an essential, static category, and as the meaning of one changed, so did the other. That some Maasai men embraced that which had been defined and stigmatized for years by Maasai and colonial administrators as not Maasai destabilized the dominant masculinity. And as the scope and pace of interventions in Maasai life increased, the meaning of *ormeek* broadened to encompass each new arena of imposed social and cultural change, further heightening the contrast between them.

Furthermore, *ormeek* refracted the opposition in gendered terms—it was rarely applied to Maasai women. If being a traditional Maasai was about being male, then its opposite, *ormeek*, was also a masculine category. Maasai women were in many ways doubly excluded from this identity dilemma: not only had they become devalued as less than Maasai, but they were also denied many of the opportunities for change available to Maasai men. Only a few Maasai women were called *emeeki* (the feminine form), either because they were one of the few to attend school during the colonial period, or more often because they married *ormeek* schoolteachers and politicians and adopted Western clothes and Swahili hairstyles. Baptized women, however, unlike the baptized men discussed earlier, were rarely called *emeeki*, in part because so many Maasai women converted to Christianity. Maasai women have always been recognized by both men and women as more religious than men, so their conversion to Christianity (after some initial objections by men) was perceived as an extension and broadening of their religiosity, not a radical change in their subjectivity (Hodgson 1999e).

Although the commentary of the senior and venerable elders marked the *ormeek*/Maasai distinction as a vast, unbridgeable gap, several Maasai men during this time struggled to reconcile the seemingly stark differences. In part because of their efforts, the configuration of Maasai masculinities, and thus the meaning of *ormeek*, are now shifting. One reason for this is that the number of *ormeek* has expanded as the first generations of *ormeek* have raised their children as *ormeek*. Like their fathers, these men use their education, knowledge of Swahili, and capacity to operate in the political realm of the nation-state to work for salaries, vie for development resources, and struggle for political power. Given the changing political economic situation of Maasai, these men (and some women) are far better situated than their uneducated cohort to adapt, survive, and even prosper. Pastoralism has collapsed in many areas, as the development props that sustained it have eroded, thereby intensifying the structural contradictions of being traditional in a modern world. Many Maasai throughout Tanzania have now turned to farming as a means to feed their families and education as the hope of their future. Maasai men of all ages desperately want to educate all of their children so that they can survive in what they perceive as a rapidly changing land: "The land is now completely wild. There are no cattle, I have only a few left. What shall I do? . . . What happened to the past when people followed the cattle?" One elder man put it quite poetically: "I want to educate all of my children, I no longer want one who is blind. I mean, the country has become darkness for everyone."

"The wisdom of the past," another elder explained, is worthless; it must be replaced by "the wisdom of the present."

Most senior and venerable elders now speak of themselves as *emodai*, or stupid, for ever having clung to a masculine mode that embraced pastoralism and rejected education, farming, and involvement with the state. "Not everyone is educated!" one senior elder exclaimed. "It is only us of the colonial period who are *emodai*." "Let me just say," remarked a junior elder, "that even I will put my child in school. I mean, I am very *emodai*, but my child will come to prosper." To be *emodai* for them is to be stupid in a particular way; it is to be ignorant of the language and practices of the nation-state; it is to be unable to operate in the world of hospitals, courtrooms, banks, and politicians. To call themselves *emodai* is to refute the prestige of the dominant Maasai masculinity by invoking its negative consequences. The irony here is striking: while *ormeek* were stigmatized by many of these same men for being ignorant of cattle, and thus not really pastoralists, this ignorance has little resonance now that pastoralism itself is increasingly less viable. Instead, it is precisely the knowledge of *ormeek* that is now valued, and the ignorance of traditional pastoralists that is discredited.

Some are aware that their impoverished condition is partly a result of their lack of access to economic resources and political power within the state. The state government is described by many as the "government of *ormeek*," and education is seen as the avenue to national political power: "Doesn't this thing called school now run the entire country?" Or, as another junior elder explained, "If you put your son in school he will study until he gets work as a member of parliament, or he'll get some other important work and he will be able to help you in the future when you are old."[11] Like Thomas's father, these men increasingly depend on their *ormeek* sons to help them understand and negotiate the stark changes in the contours of their lives.

A key symbol of the power education is believed to have is "the pen." "With the pen and the roads that now pass through the village," one elder said, "there will be no place that a person can get problems, if these two, the pen and the road, are available." "We people of the past don't know anything," another venerable elder lamented, "but these new people, these people who know the pen, they have a clear way."

And now that all men, both old and young, struggle to overcome the constraints of a dominant masculinity that rejected modernity, the category of *ormeek* is being reforged in less derogatory terms. As all elderly Maasai men embrace education as necessary to the future of their children, and as more of their children and grandchildren, the younger men, go to school, participate in national government, or even join the church, the dominant masculinity of Maasainess is being reconfigured to contain the attributes of modernity historically associated with *ormeek*. As a result, *ormeek* as a mode of masculinity is being recast to either represent minimal differences or, more commonly,

Photo 12.1. An *ormeek* man poses with his brothers and friends in his homestead. Photo by author, 1986.

becoming a category empty of any meaning at all. Younger men speak of *ormeek* as merely signaling a difference in language ("they speak Swahili") or a difference in dress ("they wear pants"). In contrast to earlier meanings of *ormeek*, such differences are more external and not mutually exclusive: one can both speak Swahili and speak Maa, or one can wear a red cloth in the morning, put on pants to go to town, then return in the evening to home and the red cloth again.

The transformation in the meaning of the term is evident in one elder man's comments:

> In the past they said that an *ormeek* did not know how to care for cattle. . . . But what do we mean now by *ormeek?* I don't know this thing called *ormeek*. I mean, I am called *ormeek* and him over here [referring to my assistant], he is *ormeek*, and this child sitting here is *ormeek*. Now what will we do with this term *ormeek?* I know that a smart person is called *ormeek*, so maybe an *ormeek* is a smart person with a white house and a tractor— that is what we are learning and that is what we want.

Other elders, junior elders, and young men shared his sense that as more and more Maasai became like *ormeek*, the term was losing any fixity of meaning, it was a sign without a referent:

I don't know what an *ormeek* is, I just don't know. I mean this name *ormeek*, if I am not wrong, we use it to slander those we meet on the road, or when we see an *Ormakaa* [junior elder] resting in his pants. That is what we mean by *ormeek*. It came in as a name, but it is a mistake. I mean look here—this woman [me] who is sitting here is an *elaisungun* [European], but although she is *elaisungun*, we don't know what kind of *elaisungun* she is. They have lots of tribes themselves—there are Americans, English, Indians, Boers. Similarly, if you look within our Maasai, there are Arusha, Sukuma, Chaga, and Meru. So if you try to find the meaning of this word *ormeek* you will fail. I am unable to know the meaning of this name called *ormeek*, I just don't know.

While the senior and venerable elders lament the past and berate themselves for having clung so desperately to a certain way of being, a masculinity they now deride as *emodai*, the junior elders and even more so the *ilmurran* seek to forge new ways of being a Maasai man that can embrace the claims of the past and the demands of the present. Unlike their more senior elders, all of the *ilmurran* and junior elders speak Swahili, and some can even converse in rudimentary English. Four of the five young men were educated through Standard VII, none of the other men interviewed had any education. But one senior elder had taught himself to read through occasional adult education classes. Whenever I visited, he would proudly bring out his Swahili Bible and read long passages to impress me with his literacy. And while the senior and venerable elders rely on their wives and sons to farm for them, the elders, junior elders, and young men eagerly cultivate maize, beans, and occasionally barley to eat and sell. And two of the younger men have salaried employment: one as a schoolteacher in a neighboring village and the other as a local government representative.

Other contrasts with the dominant masculinities described for the early twentieth century are even more remarkable. Age sets are still an organizing principle of masculine subjectivity and social relations, and their fundamental apparatus has remained much the same; male circumcision is still a prerequisite to becoming an adult man, each age set is still given a unique name, and men advance from age grade to more senior age grade together. But the experience, attitudes, and practices of being an age set member have changed. In this Maasai community, like many others, few young men have the time to spend in the numerous activities that build solidarity within their age set: the liminal period after circumcision has been dramatically shortened, as most boys must return to school; *emanyatta* (warrior-villages) are a rare occurrence; and *ilmurran* have infrequent opportunities to congregate with each other as they pursue farming, education, labor, and other opportunities to make money. Many only selectively observe the dietary prohibitions, and obviously none can sustain themselves on milk and meat alone, given the demise of the cattle herds. They wear an array of clothes, depending on the context. At home, some wear a long cloth knotted over one shoulder and fastened to the waist by a belt, while others wear blue jeans and T-shirts. All have pants, shirts, jackets, and shoes to wear to town, political meetings, and other venues.

Not all venerable elders like the interests and pursuits of the younger men. A few complain about their lack of respect, their individualistic ways. One venerable elder was quite terse in his criticism: "If you look closely, all that [the younger men] are interested in is money, what he cares about is his radio, his watch. He doesn't know cattle, and when he farms all he cares about is his radio and watch . . . he can't know if his father is hungry; he can't know if his mother is hungry; he can't know if his child is hungry." Such scathing diatribes about the selfishness of younger men challenge both the communal ideal of *ilmurran* as well as the generosity ideal of elders. It also invokes an early critique of *ormeek* (that they didn't "know" cattle), but extends and complicates it: what these young men do know is money and material goods, but their self-interested obsession with accumulating their individual property blinds them to the basic needs of their families. The radio and watch are also potent symbols of the changes that have occurred among Maasai men: listening to radio broadcasts in Swahili reinforces their links with the nation-state, and their preoccupation with their watches confirms the new salience of time in their lives.

But whatever their current survival strategy, Maasai men of all ages now assert a very modern dream: for the village, they want a hospital, a good school, a grinding machine, more cattle medicine, a better road, and cheap public transportation to the nearby district headquarters. When asked what they personally wanted, most replied with some version of "I want everything; there is nothing I don't want," then proceeded to list a house with a corrugated iron roof, a car, a tractor, a bigger farm, more cattle, and more children as the most common elements of their dream. And they hope that their sons, their warriors, become scholars and will help make these dreams come true.

But in a curious echo of the earlier British ambivalence about changing Maasai culture, they are also aware of the tensions and contradictions that such aspirations entail. "But really, I don't want our culture to be changed, because if we change our culture we will all be stupid. But I also don't want development to be lost, because if it is lost we will all go to the bush." Or as another elder complained, "I don't want our Maasai culture to be changed at all; I don't want our children to be changed; I don't want our cattle to be changed so that we don't have them anymore. . . . I don't want this area to be cultivated even though I want a farm, but I don't want it to be farmed so that the cattle have to be fenced in."

CONCLUSION

As a celebration of Western progress, civilization, and rationality, the idea of the modern, as Hall (1992), among others, has argued, is consciously built on a difference with another; the modern not only presupposes but requires the existence of the traditional to acquire its meaning (cf. Escobar 1995). The Maasai case demonstrates how such a modern/traditional dichotomy was inscribed on the categories (such as ethnic identities) that were formed as part of the imperial project of imposing a modern order on the perceived chaos of the native. Furthermore, it shows that the very development interventions that were critical to implementing the modernist project were crucial to sustaining and intensifying these oppositions. Thus paternalistic efforts in the early colonial period to design and implement development projects that would protect Maasai culture by enforcing the political-economic isolation of Maasai and sustaining them as pastoralists reified the distinction between Maasai as traditional and other Africans as modernizing. The abrupt shift in policies and practices in the 1950s, with accompanying pressures for Maasai to change rapidly, further heightened (and stigmatized) such differences. In turn, such differences were used by Tanzanian elites to further marginalize Maasai from political and economic power in the postcolonial period, and more recently to market them as relics of Africa's primitive past to lure tourists.

The Maasai case raises larger issues about the relationship between the experience of modernity and the formation of individual and collective subjectivities. Identity formation is not just a matter of individuals engaging directly with broader structural forces, but is always mediated by collective, cross-cutting allegiances such as gender, generation, ethnicity, and class. For Maasai, the imposition of the modern/traditional dichotomy has been a profoundly gendered process in its constitution, representation, and effects: the oppositional categories of modernity simultaneously valorize and stigmatize certain gender configurations, certain masculinities and femininities. Maasai masculinities have become a key site for the experience and negotiation of modernity.

Ethnohistorical analysis through the prism of masculinity demonstrates, however, that modernity is never a totalizing process, but that the contradictory structures imposed by modernist interventions can be appropriated, reshaped, and even transcended by local people in novel, if painful, ways. The combination of participant observation, life histories, interviews, and careful readings of archival documents enables us to go beyond mere textual readings of the construction of masculinity. Instead, we gain a partial understanding of how some Maasai men have experienced and coped with the contradictions produced by their encounters with modernity. Through their accounts, we learn that a dominant masculinity is less a construction than a production, and thus always in tension, always relative, and always a site of mediation and negotiation. Thus the dominant Maasai masculinity and its negative other, *ormeek*, are now being melded into a new masculinity whose meaning and practices are still being formed. So while one venerable elder still plaintively asserts that "we Maasai are people of the spear," another elder marks the shift in masculinities in similar terms: "the spear of our grandfathers is finished; the only source of power now is the power of the pen."

NOTES

1. This chapter is a significantly shortened and revised version of an article first published under a different title in *Ethnology* and is republished here with their kind permission.

2. The preferred spelling is "Maasai." "Masai" is retained here when used by others in writings, letters, and other quotations.

3. I recognize, of course, the historical production and presence of other modernities besides that developed in the Enlightenment period in Europe, as well as the production of multiple modernities through specific local–translocal interactions (Hodgson 2001b).

4. For an analysis of the articulation of colonialism, modernity, and development with female Maasai subjectivities, see Hodgson (1997).

5. The following is largely based on the detailed ethnography of Merker (1910 [1904]), supplemented by Baumann (1894), Hollis (1905), Fosbrooke (1948), and archival records. Spencer (1988) offers a rich and compelling portrait of dominant Maasai masculinity in contemporary times. Although he briefly discusses the many historical and political-economic changes that have influenced Maasai life, his ethnographic description presents Maasai masculinity as shaped by the age set system as timeless, unchanging, and unaffected by broader changes (but see Spencer 1998).

6. Revington, Acting PC, NP, "Olkiama Address 25th August 1947," TNA 17/252.

7. See, for example, Galaty (1982a), in which his symbolic analysis of contemporary Maasai ideology shows that Maasai men are the real pastoralists, and Maasai women are equated with lower-status hunter-gatherers. Elsewhere I have challenged the ahistoricity of his model by demonstrating the historical emergence of patriarchy and its concomitant devaluation of women among Maasai (Hodgson 1999a).

8. The men reside in one of three research communities among the Kisongo section of Maasai living in Monduli District, Tanzania. Socioeconomic data were collected from a 1992 census of all households and individuals, and the narrative excerpts are from semi-structured interviews in 1992 and 1993 with a stratified random sample of five members of each age/gender category of adults. All of the English translations are my own, based on the original tapes and transcripts, as well as sections translated into Swahili by my assistant, Morani Poyoni. For the sake of simplicity, I refer to age grades by categories, corresponding, in 1991–93, to the following: *ilmurran* (*Illandissy*), junior elders (*Ilmakaa*), elders (*Seuri*), senior elders (*Ilnyangusi*), or venerable elders (*Ilterito*).

9. One of the earliest archival occurrences of the term is by Merker (1910 [1904]:116), who reports that in the 1890s, *el meg* (sing. *ol megi*) referred to all non-Maasai, and he translated the term as "unbeliever." Galaty (1982b) notes that *olmeek/ilmeek* was used by Kenyan Maasai in the 1970s to refer to non-Maasai agriculturalists, who were disparaged in terms of their diet, labor, and character. According to Galaty (1982b: 3–4), Maasai (men) perceived *ilmeek* as people of labor and themselves as people of leisure.

10. See, for example, Acting PC, NP to Chief Secretary, Dar es Salaam, 21 July 1934, TNA 69/27/MS.

11. This quotation refers indirectly to Edward Sokoine, one of the few Maasai to attain prominence in national politics. After becoming a Member of Parliament, Sokoine became Prime Minister in 1977. He died under suspicious circumstances in a car accident in 1984 (Halimoja 1985).

REFERENCES

Appadurai, A. 1996. *Modernity at Large: Cultural Dimensions of Globalization.* Minneapolis: Univ. of Minnesota Press.

Baumann, O. 1894. *Durch Massailand zur Nilquelle: Reisen und Forschungen der Massai-Expedition des deutschen Antisklaverei-Komite in den Jahren 1891–1893.* Berlin: D. Reimer.

Bernsten, J. 1979. "Pastoralism, Raiding and Prophets: Maasailand in the Nineteenth Century." Ph.D. dissertation, University of Wisconsin–Madison.

———. 1980. The Enemy Is Us: Eponymy in the Historiography of the Maasai. *History in Africa* 7: 1–21.

Escobar, A. 1995. *Encountering Development: The Making of the Third World.* Princeton: Princeton University Press.

Fosbrooke, H. 1948. "An Administrative Survey of the Masai Social System." *Tanganyika Notes and Records* 26: 1–50.

Galaty, J. 1982a. "Being 'Maasai'; Being 'People of the Cattle': Ethnic Shifters in East Africa." *American Ethnologist* 9, 1: 1–20.

———. 1982b. "Maasai Pastoral Ideology and Change." *Studies in Third World Societies* 17: 1–22.

———. 1993. "Maasai Expansion and the New East African Pastoralism." In *Being Maasai: Ethnicity and Identity in East Africa*, T. Spear and R. Waller, eds., pp. 61–86. London: James Currey.

Halimoja, Y. 1985. *Sokoine: Mtu wa Watu* (Sokoine: Man of the People). Dar es Salaam: Tanzania Publications.

Hall, S. 1992. "The West and the Rest: Discourse and Power." In *Formations of Modernity*, S. Hall and B. Gieben, eds., pp. 275–320. Cambridge: Cambridge University Press.

Hodgson, D.L. 1996. "'My Daughter . . . Belongs to the Government Now': Marriage, Maasai, and the Tanzanian State." *Canadian Journal of African Studies* 30, 1: 106–23.

———. 1997. "Embodying the Contradictions of Modernity: Gender and Spirit Possession among Maasai in Tanzania." In *Gendered Encounters: Challenging Cultural Boundaries and Social Hierarchies in Africa*, M. Grosz-Ngate and O. Kokole, eds., pp. 111–29. New York: Routledge.

———. 1999a. "Pastoralism, Patriarchy and History: Changing Gender Relations among Maasai in Tanganyika, 1890–1940." *Journal of African History* 40, 1: 41–65.

———. 1999b. "Images and Interventions: The Problems of Pastoralist Development." In *"The Poor are not Us": Poverty and Pastoralism in East Africa*, D. Anderson and V. Broch-Due, eds. Oxford: Oxford University Press.

———. 1999c. "Critical Interventions: The Politics of Studying 'Indigenous' Development." *Identities* 6, 2/3: 201–24.

———. 1999d. "Women as Children: Culture, Political Economy and Gender Inequality among Kisongo Maasai." *Nomadic Peoples* (n.s.) 3, 2: 115–30.

———. 1999e. "Engendered Encounters: Men of the Church and the 'Church of Women' in Maasailand, Tanzania, 1950–1993." *Comparative Studies in Society and History* 41, 4: 758–83.

———. 2000a. "Taking Stock: Ethnohistorical Perspectives on State Control, Ethnic Identity and Pastoralist Development in Tanganyika, 1930–1961." *Journal of African History* 41, 1: 55–78.

———. ed. 2000b. *Rethinking Pastoralism in Africa: Gender, Culture and the Myth of the Patriarchal Pastoralist.* Oxford and Athens, OH: Ohio University Press.

———. 2001a. *Once Intrepid Warriors: Gender, Ethnicity and the Cultural Politics of Maasai Development.* Bloomington, IN: Indiana University Press.

———. ed. 2001b. *Gendered Modernities: Ethnographic Perspectives.* New York: Palgrave.

———. n.d. "Rethinking Indigenous Development." Unpublished manuscript.

Hodgson, D.L. and S. McCurdy, eds. 2001. *"Wicked" Women and the Reconfiguration of Gender in Africa.* Portsmouth, NH: Heinemann.

Hollis, A.C. 1905. *The Masai: Their Language and Folklore.* Westport, CT: Negro Universities Press.

Johnston, H.H. 1886. *The Kilima-Njaro Expedition: A Record of Scientific Exploration in Eastern Equatorial Africa.* London: Kegan Paul.

Kilusu (pseud.). 1956–57. "Masai and Their Finery." *East African Annual* 1956–57: 135–7.

Kituyi, M. 1990. *Becoming Kenyans: Socio-Economic Transformation of the Pastoral Maasai.* Nairobi: Acts Press.

Krapf, J.L. 1968 [1860]. *Travels, Researches and Missionary Labours during an Eighteen Years' Residence in Eastern Africa.* London: Cass.

Llewelyn-Davies, M. 1978. "Two Contexts of Solidarity among Pastoral Maasai Women." In *Women United, Women Divided*, P. Caplan and J. Bujra, eds., pp. 206–37. Bloomington: Indiana University Press.

———. 1981. "Women, Warriors and Patriarchs." In *Sexual Meanings: The Cultural Construction of Gender and Sexuality*, S. Ortner and H. Whitehead, eds., pp. 330–58. Cambridge: Cambridge University Press.

Merker, M. 1910 [1904]. *Die Masai. Ethnographische Monographie eines ostafrikanischen Semitenvolkes.* Berlin: D. Reimer.

Ndagala, D. 1982. "Operation Imparnati: The Sedentarization of the Pastoral Maasai in Tanzania." *Nomadic Peoples* 10: 28–39.

Saitoti, T. ole. 1986. *The Worlds of a Maasai Warrior: An Autobiography.* Berkeley: University of California Press.

Sommer, G., and R. Vossen. 1993. "Dialects, Sectiolects, or Simply Lects? The Maa Language in Time Perspective." In *Being Maasai: Ethnicity and Identity in East Africa*, T. Spear and R. Waller, eds., pp. 25–37. London: James Currey.

Spencer, P. 1988. *The Maasai of Matapato: A Study of Rituals of Rebellion.* Bloomington, IN: Indiana University Press.

———. 1998. *The Pastoral Continuum: The Marginalization of Tradition in East Africa.* Oxford: Oxford University Press.

Sutton, J. 1990. *A Thousand Years in East Africa.* Nairobi: British Institute in Eastern Africa.

———. 1993. "Becoming Maasailand." *Being Maasai: Ethnicity and Identity in East Africa*, T. Spear and R. Waller, eds., pp. 38–60. London: James Currey.

Thomson, J. 1968 [1885]. *Through Masai Land.* London: Cass.

Waller, R. 1978. "'The Lords of East Africa': The Maasai in the Mid-Nineteenth Century (c. 1840–1885)." Ph.D. dissertation, Cambridge University.

———. 1988. "Emutai: Crisis and Response in Maasailand 1883–1902." In *The Ecology of Survival: Case Studies from Northeast African History*, D. Johnson and D. Anderson, eds., pp. 73–112. Boulder, CO: Westview Press.

13

TO BE A MAN IS MORE THAN A DAY'S WORK: SHIFTING IDEALS OF MASCULINITY IN ADO-ODO, SOUTHWESTERN NIGERIA

Andrea A. Cornwall

Sitting around with a group of young men in Ado-Odo, a small southwestern Nigerian town close to Lagos, chewing over the latest turn in the political events that were so powerful a presence in Nigeria in 1994, the conversation turned abruptly to women. The cloud of gloom hanging over our discussion deepened. Bayo, whose attempts at business continued to fail, began to bemoan the kind of wife who takes a man for granted. Others narrated tale after tale of women mocking the little husbands could offer, spending on finery to parade at parties, trailing after men with money, and leaving their penniless husbands behind. Later, in the kitchen, teenage Agnes told stories of "eat and run" girls who played with men to get their cash, of women for whom satisfaction had a price.

At the time, I interpreted these tales as sour grapes. Women, it seemed, were in the ascendancy: getting on, as well as making do with scant resources in hard times. I spent hours talking to men. But my quest for answers to other questions, about how and why women "endured" marriages in the absence of support from their husbands (see Cornwall 1996), persistently eclipsed men's own experiences. Only when I listened more closely did I start to pay attention to what men were telling me about what it meant to be a man in such turbulent times.

This chapter draws on case material from interviews, oral histories, and participant observation in everyday life in Ado-Odo to explore the negotiation of ideals of masculinity by men of different generations.[1] In it, I tell stories of men for whom becoming a man was "more than a day's work," as the popular adage goes. My point of departure is a present that is now past, 1992–4: a time when structural adjustment, political instability, and economic decline had left many men vulnerable in ways they could not have imagined a few years before.[2]

I begin by sketching a context in the ebb and flow of people, options, and images of what it is to be a man. I go on to focus on the marital careers of men of different generations, highlighting some challenges posed for their sense of themselves as men as they negotiated relationships with women in changing times.

MALE IDENTITIES IN CHANGING TIMES

Close enough both to the ring of markets serving Lagos, and the Benin–Nigeria border with its flows of contraband goods—a source of lucre many highlight as influencing changes in gender relations—Ado-Odo straddles urban and rural economies, sustaining a diversity of occupations. Retreating from war or seeking new fortunes, members of other Yoruba sub-ethnic groups have migrated to and settled in Ado since the late nineteenth century. Improved transport and trade connections in the mid-twentieth century brought further waves of immigrants, more recently from the north and east of the country. Since the 1920s, Ado people have migrated for work, mostly to Lagos; some have sought education and fortunes in the United States, the United Kingdom, or other African countries. Those who are not regarded as "indigenes" of the town maintain networks in other places; and those whose families moved away remain part of national and transcontinental networks, a source of pride for some and loss for those whose sons never returned to stay. With these flows of people have come new ideas and ways of being that extend the spectrum of possibilities for contemporary identities.

Migration and the influx of diverse images of masculinity have made available ever more complex masculine identities. Barber's (1991) analysis of Yoruba "big men"—men with the clout to, as people in Ado put it, "do and undo"—shows how crucial the ability to draw followers is to the maintenance of a man's standing. Amid the changes wrought by the opening up of opportunities for men beyond "traditional" forms of wealth and authority have come different routes to "bigness," which in turn depend on and give rise to changing ideals of masculinity (see Peel 1983, Barber 1991). Where once a man acquired status by virtue of lineage and generation, there are now other routes to success. People often spoke of "enlightenment" (*olaju*) as the distinction that produced new aspirations and identities among men, and changing economic and conjugal relations (Cornwall 1996).

For younger men, older cultural referents barely hold in these changing times. With aspirations that lie beyond the backwater that many think Ado to be, their concerns are less with the forms of prestige and authority available to their fathers or grandfathers than with more directly material opportunities for self-assertion. Few engage in farming—most are in risky informal sector employment. Men who have returned from careers in the cities may also return to family farms, but their relations are permeated with referents from beyond Ado. For the older generation, the old certainties are out of reach. Complaining about young men's rudeness and with faltering bases of respect and authority, some also struggle with younger wives whose expectations are as foreign as the images of sexuality and intimacy from the pages of popular magazines. And younger men talk less of obedience and endurance than of love and romance; their anxieties about satisfying women's sexual and material desires are all too much a part of their everyday relationships. Men's agency and identities within everyday life are imbricated with the contrasts evoked by these changes. Perhaps the most acute and dissonant arena is sexual and marital relationships, portrayed by men and women alike as a dramatic breach with the past (Cornwall 2000). No longer can compliant wives be relied on to shore up a man's sense of his own potency. Women contest male authority, voting with their feet if dissatisfied. Amid grumbling about women's waywardness and lack of endurance, a set of new anxieties and ambivalences has arisen among men. Younger men talk of how love now has a price; older men find the once unquestioned patriarchal prerogative has been undermined, telling of disobedient wives who took lovers and "packed out" as it suited them. Amid contested and competing discourses on what "being a man" entails, everyday struggles within marital relationships make being a man more than a day's work. The reconfiguration of male identities among changing work opportunities, movements across different spaces and places, and an ever more complex palate of cultural referents is thrown into sharp relief within heterosexual relationships.

CONTEST AND CHANGE IN CONJUGAL RELATIONS

Over the last century, marital forms and practices in the region have changed significantly (Fadipe 1939 [1970], Mann 1985; Lindsay 1996). While continuities and the reinvention of "traditional" practices within them remain evident in some contemporary conjugal relationships, the diverse influences noted above have shaped forms of marriage that offer entirely different modes of interaction, both between partners and within families. Discourses on intimate relationships in Ado often counterpose a present disquiet against a past in which female compliance and male responsibility were assured. In nostalgic representations of the past invoked by older men and women alike, women knew their place, obeyed men, and treated them with respect, and people lived peacefully and happily. The present is represented as rupture, in which men almost expect their wives to disregard their authority, and women complain if they are not satisfied sexually or financially, seeking other men if their husband fails to come up to scratch. A picture of divorce, deviance, and resistance is often presented by men, with pain and bemusement as part of the struggle of living in contemporary Nigeria (Cornwall 1996). Residues of the "olden days" remain salient in contemporary conjugal relationships. They are lived out in contests over expectations and battles of will and wit, persisting despite attenuated endurance by once-compliant wives. Men for whom marriage has proved a battlefield continued to frame "good marriage" in terms of women's obedience and "endurance," sometimes conveniently forgetting that these "bad" wives are the ones to put food on the table. In their evocation of compliant wives, they also made spaces for themselves as husbands whose claims to authority resided in fulfilling their part of the "conjugal bargain" (Whitehead 1981)—spaces now marked by their absence in many younger people's intimate relationships.

What has this shifting landscape of gender relations meant for men's identities? Contemporary struggles "to be a man" are framed by expectations that began to fragment in colonial times and were increasingly contested with the advent of adversity. These contests are rooted in recourse to normative ideals of masculinity that have been displaced by recent changes and actively contested as alternative ways of being a man emerged. These identities are formed over biographical time and set within historical time; over the course of a man's life, relationships change as gender intersects with other dimensions of difference, most notably seniority. Accounts of men in general obscure these differences and their implications for men's identities and relationships with other men, as well as women.

Carrigan et al. suggest that certain ways of being a man come to be "culturally exalted" and, thus, "hegemonic" (1985: 92). They argue that while it may describe few actual men, the "hegemonic model" of masculinity is sustained through the complicity of many and is intimately bound up with the subordination of women. Connell (1995) takes this notion of "hegemonic masculinity" further, exploring how relations of male dominance are reproduced. Distinguishing "hegemonic" from other forms of masculinity crucially highlights the multiplicity of ways of being a man, rather than a single, fixed, masculine identity. It enables us to unpack the associations often made between men, masculinity, and power, revealing the fluid, situational, and relational aspects of men's identities (Cornwall and Lindisfarne 1994).

Taking a closer look at what exactly *is* "hegemonic" about a particular style of being a man raises the question of whether "hegemonic masculinity" is in fact simply a popular stereotype, rather than something men in all their diversity would exalt unquestioningly. Accordingly, I focus here on *ideals* rather than models of masculinity: on attributes persistently associated with idealized versions of being a man, rather than on the identities that they describe. As I suggest here, particular ideals of masculinity may be enacted and identified with in different ways by different men and by the women with whom they have relationships.

ENDURING IDEALS?

Curious to find out what different generations of men and women thought being a man was about, I asked men and women whether, if they had the chance to be born again, they would choose to be a man or a woman.[3] Their answers revealed a preoccupation with one subject position: that of "husband." "Husband" was commonly elided with "man," capturing with it significant elements of an idealized version of masculinity that appeared to span generations. Complaints voiced by women about men in general and their husbands in particular and by men, as husbands, about women's behavior were insistently situated within discourses that positioned men/husbands as owners, controllers, deciders and providers. Tunde, a shopkeeper in his late fifties, declared:

> A man is—according to how we put it—the husband and the landlord. Men marry women and they control them. They are their masters. We control our children and anything they want to do. Women suffer a lot with children, yet men are the ones to control the children. If my wife wants to go I won't allow her to take them, because I have more power over the children than her. That is the custom. Men are the owners of the children and the wife, and the wife should not do anything without the knowledge of the man. If the wife wants to do something and doesn't tell me, I won't be happy as she doesn't regard me as a husband.

None of the men I spoke with chose to be women. And most women said they would rather be a man. Bolaji, in her thirties, argued:

> The man is supposed to have responsibility in the family, but the woman always helps as well, so I would rather be a man. It's better to be the head of the family than to be under someone. The wife will fear the husband. The husband gets up and goes to work, often without giving any money for feeding, while the wife has to clean the house, wash the children, cook and take financial responsibility.

Yemisi, an unmarried woman in her early twenties, gave being in control as her reason. Peter, in his fifties, said he wouldn't want to be a woman, as the man would be dominating him all the time: "Men usually command women as they like; if they want them to do anything, if they don't want them to go out anywhere, they can stop them from going. Women are under the husband's control for as long as they are in the house." Bola, in her thirties, put it even more directly. She'd be a man, she said, and would marry many wives. Then she would just sit in her chair ordering her wives around: "Get me this! Get me that!" And Bose, a teenager, concurred. She would marry many wives and beat them thoroughly if they didn't obey her.

For men and women alike, being a husband meant being vested with control over the household. Affirming their desire to be male, however, some men talked about the challenges of living up to the ideals they described. One talked of how men cannot control women. Another said, "Men don't like women to earn more than them as the women may then refuse their orders." Another talked of how he'd like to be a real man, stronger, able to work hard. Women's versions of being a husband, voiced not in idealized statements but in everyday complaints, were different. "Good husbands," rare as they seemed to be, were men who took their responsibilities seriously, rather than those who used their rights to enforce control. One woman in her forties complained: "In the olden days, the husband was responsible for everything. But now you're lucky if he gives half. That's why women are running here and there trying to make money." And, one woman in her fifties grumbled, "In Nigeria, there are no husbands anymore. No men are catering properly for their wives and children." In the face of the lack of support women receive, husbands are eclipsed either by the woman's own capacity to maintain her family herself or by "helpers," lovers whose money helps sustain and nurture.

Drawing on snapshots from the lives of Ado men of different generations, I explore in the following sections how particular ideals of masculinity emerge and are played out. I trace some of the options available to two pairs of brothers of different generations and to men the age of their sons to explore some of the dilemmas they faced in being and becoming men.[4] These men and their stories are not intended to be representative. Rather, I have chosen men who are both "typical" of a particular kind of man and yet also distinctive in the particularity of their experiences. Their stories offer examples that shed light on continuities and changes in ideals of masculinity in Ado and insights into the dilemmas of being and becoming men.

MAN THE CONTROLLER, MAN THE PROVIDER

Shakiru and his older brother Muji were born to an established Yoruba Muslim family almost a decade apart, in the 1920s. Their options as young men were in many ways identical; growing up when most men farmed,

Shakiru and Muji were brought up to expect they would do the same. Muji did, living his life within the surrounds of Ado, a moderately successful farmer, marrying three wives and fathering a large family. Muji's authority over his wives and family came simply from being a man. His wives processed and marketed the produce he grew, occasionally helping him on the farm; their lives were intertwined in this sense, their work complementary, their obligations to each other predictable and unquestioned. Even then, men's neglect of their wives—especially if they had more than one—was already a complaint among women. The expectation of male contributions to sustenance, if not as principal provider, was embodied in the ideal of complementarity. But as one woman who married a farmer of Muji's generation pointed out; "Some women will marry the husband and be responsible for their feeding and everything. That has been my fate."

In those days, older women told me, they had few options. They would be told whom to marry. If they stepped out of line, they might be sent back, to the shame of their families. Dependent on their husbands, they had little choice but to get on and get by. Just as over the next decades women's options began to broaden, enabling them to exercise more agency and leave unsatisfactory relationships, so too the subject position "husband" underwent changes that meant the previously unquestioned authority of older men came to face new challenges (Cornwall 1996). As men like Muji found as they took younger wives, the subservience they took for granted was more fragile than they thought. Indeed, as one man of Muji's generation who opted for celibacy after five (serial) marriages commented, "Having wives shortens your life."

For Shakiru, things were very different. Schooling, for their illiterate father, represented the prospect of a better life. While for Muji, school was an interlude in a life punctuated by the everyday concerns of farming, Shakiru's imagination was fired by men whose fluency in English had provided routes to other places, beyond Ado. For Shakiru's generation, education offered young men a sense of agency and choice that previous generations could barely dream of having, one that frustrated the older patriarchs who could no longer control them as they wished (Peel 1993).

Muji's father chose his wife, to whom he hardly spoke before marrying in 1944. That he would work on the family farm was barely even a choice. For Shakiru, making his own choices—of career, wife, lifestyle—came as a result of education: "People who had been schooled, they were not able to control us, we didn't go to farm again. If we liked, we went to visit; if not, we didn't. If we liked things we did them in our own way." With the kind of jobs schooling offered, men like him gained new sources of prestige. He attributed this to earning a salary. With this came the capacity to provide regular money for his family. He said, "At that time, if you were able to put 5sh down, you were a man." He set his wife up in business, but still felt he should give her an allowance to secure his rights: "I had to put something down to show that I was the head of the household." The image of the responsible breadwinner shaped his sense of himself as a man. In his commentary on the contemporary state of affairs, he emphasized the importance of men fulfilling financial obligations to their families as a means of asserting control—in the absence of this, he argued, "you can expect anything to happen."

Notions of legitimate control embedded in a man's capacity to be the responsible provider became increasingly salient under colonialism (Lindsay 1996 and this volume). With it came an effective shift from complementary contributions by husband and wife (see Sudarkasa 1986) to the ideal of the man as principal provider. For all but the wealthiest families, this ideal remained distant from a reality in which women have consistently provided for their hearthholds, sometimes with little if any contribution from their husbands. Yet it provided a sustaining ideal on which male authority became contingent. In one exceptional case, a husband was so insistent in affirming this ideal—and asserting the rights associated with it—that he barred his wife from working as a trader. She found other ways of making her own money. The image of the male provider whose authority came not only from being a man, but from behaving as a man ought to by "catering properly" for his family, has had powerful repercussions in hard times.

RECONFIGURING IDEALS OF MASCULINITY

Shakiru and Muji were among the first to use education to carve out "new" ways of being a man, associated with worldly sophistication. Many of those who preceded them were Christian converts, like the father of Samuel and Ade, born roughly the same number of years apart some twenty years after Shakiru and Muji.[5] For them, routes out of Ado and the influx of people into the town offered broader horizons. Samuel and Ade went to school as a matter of course. Some of Samuel's peers sought fortunes in Lagos, leaving arranged marriages, farms, and families behind. Like Muji, however, his life was punctuated by the rhythms of farm life; he never strayed far beyond the town, assuming the part of the quiet, relatively ineffectual patriarch at home and marrying one wife, with whom he remains.

Samuel became a man during a time of rapid social change. Yet for him, as for so many other men of his age, continuities, rather than rupture, marked his coming into manhood: his career as a farmer and his social network appeared little different from those of generations before him. Samuel remained in the interstices between the "old" and the by then not so "new." Indeed, it was hard to associate anything about him with either the older form of male authority that was vested in indigenous governance structures or that of the newer educated elites. Being a man, for Samuel, was about making do with what he had and getting along day by day, going to church on Sundays, chatting over palm wine. Like numbers of men of his age whom I knew in Ado, it seemed Samuel simply wanted a quiet life, enough to eat and peace at home. Men like these were simply not interested in pursuing the course of becoming a "big man," the world of politics that preoccupied those concerned with power and prestige, and the uncertainties of city life. They didn't want lots of women or wives: they didn't want any *wahala* (trouble).

While Muji might have expected unquestioning obedience from his wives, and Shakiru talked about a bargain through which regular contributions showed who was boss, Samuel's relationship with his wife seemed pretty complementary. They had chosen each other and lived together for decades. She was recognized independently of him as a moderately successful trader, and both worked hard. To talk of Samuel in relation to "hegemonic masculinity" seems quite inappropriate. Certain aspects of Samuel's life were, of course, clearly defined by his sex. But there was little that conformed to attributes evoked by the association of men with power, prestige, and authority that would seem to be key to a "culturally exalted form of masculinity, the hegemonic model" (Carrigan et al. 1985: 92). He was no authoritative patriarch, not excessively controlling, and no one feared him. He had little interest in exercising one aspect of masculinity that younger men talked about, men's irresistible urge for sexual satisfaction. Indeed, Samuel's very ordinariness contrasted with the images of powerful controllers and responsible providers that men and women evoked when speaking of ideals of masculinity.

For Ade, Samuel's younger brother by a decade, what he was *not* as a man was as significant in shaping his sense of self as what he *was*. In Ade's case, those very notions of control, dominance, and masculine strength provided an overarching image against which he judged himself to be lacking. Yet Ade's frame of reference was different; growing up when the route out of Ado had become the choice of many young men, Ade never contemplated farming. After school, he joined the army, and it was in the city that he came up against a model of masculinity that embodied all that he was not. "Being a man" among his army colleagues meant displays of hypermasculinity that Ade found uncomfortable to emulate. A quiet and gentle man, he preferred reading to going out. Laughed at by his colleagues and accused of being impotent for not wanting to chase women, he struggled to become a man in their terms, learning to mask his shyness with alcohol and eventually to blot out his disquiet. For Ade, "being a man" according to those around him was much more than a day's work. He married a woman in Lagos who showed him she would tolerate nothing less than being properly provided for. His attempts to earn enough faltered as time went on. When she "misbehaved," taking lovers and going to parties, friends advised him to beat her or to use *juju* to prevent her from sleeping with other men.[6] He couldn't do this, he said, "for after all, she is the mother of my children. I couldn't harm her."

Ade's wife increasingly contested any semblance of his authority. When she left to go to a nearby town on the grounds that her trade was not moving well in Ado, a familiar euphemism to mask a split, he was bereft. With her went the children and all their household possessions, which she had bought. He had no idea what to do. In theory, he should have been able to withhold the children; in practice, he had no means to look after them himself and barely any agency to insist on their return, until his relatives intervened to support him. When she later tried to reconcile with him and invited him to move in with her, he said: "I can't control that woman here. And now she wants me to go and live with her. How will I control her there? I'm useless. What does she want me there for?"

For Ade, being able to control his wife was a marker of masculinity that he felt he lacked. When he talked about their relationship, however, he spoke more of love and care than of power and control. When things were going well, they enjoyed life together. If she had really cared she would have stayed with him, he said. When the money ran out, he bemoaned, so did her "endurance." This wasn't strictly true, as he knew I knew. She had stuck it out for years longer than she might have had she been looking only for material provision and had been supporting him and the family for all that time. But the vehemence of his feelings was best channeled through this all too familiar complaint. And his declaration of himself as "useless" mirrored the complaints of women all around about the failure of their men to provide properly for them and their families. Robbed of economic potency and the means to control, Ade felt emasculated. His tenderness with his children and his gentle kindness did him no favors either. Against an ideal that was about being able to secure and enforce control, Ade lacked any cultural referent with which to rescue his self-esteem.

Ade's pain and bewilderment were echoed by other men of his generation who had entered into marriage with other ideals in mind. Basiru, a driver about the same age as Samuel, told a woeful tale of a woman he'd married who was wealthy in her own right. She'd built her own house and he visited her there; he didn't want to live with her, as he felt he'd have no control over her there. She was desperate to become pregnant and he spent thousands of naira taking her to herbalists for treatment. And one day he walked in to find her in bed with another man. Joseph, in his late forties, talked of how wife after wife had disappointed him: the first had run off with a wealthier man, the second he accused of "making nonsense, going after men." The third was so jealous he had to divorce her. Of the fourth, he said, "She said she's going out, but goes to meet men at the river; she says she's going to farm, she goes to meet men at the market. She wanted to kill me [by using *juju* on him]." After two more wives, he found the woman he wanted: quiet, compliant, and, above all, faithful.

These tales are redolent with anxieties echoed more widely, revealing the preoccupation with sex and sexuality that permeates the landscape of heterosexual relationships. What emerges from these tales is men's frustration with threats to their occupancy of the subject position "husband," displacing them from the exercise of exclusive rights to sexual access and control, and the responsibilities of provisioning. For younger men and those with younger wives, these concerns became even more acute in an era of austerity.

BEING AND BECOMING A MAN IN A TIME OF SCARCITY

Love and money have become more closely intertwined over the last few decades (see Cornwall 2002). The ability to spend money on a woman, to sustain her and the family, has featured more and more prominently in men's accounts of what women want. From Agnes' "eat and run" girls to the images of desirability that young men painted, with cars, elegant clothes, and the means to impress, money represents a form of power that reconfigures discourses of man the controller and man the provider. This discourse has been infused with new cultural influences that emphasize sexuality, especially female sexuality, in entirely new ways. Nackson, the cartoon rapist who is driven by insatiable sexual desire; male posturing in imported pornographic movies; and the insistent sexuality of Nigerian popular music (see, for example, Adeleye-Fayemi 1995) are echoed in young men's eagerness for sexual adventures and their recognition of the potency of female desire.[7]

One central issue for young men was that "there is no romance without finance." Deji, 24, summarized the dilemmas his peers face: "Love is money: if there is no money, there is no love." As structural adjustment took its toll on younger men's earning power, some men began to feel they had to wait until they could afford to marry to avoid "disappointment." Amos, son of an Egbado man of the same generation as Samuel, 30 at the time, expected to attend university after secondary school. But there was no money, and he trained as a vulcanizer, mending worn-out tires. Amos had been going out with the woman he wanted to marry for five years but felt that he could not marry her yet as he did not want her or his children "to suffer." He gave her as much money as he could manage, around a quarter of his income, to sustain their relationship.

Other young men talked less about the means to marry than about having any sexual relationships at all with the women they desired. As Lasisi, aged 25, commented, having a relationship without any money is extremely hard: "A man must spend to satisfy her." Segun, aged 19, gave a picture of what a woman might look for in a man: "Following the situation this country is in now, most ladies do not want to suffer with any man again. The man must be dressing gorgeously and proving a high class. The man must also be wealthy and popular." This is a bit of a tall order for men who can barely find employment. Among younger men, the prospects of romance without finance are threatened by the superior purchasing power of "sugar daddies," married men wanting an "outside wife" (see Karanja 1987), or petrol smugglers who treated their gains, one man suggested, as danger money that needs to be enjoyed. This contrasted with the virtual unanimity from surveys of young women and men that their choice of marital partner would rest, most of all, on being loved by them; wealth came lower on a list of priorities than being "serious," educated, and kind (see Cornwall 1996).[8] Other young men told of "sugar mummies," about whom lurid stories circulated, of their luring toy-boys so as to steal their semen for magical money-making preparations. An article in the popular press some years previously captured an important dimension of these relationships: "I don't demand any financial favours from him so he doesn't feel threatened," said the older woman being interviewed (*Lagos Weekend*, 13 October 1989).

REVERSED REALITIES

Where does all this leave normative ideals of control and provision? Bayo and his friends, with whom I began this article, initially invoked the ideal of man as provider and controller when I asked about their views on marriage. Yet it was a version with a twist. After outlining the obligations of a wife to cook, clean, and care for the children, Bayo went on to talk about his own wife's work as a trader. The long hours she worked meant she was unable to fulfil these obligations if she was to bring in the income on which the family survived. And he'd adjusted his side of the bargain to compensate: "My wife is not a slave," he insisted, telling me how he helped her cook, bathe the children, and wash the clothes when she was really busy. The public setting in which Bayo named activities such as these, so strongly associated with "women's work" that a middle-aged friend of mine admitted he only did them in secret, is revealing.

This, it seemed, was role reversal in the extreme: men tending to the children, women bringing in the money—and using their positions as de facto "husbands" to refute men's claims to authority. And Bayo and his friends had more stories to tell. One told of how he couldn't give his wife regular amounts as he struggled to get work; when he did venture whatever he could afford, she'd refuse to go to market with it. So he went himself. Both he and Bayo insisted they were thriftier than their wives and could make these small amounts of money stretch further. And next market day I realized that, sure enough, there were some men among the throngs of women buying food. These were invariably younger men, of Bayo's age group, for whom the indignity of doing "women's work" was clearly less of an issue than making sure there was food in the house.

Men voiced further complaints about how expectations associated with their provider role were being challenged by women. One story summed up how far things had gone. A farmer in his thirties offered some cassava to his and his brother's wife to make *gari* (roasted cassava meal) for the family.

Both refused, saying he should sell the cassava and give them the money to buy *gari* instead. Neither wanted to spend long hours peeling, grating, and frying the cassava: they had their own work to attend to. Their mothers would have been expected to do this; indeed they themselves would have expected the man to provide for them in kind from the farm. But now women want none of the hassle. Indeed, others told me of men who are forced to fry *gari* for the household as the women are too busy. The men were more resigned than outraged, nodding their heads as if it further proved women's unruliness.

That young men had added to their list of desirable attributes in a woman her ability to earn a decent living is hardly surprising in this economic climate. Yet this was a sign of the crumbling of the provider ideal that Amos and others upheld. It meant, perhaps, a return to notions of complementarity that older people evoked, one driven by exigencies of contemporary life and the pragmatic realization that men couldn't possibly support their families alone. But it might also have related to the expectation many women had of the effective absence of male support and hence the crucial importance of independent means to support themselves and their children. As some women pointed out, men's standing may depend on the wife who masks his poverty from public view and provides him with the means to seem to be a "somebody."

For some men, the strategic use women were seen to be making of the man-as-provider discourse was a source of considerable bitterness. One man of Samuel's generation argued that "these days there are a lot of women who don't want to work. They believe if a man has a lot of money to play with they'll follow him rather than staying with the husband who is struggling in the house." This, of course, was Ade's line on his failed marriage. The complaint of another man of his generation revealed a definite whiff of sour grapes:

> A lot of men now think that women are cheating them, because they are richer than the husband. Some women build themselves a house when the husband himself doesn't have one. Some women have fine clothes and attend many social occasions when the husband can't do this and is spending his money on feeding the wife and children. Some women use the money they earn from work together with money from the amount the husband gives her. So men will feel cheated and will caution the wife and refuse to give her money.

Withdrawing from the provider role has risks. By failing to provide for a woman, a man loses his opportunity to exert leverage over her. For, as one woman pointed out, "he doesn't cater for you, so he can't ask where you get your money from."

But men still have the prerogative afforded to them by being male, and the ultimate weapon—as the "owners" of children, they can threaten to turn their wives out and keep the children. This, I was told, deterred many women from escaping unhappy marriages and taught them the error of their ways. Some men, however, failed to reform wayward wives. Reliant on women's earnings, the use of threats might backfire if women took men at their word and "packed out." The numbers of women receiving custody in divorce proceedings might suggest either men's unwillingness or inability to support their children themselves, or indeed their inability to effectively mobilize this threat.[9]

Customary courts in and around Ado have dealt with wave after wave of marital dissolution over the course of the twentieth century. The vast majority of divorce cases continue to be brought to court by women, who often cite grounds of not being properly provided for by their husbands (Cornwall 1996).[10] One, if extreme and unusual, court case from 1993 gives a glimpse of what is at stake. In answer to the accusation of "lack of control, uncontrollable wife, fornication," the wife pointed out that she paid for everything: she even brought the schnapps that was given to her own parents when they married, spent a large sum on her husband while he was training, and bought furniture, beds, a TV, and fan for his house.[11]

These days, people told me, relationships are so fragile that it had become common for some young women not even to bother to move in properly, keeping most of their possessions in their father's house as a precaution. Regardless of whether this is actually the case, repeated citings of this kind of behavior further fueled young men's insecurities. The normative ideals of the provider/controller discourse provoked contests and anxieties that pervade conjugal relationships, while the sexualized images evoked in contemporary media give rise to further anxieties. Amid all this, men continue to assert their prerogative but on ever weaker grounds, and women adopt covert or directly confrontative measures in negotiations on the contested terrain of intimate relationships.

IDEALS OF MASCULINITY ON SHIFTING GROUND

Tunde's evocation of a masculinity that elides being a man with being a husband, equating both with being the controller, captures a pervasive ideal. Men and women of different generations make recourse to a version of this ideal, even if only in terms of framing options for dissent and exit. The cultural salience of this ideal of masculinity appears on the face of it to have enduring, even "hegemonic" features. Yet closer attention to the lives and stories of individual men suggests that it is how men and women relate to and make use of this ideal that determines distinctive shifts that have taken place over the twentieth century. Identities and identifications have changed significantly over this period. The idealized version of masculinity embodied in the man-as-controller discourse has come to be bound up with the capability of husbands to fulfil obligations as providers: "taking proper care," bringing in the bread, spending money to secure women's happiness, and, of course, compliance.

Whereas simply being a man brought with it privileges and prerogatives in Muji's days, the appearance of masculine ideals that were tied to provision—as vividly conveyed in Shakiru's image of putting down money to secure his prerogative—shifted the frame. Being a man was not enough to maintain authority; much came to depend on a more performative identity as man, through which men asserted dominance through enacting the role of provider. Cast as part of a "conjugal bargain" (Whitehead 1981) that requires constant maintenance, men's control thus becomes open not only for negotiation but also for realignment. The impact of shifts in responsibilities for provisioning, whether through deliberate choices or as a product of circumstance, have impinged on men's ability to retain those aspects of identities associated with having the means to exert authority. Where women do what "husbands" ought to do, men are left with little effective exercise of control through the giving or withdrawing of resources. Resorting to other tactics, such as domestic violence, can backfire when a woman withdraws her economic support and "packs out."[12]

While the notion of "hegemonic masculinity" may serve as a useful way of exploring identities in an era where influences were more limited, the very fluidity and hybridity of contemporary identities reveal its instability. Plural versions of what "to be a man" can or should involve suggest, in turn, less a distinction between a "hegemonic masculinity" and other residual variants than a spectrum of ways of being that are more or less valued by different kinds of people. Across this spectrum, ideals of masculinity can be actively deployed to maintain, challenge, or defend particular positions of power. It is this active negotiation of ideals of masculinity to evaluate men's performance that has framed the most insistent challenges and changes over time.

Butler argues that gender is not "a stable identity or locus of agency from which various acts follow; rather, gender is an identity tenuously constituted in time, instituted in an exterior space through a stylised repetition of acts" (1990: 140). Recourse may be made to a set of ideals with broader cultural resonance, but the ways in which particular men negotiate these ideals in shaping their own relational identities sits uneasily with the idea of them simply performing "hegemonic masculinity." While discourses make available subject positions for men to take up, as Hollway (1994) shows, men as agents actively make and shape these identities, rather than simply play out scripts that are given to them. To be a man is more than a day's work; it requires active maintenance, which in the face of economic change has become something that takes more than a day's work to be able to sustain.

ACKNOWLEDGMENTS

I dedicate this chapter to the memory of a dear friend, Adebowale Akinsowon, who taught me so much about men's lives and struggles, and whose untimely death brought me such profound sadness. To all of those men and women who spent so many hours with me telling me about their lives, I am very grateful. Special thanks go to Adebowale Akinsowon, Dorcas Odu, Tunde Olaosebikan, and Paul Fadairo for their assistance with interviews and my funders, the Economic and Social Research Council and the Royal Anthropological Institute. And I am very grateful to Naomi Hossain for incisive pruning of a longer version. Had Lisa Lindsay not first asked, then insisted, and then determinedly prodded me to get it done, this piece would never have been written; many thanks are due to her for her patience and encouragement.

NOTES

1. Fieldwork in Ado-Odo was carried out between December 1992 and June 1994. The interviews on which this account is based were conducted in English and Yoruba, from which they were translated into and recorded in English. With appropriate caveats, I use these translations here. A number of the interviews I draw on here were conducted with the assistance of a series of other people. Mrs. Dorcas Odu (in her fifties) worked with me throughout the research. She not only translated for me, she also took an active part in discussions. Although I strove initially for us to present ourselves as entirely neutral, Mrs. Odu's own censure of women's behavior and her sympathy with men's predicaments opened important spaces for men to express their feelings more confidently. That this did not in itself "bias" men's responses became clear from interviews I conducted independently and from further work carried out independently by Wale Akinsowon (in his forties), Paul Fadairo (in his late teens), and Tunde Olaosebikan (in his early twenties) on my behalf.

2. Sarah Berry's (1975, 1985, 1993) work on agrarian change, spanning three decades, contains vivid evocations of the changing landscape of occupational identities. It provides a rich ethnographic backdrop against which to situate plummeting fortunes and consequent social change in the last decade. See also Adepoju's (1993) edited volume on the impact of structural adjustment across a spectrum of sectors and aspects of people's livelihoods.

3. I am grateful to Mark Hobart for suggesting this idea.

4. I have changed the names and taken some measures to obscure the identities of the men whose life stories I draw on here to preserve confidentiality as far as possible.

5. See Ajayi (1965) and Ayandele (1966) on the missionary impact and the emergence of a Christian educated elite in southern Nigeria.

6. Herbalists in Ado told me of a number of such preparations that may be sought by men and women alike to constrain the sexual misbehaviour of their partners and secure peace in their relationships. These range from medicines that affect men's ability to have an erection with another woman or dampen their desire, to those that make men pay excessive attention to their wives, to the extent of doing household tasks to please them (see Cornwall 1996). In turn, men who did behave in this way toward their wives might be suspected of having been "given something," as it was such unusual behavior.

7. Survey work with young men in Ado revealed great interest in sexual experimentation, especially with different sexual positions—many of which they'd seen or heard of through access to pornographic films. Letters to Planned Parenthood of Nigeria by adolescent boys from all over the country revealed numerous young men who were concerned

about their ability to satisfy women sexually. I am extremely grateful to PPFN for giving me access to their archive of letters.

8. A questionnaire was administered to fifty boys and fifty girls in the last year of secondary school to explore their views on changing ideals in relationships. This included ranking criteria of what they would look for in a future spouse.

9. In those cases I came across, it was often down to the family to decide whether or not they would seek to take the children. In a couple of cases, the man seemed to have little if any agency in the matter and was not charged with any responsibility either as the children were then farmed out to other relatives. Very rarely did I ever come across children living with their fathers in the absence of other women to care for them.

10. An analysis of a sample of cases brought to Ado's customary court in 1991 is revealing. Ninety-six percent of cases were brought by women, 86% of which mentioned as a principal ground "lack of proper care," 50% neglect (which usually means no sex either), and 42% domestic violence. Ten percent of cases named "no love" as a ground for divorce. Other reasons included no child (14%), husband told the woman to leave (8%), and problems with others in the house, such as co-wives (4%). These figures include more than one mention of each reason.

11. Case AD2/129/93 of 18/8/93, Ado Customary Court records.

12. That many women remain and "manage" with no love and no money defies the logic of economistic arguments that would imagine every woman leaving if only she had the means to do so (see, for example, Blumberg 1993). I explore these issues further in Cornwall (1996). What is significant however, is that numbers of women now have the means to leave unsatisfactory relationships if they want to.

REFERENCES

Adeleye-Fayemi, Bisi. 1995. 'Shinamania: Gender, Sexuality and Popular Culture in Nigeria.' In *Images of African Women: The Gender Problematic*, Stephanie Newell, ed. University of Stirling Occasional Paper No. 3.

Adepoju, Aderanti. 1993. *The Impact of Structural Adjustment on the Population of Nigeria*. London: James Currey.

Ajayi, J.F. Ade. 1965. *Christian Missions in Nigeria 1841–91: The Making of a New Elite*. London: Longman.

Asiwaju, Anthony. 1976. *Western Yorubaland under European Rule 1889–1945*. London: Longman.

———. 1991. 'The Nigeria/Benin Transborder Trade, Border Control and the Nigerian SAP Programme,' Working Paper No. 155. Boston: Boston University African Studies Centre.

Ayandele, E.A. 1966. *The Missionary Impact on Modern Nigeria 1842–1914: A Political and Social Analysis*. London: Longman.

Barber, Karin. 1991. *I Could Speak Until Tomorrow: Oriki, Women and the Past in a Yoruba Town*. London: International African Institute.

Belasco, Bernard. 1980. *The Entrepreneur as Culture Hero: Preadaptations in Nigerian Economic Development*. New York: Praeger.

Berry, Sara. 1975. *Cocoa, Custom and Socio-economic Change in Rural Western Nigeria*. Oxford: Clarendon Press.

———. 1985. *Fathers Work for Their Sons: Accumulation, Mobility and Class Formation in an Extended Yoruba Community*. Berkeley: University of California Press.

————. 1993. *No Condition Is Permanent: The Social Dynamics of Agrarian Change in Sub-Saharan Africa*. Madison, WI: University of Wisconsin Press.

Blumberg, Rae Lesser. 1993. "Poverty versus 'Purse Power': The Political Economy of the Mother-Child Family." In *Where Did All the Men Go?* Joan P. Mencher and Anne Okongwu, eds. Boulder, CO: Westview.

Burnham, Phil. 1987. "Changing Themes in the Analysis of African Marriage." In *Transformations of African Marriage*, David Parkin and David Nyamwaya, eds. Manchester: Manchester University Press.

Butler, Judith. 1990. *Gender Trouble: Feminism and the Subversion of Identity*. New York: Routledge.

Carrigan, Tim, Bob Connell, and John Lee. 1985. "Toward a New Sociology of Masculinity." *Theory and Society* 14:551–604.

Connell, R.W. 1995. *Masculinities*. Berkeley and Los Angeles: University of California Press.

Cornwall, Andrea. 1996. "For Money, Children and Peace: Everyday Struggles in Changing Times in Ado-Odo, Southwestern Nigeria." Ph.D. dissertation, University of London.

Cornwall, Andrea. 2000. "Wayward Women and Useless Men: Contest and Change in Gender Relations in Small Town Southwestern Nigeria." In *Wicked Women and the Reconfiguration of Gender in Africa*, Dorothy Hodgson and Sheryl McCurdy, eds. Westport, CT: Greenwood Press.

Cornwall, Andrea. 2002. "Spending Power: Love, Money and the Reconfiguration of Gender Relations in Ado-Odo, Southwestern Nigeria." *American Ethnologist* 29, 4.

Cornwall, Andrea and Nancy Lindisfarne. 1994. *Dislocating Masculinity: Comparative Ethnographies*. London: Routledge.

Ekundare, E.O. 1973. *An Economic History of Nigeria 1860–1960*. London: Methuen.

Fadipe, Nathaniel A. 1939 [1970]. *The Sociology of the Yoruba*, Francis Olu Okediji and Oladejo O. Okediji, eds. Ibadan: Ibadan University Press.

Galletti, R., K.D.S. Baldwin, and I.O. Dina. 1956. *Nigerian Cocoa Farmers: An Economic Survey of Yoruba Cocoa Farming Families*. Oxford: Oxford University Press.

Hollway, Wendy. 1994. "Gender Difference and the Production of Subjectivity." In *Changing the Subject: Psychology, Social Regulation and Subjectivity*, J. Henriques, W. Hollway, C. Urwin, C. Venn, and V. Walkerdine, eds. London: Methuen.

Karanja, Wambui wa. 1987. " 'Outside Wives' and 'Inside Wives' in Nigeria: A Study of Changing Perceptions of Marriage." In *Transformations in African Marriage*, David Parkin and David Nyamwaya, eds. Manchester: International African Institute.

Lindsay, Lisa A. 1996. "Putting the Family on Track: Gender and Domestic Life on the Colonial Nigerian Railway." Ph.D. dissertation, University of Michigan.

Mann, Kristin. 1985. *Marrying Well: Marriage, Status and Social Change among the Educated Elite in Colonial Lagos*. Cambridge: Cambridge University Press.

Matory, J. Lorand. 1994. *Sex and the Empire That Is No More: Gender and the Politics of Metaphor in Oyo Yoruba Religion*. Minneapolis, MN: University of Minnesota Press.

Mohanty, Chandra Talpade. 1988. "Under Western Eyes: Feminist Scholarship and Colonial Discourses." *Feminist Review* 30: 61–88.

Moore, Henrietta. 1993. "The Differences Within and the Differences Between." In *Gendered Anthropology*, Teresa del Valle, ed. London: Routledge.

Peel, J.D.Y. 1976. "*Olaju*: A Yoruba Concept of Development." *Journal of Development Studies* 14: 135–65.

————. 1993. *Ijeshas and Nigerians: The Incorporation of a Yoruba Kingdom 1890s–1970s*. Cambridge: Cambridge University Press.

Sudarkasa, Naira. 1986. "'The Status of Women' in Indigenous African Societies." *Feminist Studies* 12, 1: 91–103.

Whitehead, Ann. 1981. "'I'm Hungry Mum': The Politics of Domestic Budgeting." In *Of Marriage and the Market: Women's Subordination in International Perspective*, Kate Young, Carol Wolkowitz, and Roslyn McCullagh, eds. London: CSE Books.

14

AFTERWORD

Luise White

I find myself in an odd position, asked to write the afterword for a book that I kept pestering the two editors to edit so that I could get one of my favorite articles reprinted. But the series editors or the publishers' readers or both thought that this book needed a final frame, a commentary on how far the field of African men's history had come in the last decade or so, and they asked me, and with some hesitation I said yes. I'm probably as qualified as anyone; I have good credentials in women's history: "Separating the Men from the Boys" is an early piece on the history of masculinity in Africa, when I was still at the University of Minnesota I organized a conference on "Men and Masculinity in Africa" in the spring of 1990, and I was an invited speaker at the 1997 conference on masculinity in Africa at the University of Natal at Durban. All of these qualifications, however—and however lame they might be—make me think this collection does not need a final frame, does not need closing remarks that somehow announce that here, at long last, is the history of masculinity in a teachable, orthodox form: the edited collection.

Let me explain: when I started organizing the 1990 conference, I joked that I could take my old grant proposals, cross out the words "women" and "gender," replace "women" with "men," and I would have a case for a conference on historicizing masculinity in Africa. That's not quite what I did, but whatever I wrote it suggested that the gendering of men and that of women were complementary processes, that they took place in the same situations and venues. (It was 1989 when I requested funding for this conference; it never occurred to me then that anyone's gender was inscribed.) The conference itself revealed how wrong I had been, even in my preliminary thinking, and how complicated the construction of men was in Africa or indeed anywhere. Even the terms *masculinity* and *femininity* were not commensurate: they were both gendered categories, but that gendering took markedly different forms. For reasons that I still find hard to articulate, women and gender do not translate easily to men and masculinity. The parallels between the two categories are there, but those parallels do not reveal very much, and they certainly do not tell us much about the historical specificity of men or why men are—and are not—so different from women. Once we got beyond the point that male and female genders were constructed, the sheer variety of places, spaces, and situations in which masculinities were constructed and reconstructed made the task of understanding and unpacking something called "masculinity" seem overwhelming. The conference papers demonstrated how the social construction of masculinity took place in so many sites—families, kraals, schools, missions, gangs, and then workplaces, hostels, union halls, beer halls, and what we now call the public sphere—that the generalizations we made simply underscored their own inadequacy. But the conference papers also addressed how the construction of masculinity took place on men's bodies, and not just on genitals but on faces, arms, and backs. (Even though I pretended to be surprised that in 1990 we had no paper historicizing the physicality of men's initiations, I don't think such a study was done in the next decade. Nevertheless, we had a paper on eunuchs.) Again, generalizations about the embodied markings of puberty or adulthood and their meanings seemed to obscure more than they illuminated. But what I had not realized when I planned the conference was this: that the social construction of men did not stop with marriage, with adult life, with old age. What became perfectly clear as we listened to the ten papers was that it was in the very spaces where masculinity was supposed to be solidly established—in the household, in the kraal, in the palace—that masculinity was the most contested and the most actively constructed and reconstructed.

I did not even attempt a conference volume of the papers—although several were later published, including Cooper's piece in this collection—in part because they did not really hang together, but mainly because all the conference had done was to humble my initial ideas. Men and masculinities—*if* masculinities encompassed all of the alterations and genders that men were in Africa—were so complexly imagined and constructed, and then reconstructed, that it didn't make much sense to publish a few articles in which scholars had studied men carefully and thoughtfully, but not necessarily as gendered and constructed beings. I went on to other things and did not really think about these issues until I got invited to Durban in 1997. I'm not about to comment on anyone else's conference, but by comparison with what I had done in 1990, this was a celebration of the rich complexity of men's experiences. Robert Morell, the organizer, was well versed in the theoretical and sociological literature on men and masculinity, and the conference had some extraordinarily theoretical pieces and an enormous range of empirical studies. I think two collections have come out of the conference, but once again, I was struck by the enormity of the undertaking: men were simply too visible, too much a part of the world, too naturalized to be studied with any ease.

The reasons have to do with all of the complications of men's place in broader histories: if women's history had been content to spend years finding famous women in the past and excavating women's historical activities, men's history could hardly do that—that's what much history had already been. Men's history, and men's studies more or less, had to begin with the question of how to problematize what had been considered universal. But for reasons that may have as much to do with the academic production of knowledge as with the practice of gendering anyone, the term *gender* has, despite the most earnest efforts of several scholars, continued to mean women. It was as if no one doubted that masculinity was gendered, but no one wanted to say it out loud. At a recent, ambitious conference on "Africa after Gender? An Exploration of New Epistemologies for African Studies" at the University of California at Santa Barbara in April 2001, organized by Catherine Cole and Stephan Miescher, there were five (out of fifteen) papers on men—by Rudolf Gaudio, Lisa Lindsay, Stephan Miescher, Helen Mugambi, and myself.

This is why I do not think this volume needs an afterword. Lindsay and Miescher have met head-on the problems that confronted earlier conferences, I think: they start from the complexity of men's experiences and the ways in which men reconstruct themselves as they live and work. The papers presented here argue that men in the royal compound, men in the workplace, soldiers and ex-soldiers, schoolteachers and students were not only constructed as men by the institutions in which they lived and worked, but all thought seriously about what it was to be a man, and rethought it again and again as their lives and ideas changed. Indeed, many of these men seemed more aware of the fluidity of African gendered categories than a generation of scholars were, and so they not only invented themselves as men, but played with gendered concepts and categories that allowed them to problematize their own inventions. There is no single reason that African men did this, in the past or in the present, but the wealth of meanings that men brought to their various selves—in the various sites in which men had to be, or wanted to be, or thought it was a good thing to be, manly—trouble any frame, any afterword, and any sense of closure this collection might aspire to. There's a sanctioned untidiness to masculinity in Africa, an encouraged (or at least not discouraged at all) freedom for men to fashion themselves into the man with the masculinity a situation requires. Sometimes these masculinities are socially constructed—through initiation, marriage, or aging—and sometimes they are consciously constructed and interrogated choices—in the workplace or the mosque—but they are never linear, never so stable and constrained that they can be easily fixed in scholarship.

Indeed, if this collection ends abruptly, if readers are left with a sense that they do not quite know where this field is going or what its trajectory is, I think this is a good thing. This is the first collection of essays on men in

Africa that has begun with the premise that African men forge their masculinities in complicated ways, and, as such, it does not require any statement on the state of the field or how we got to the edited collection stage of men's history. Instead, this collection locates men in the lives and societies in which and for which they forged their various masculinities, and as such it serves as an opening, a loosely conceived direction from which the historical study of men and masculinity in Africa can move on.

INDEX

ABOUT THE CONTRIBUTORS

Nwando Achebe received her Ph.D. in African History from the University of California, Los Angeles, where she is currently a visiting assistant professor of history and research associate/visiting scholar at the Institute for the Study of Gender in Africa, James S. Coleman African Studies Center. She served as a Ford Foundation and Fulbright-Hays Scholar in Residence at the Hansberry African Studies Institute and History Department of the University of Nigeria, Nsukka, in 1996 and 1998. Her research interests include the use of oral history and the study of women, gender, and power in eastern Nigeria.

Carolyn A. Brown is an associate professor of history at Rutgers the State University of New Jersey. Her book, *We Were All Slaves: African Miners, Culture and Resistance at the Enugu Government Colliery, Nigeria,* is being published as part of the Heinemann Social History of Africa series. She is currently working on a social history of Enugu, the site of the coal mines that she has studied and an oral history project on the slave trade in southeastern Nigeria.

Frederick Cooper teaches African history at New York University. His most recent books include *Decolonization and African Society: The Labor Question in French and British Africa* (1996), *Beyond Slavery: Race, Labor, and Citizenship in Postemancipation Societies* (with Rebecca Scott and Thomas Holt, 2000), and two co-edited collections, *Tensions of Empire: Colonial Cultures in a Bourgeois World* (with Ann Stoler, 1997) and *International Development and the Social Sciences: Essays on the History and Politics of Knowledge* (with Randall Packard, 1997).

Andrea A. Cornwall is a fellow of the Institute of Development Studies, University of Sussex, UK. A social anthropologist by training, her current work includes research and writing on participation, social policy, and men and masculinities in development. Her publications on men and masculinities include *Dislocating Masculinity: Comparative Ethnographies* (co-edited with Nancy Lindisfarne, 1994) and "Missing Men? Reflections on Men and Masculinities in Development" (IDS Bulletin, 2000).

Dorothy L. Hodgson teaches anthropology at Rutgers University. She is the author of *Once Intrepid Warriors: Gender, Ethnicity and the Cultural Politics of Development among Maasai, 1890s–1990s,* editor of *Rethinking Pastoralism in Africa: Gender, Culture and the Myth of the Patriarchal Pastoralist,* and co-editor of *"Wicked" Women and the Reconfiguration of Gender in Africa* (Heinemann). She is currently completing a book on the Maasai experience of Catholic evangelization since 1950 and how it has affected gender relations.

Lisa A. Lindsay is an assistant professor in the history department at the University of North Carolina, Chapel Hill. Her research interests include gender, labor, colonialism, and popular culture in West Africa. She is currently completing a monograph titled *Working with Gender: Wage Labor and Social Change in Southwestern Nigeria,* which will be published in Heinemann's Social History of Africa series.

Gregory Mann recently completed his Ph.D. in African history at Northwestern University and currently teaches at Columbia University.

Meredith McKittrick is an assistant professor in the Department of History and the School of Foreign Service at Georgetown University. She is completing a book on the creation of a Christian community in northern Namibia. Her other research interests include gender, generational relations, and environmental history.

Stephan F. Miescher teaches African history at the University of California, Santa Barbara. His research focuses on gender, colonialism, law, personhood, and migration in southern Ghana. He is co-editor of *African Words, African Voices: Critical Practices in Oral History* and is preparing a monograph on the construction of masculinities in twentieth-century Ghana.

Pashington Obeng is an assistant professor of Africana studies at Wellesley College and adjunct professor at Harvard University. He has done postdoctoral studies at the Center for the Study of World Religions and Afro-American

Studies department at Harvard and Oxford Universities. In addition to scholarly articles, he is the author of *Asante Catholicism: Religious and Cultural Reproduction among the Akan of Ghana* (1996).

Keith Shear teaches African history and politics at the Centre of West African Studies, University of Birmingham, England. His contribution in this volume is part of a larger work on policing and state formation in early twentieth-century South Africa, portions of which have also been published in *Gender and History*, and in Saul Dubow (ed.), *Science and Society in Southern Africa* (2000).

Luise White teaches African history at the University of Florida. Her first book, *The Comforts of Home: Prostitution in Colonial Nairobi* (1990), won the Herskovits Prize of the African Studies Association in 1991. Her second book, *Speaking with Vampires: Rumor and History in Colonial Africa*, was published in 2000.